桐昆·中国纤维
流行趋势报告
TONGKUN·CHINA FIBERS
FASHION TRENDS REPORT
2025 / 2026

端小平　陈新伟　陈　蕾　主　编
王华平　靳高岭　　　　　副主编

中国化学纤维工业协会
东华大学
中国棉纺织行业协会
桐昆集团股份有限公司
组织编写

内 容 提 要

本书是在工业和信息化部消费品工业司指导下，由中国化学纤维工业协会、东华大学、中国棉纺织行业协会、桐昆集团股份有限公司组织编写而成。本书紧密结合政治、科技、经济等热点及中国纤维行业宏观发展趋势，围绕"质尚与致远"主题，划分纤·境界、纤·破界、纤·跨界、纤·无界四大篇章，汇集2025/2026年度科技、绿色、时尚、健康等方面最具前瞻性的纤维品种，深度剖析中国纤维多维度创新方向、制备技术、性能优势及其在服装用、家用、产业用等领域的应用趋势，明晰市场需求，为企业研发提供思路，为纺织、化纤产业链相关企业提供战略发展方向，助力企业在复杂市场环境中实现创新与转型升级，同时为中国纤维品牌带来更广阔的市场空间。

本书可供纺织、化纤行业企业管理者、研发人员、市场人员、服装设计师、品牌运营商及纺织院校师生、科研机构研究人员等阅读。

图书在版编目（CIP）数据

桐昆·中国纤维流行趋势报告. 2025/2026 / 端小平，陈新伟，陈蕾主编；王华平，靳高岭副主编；中国化学纤维工业协会等组织编写. -- 北京：中国纺织出版社有限公司，2025.3. -- ISBN 978-7-5229-2613-1

Ⅰ．F426.7

中国国家版本馆 CIP 数据核字第 20250SA576 号

TONGKUN·ZHONGGUO XIANWEI LIUXING QUSHI BAOGAO 2025/2026

责任编辑：由笑颖　范雨昕　责任校对：高　涵
责任印制：王艳丽

中国纺织出版社有限公司出版发行
地址：北京市朝阳区百子湾东里 A407 号楼　邮政编码：100124
销售电话：010—67004422　传真：010—87155801
http://www.c-textilep.com
中国纺织出版社天猫旗舰店
官方微博 http://weibo.com/2119887771
廊坊佰利得印刷有限公司印刷　各地新华书店经销
2025 年 3 月第 1 版第 1 次印刷
开本：787×1092　1/16　印张：16.5
字数：360 千字　定价：288.00 元
京朝工商广字第 8172 号

凡购本书，如有缺页、倒页、脱页，由本社图书营销中心调换

主编：
端小平　陈新伟　陈蕾

副主编：
王华平　靳高岭

顾问（按姓氏笔画排序）：
王伟　许坤元　朱美芳　孙瑞哲　李陵申　杨兆华　何亚琼　陈士良　陈大鹏　赵庆章
俞建勇　贺燕丽　高勇　曹学军　董奎勇　蒋士成

特邀参编（按姓氏笔画排序）：
王玉萍　王乐军　王府梅　王锐　吕佳滨　关晓瑞　齐梅　庄毅　李圣军　李杰　李斌红
杨金纯　陈邦伟　邵新艳　武学凯　郝新敏　梅锋

执行编委：
杨涛　陈向玲　王永生　窦娟　王祺

组织策划：
张冬霞　戎中钰

编委：
张玉梅　陈仕艳　王朝生　陈龙　李戎　陈烨　乌婧　柯福佑　吉鹏　谢锐敏　张圣明
王彪　李建武　邵正丽
杨涛　陈向玲　王永生　窦娟　王祺　张冬霞　靳昕怡　李增俊　戎中钰　宁翠娟　王军锋
苗泓瑛　王朝乾
李杰　贺文婷　盖丽轩　冷景钢　王春红　石零平
李国元　陈超　孙燕琳　范辰霞　沈建松
张涛　王壮飞　安毅恒　张嘉

前言

当人类文明与自然生态的共生议题成为全球共识，当科技创新与可持续发展交织为时代命题，纤维——这一承载人类衣、住、行、用的基础材料，正以颠覆性的姿态重新定义未来的可能性。作为纺织产业链的源头，中国纤维产业不仅是技术革命的试验场，还是绿色未来的探路者，更是满足人民美好生活的践行者。

中国纤维产业经历了从规模数量扩张到质量效益增长、品牌价值重塑的深刻转型。在"双碳"目标驱动下，中国纤维产业的绿色、可持续发展成为必然；与此同时，智能穿戴、医疗健康、航空航天等新兴领域对纤维性能提出更高维度的要求，轻量化、功能化、可循环、数字化正成为产业升级的必答题。

在工业和信息化部消费品司的组织和指导下，在主办单位中国化学纤维工业协会、东华大学、中国棉纺织行业协会等的推动下，中国纤维流行趋势伴随中国纤维产业的发展变迁，成为发布差异化、高附加值、高性能和多功能新型纤维的平台，每年都要向世界展示中国纤维产业最有热度、最富科技性、最有市场潜力的纤维品种，并将其汇编为每一年度的《中国纤维流行趋势报告》。

自 2012 年创立以来，历经 14 年的积淀与发展，中国纤维流行趋势开创了原料端流行趋势研究的先河，成为中国化学纤维行业发展的风向标，引领中国纤维在科技创新、绿色发展、时尚跨界、国际影响力等方面全方位提升。中国纤维流行趋势提出的核心理念从"纤动世界，美丽中国""纤维改变生活"，到"纤维新视界"，已深入人心。可以说，中国纤维流行趋势为纺织行业全产业链践行供给侧结构性改革、实施"三品"战略发挥了重要作用，如今中国纤维流行趋势正在为行业践行党的二十大报告精神和建设纺织现代化产业体系贡献重要力量。

2025年是"十四五"规划的收官之年，"十五五"规划的谋划之年。面对百年变局加速演进、国际局势变乱交织，如何提升产业链供应链韧性，如何进一步聚焦纺织现代化产业体系建设的价值高点，系统推进中国纤维产业科技、绿色、时尚、健康发展？《桐昆·中国纤维流行趋势报告2025/2026》以"纤"为眼，紧密结合政治、科技、经济等热点及中国纤维行业宏观发展趋势，围绕"质尚与致远"主题，划分纤·境界、纤·破界、纤·跨界、纤·无界四大篇章，汇集2025/2026年度科技、绿色、时尚、健康等方面最具前瞻性的纤维品种，深度剖析中国纤维多维度创新方向、制备技术、性能优势及其在服装用、家用、产业用等领域的应用趋势，明晰市场需求，为企业研发提供思路，为纺织、化纤及产业链相关企业提供战略发展方向，助力其在复杂市场环境中实现创新与转型升级，同时为中国纤维品牌带来更广阔的市场空间。纤维的故事，从来不只是技术的迭代史。当"质尚"成为产业信仰，当"致远"化作文明自觉，那些穿梭于天地与星海之间的纤维，终将成为人类与未来对话的密码。我们愿每一次跨界融合，都在拓展认知的维度；每一重境界攀登，都在追问美的本源；每一场破界冒险，都在重塑可能的边界；每一次无界畅想，都在编织文明的永恒。

　　本书是在工业和信息化部消费品工业司指导下，由中国化学纤维工业协会、东华大学、中国棉纺织行业协会、桐昆集团股份有限公司组织编写而成。本书的出版凝聚了众多参与者的智慧和汗水，在此一并向所有为本书付出辛苦和努力的组织者、策划者、编写者、审稿者致以诚挚的谢意，向所有为本书提供入选纤维、入围纤维产品文字和图片资料的企业致以诚挚的谢意。

　　由于编者水平有限和时间关系，书中难免有疏漏与不足之处，请读者批评指正。

编委会
2025年2月

FOREWOED

As the symbiosis of human civilization and natural ecology becomes a global consensus, and as technological innovation intertwines with sustainable development to form the defining questions of our era, fiber—this fundamental material that carries the weight of human clothing, shelter, transportation, and utility is redefining the possibilities of the future in a disruptive manner. As the source of the textile industry chain, China's fiber industry is not only a testing ground for technological revolutions and a pioneer for a green future but also a practitioner in fulfilling the people's aspirations for a better life.

China's fiber industry has undergone a profound transformation from expanding scale and quantity to enhancing quality and efficiency, and reshaping brand value. Driven by the "dual carbon" strategy, the green and sustainable development of China's fiber industry has become inevitable. Meanwhile, emerging fields such as smart wearables, medical health, and aerospace are demanding higher dimensions of fiber performance, lightweight, functional, recyclable, and digital features are becoming essential answers to industrial upgrading.

Under the organization and leadership of the Department of Consumer Goods of the Ministry of Industry and Information Technology, and propelled by the China Chemical Fibers Association, Donghua University, and the China Cotton Textile Association, the trend of Chinese fibers has evolved alongside the development of China's fiber industry, becoming a platform for releasing differentiated, high-value-added, high-performance, and multifunctional new fibers. Each year, it showcases to the world the most popular, technologically advanced, and market-potential fiber varieties from China's fiber industry, compiled into the annual *China Fibers Fashion Trends Report*.

Since its inception in 2012, after 14 years of accumulation and development, the China Fibers Fashion Trends has pioneered trend research at the raw material end, becoming a bellwether for the development of China's chemical fiber industry, leading comprehensive improvements in technological innovation, green development, fashion crossover, and international influence. The core concepts proposed by the China Fibers Fashion Trends, from "More than Fibers, Beyond China" to "Fibers Change Life" and "New Fiber New World," have deeply resonated. It can be said that the China Fibers Fashion Trends has played a significant role in implementing supply-side structural reforms and the "Three Products" strategy across the entire textile industry chain. Today, the China Fibers Fashion Trends is contributing important strength to the industry's practice of the spirit of the 20th National Congress of the Communist Party of China report and the construction of a modern textile industry system.

The year 2025 marks the conclusion of the 14th Five-Year Plan and the planning phase for the 15th Five-Year Plan. Faced with the accelerated evolution of a century of changes and the intertwined turmoil of international situations, how to enhance the resilience of the industrial and supply chains, and how to further focus on the high-value points of building a modern textile industry system, systematically advancing the technological, green, fashionable, and healthy development of China's fiber industry? The *Tongkun · China Fibers Fashion Trends Report 2025/2026* uses "fiber" as a lens, closely integrating with political, technological, and economic hotspots and the macro development trends of China's fiber industry. Centered around the theme of "Upholding Excellence and Pursuing Endurance", the report is divided into four chapters: Fiber · At the Limit, Fiber · Beyond the Limit, Fiber · Outside the Limit, and Fiber · Without Limit, gathering the most forward-looking fiber varieties in technology, green, fashion, and health in 2025/2026. It deeply analyzes the multi-dimensional innovation directions, preparation technologies, performance advantages of Chinese fibers, and their application trends in clothing textiles, home textiles, and industrial textiles, clarifying market demands, providing ideas for enterprise R&D, and offering strategic development directions for textile, chemical fiber, and related industrial chain enterprises, aiding their innovation and transformation in complex market environments, while also bringing broader market space for Chinese fiber brands. The story of fibers is never just a history of technological iteration. When "Upholding Excellence" becomes an industrial belief, and "Pursuing Endurance" transforms into a civilizational consciousness, those fibers traversing between heaven and earth, and stars and seas, will ultimately become the code for humanity's dialogue with the future. We hope that every crossover fusion expands the dimensions of cognition; every ascent to a new realm questions the origin of beauty; every boundary-breaking adventure reshapes the boundaries of possibility; and every boundless imagination weaves the eternity of civilization.

This book was compiled under the guidance of the Department of Consumer Goods Industry of the Ministry of Industry and Information Technology, by the China Chemical Fibers Association, Donghua University, the China Cotton Textile Association, and Tongkun Group. The publication of this book embodies the wisdom and sweat of numerous participants. We hereby extend our sincere gratitude to all the organizers, planners, writers, and reviewers who have worked hard for this book, and to all the enterprises that provided the text and image materials for the issue fiber and commended fiber products.

Due to the limited level of the editors and time constraints, there may be omissions and shortcomings in the book. We welcome readers to criticize and correct it.

Editorial Committee
Feb. 2025

目录 CONTENTS

10 序与主题
PREFACE AND THEME

11 纤世代　质未来
THE GENERATION OF FIBER, A FUTURE OF QUALITY

中国纤维流行趋势主题解读 2025/2026
THE INTERPRETATION ON CHINA FIBERS FASHION TRENDS 2025/2026
17 质尚与致远
UPHOLDING EXCELLENCE AND PURSUING ENDURANCE

25 中国纤维流行趋势 2025/2026 入选纤维
CHINA FIBERS FASHION TRENDS 2025/2026 ISSUE FIBERS

　　纤·境界　　　　　　　　纤·破界
27 FIBER · AT THE LIMIT　　**61** FIBER · BEYOND THE LIMIT

　　纤·跨界　　　　　　　　纤·无界
91 FIBER · OUTSIDE THE LIMIT　**113** FIBER · WITHOUT LIMIT

134 中国纤维流行趋势 2025/2026 入围纤维
CHINA FIBERS FASHION TRENDS 2025/2026 RECOMMENDED FIBERS

161 白鲨·中国纱线流行趋势 2025/2026
WHITE SHARK · CHINA YARNS FASHION TRENDS 2025/2026

218 纤·破界 / 无界入选纤维应用趋势
ISSUE FIBER APPLICATION TRENDS OF FIBER · BEYOND THE LIMIT/FIBER · WITHOUT LIMIT

249 入选、入围纤维表及下游应用推荐表
ISSUE AND RECOMMENDED FIBERS LIST AND DOWNSTREAM APPLICATION FORM

序与主题
PREFACE AND THEME

仿佛就在眼前，青年一代昂扬自信拼搏在各大赛场。仿佛就在昨天，我们回首中华人民共和国七十五载风雨沧桑。时光已静静来到了 2025 年。

回望 2024 年，中国纤维工业积极应对经济发展新常态，直面困难，循光而行。供应链产业链安全进一步加强，总体呈现恢复性增长态势，全面实施创新驱动发展战略，高质量发展扎实推进，新质生产力稳步发展。"二氧化碳捕集利用—绿色乙二醇—功能性聚酯纤维"生产线建成，Reocoer 芮控碳捕集纤维获得了下游客户的高度认可。生物基化学纤维及原料产业快速发展，关键技术不断突破，产品品种日益丰富，进入新质发展的新赛道。锦纶 66 单体突破国产化瓶颈，迎来了扩产大年，高品质锦纶 66 长丝在纺织服装领域的需求持续增长，在高端运动服和羽绒服、泳衣、瑜伽服、内衣、职业装等领域的应用不断拓展，需求稳步释放。科技创新迸发活力："机电转换纤维及其织物的能量与湿热管理功能调控"获中国纺织工业联合会科学技术奖自然科学奖一等奖；"热湿刺激响应型聚酯纤维及舒适性智能调节织物制造关键技术"获技术发明奖一等奖；"防弹防切割用超高分子量聚乙烯（UHMWPE）纤维及其轻量化复合材料制备关键技术与产业化""聚酯复合纤维熔体直纺工程化技术研发与产业化""聚酯纤维全产业链全局可视可析智能大数据平台及集成技术"获科技进步奖一等奖。中国纤维产品，品质高精，品种丰盈；中国化纤人，奉献担当，巧手慧心；中国纤维工业，乘风破浪，永立潮头。

迎接 2025 年，"十四五"规划收官之年，中国化纤人将呈现一场高质量饕餮盛宴。

THE GENERATION OF FIBER, A FUTURE OF QUALITY

质纤
未世
来代

The young generation's fierce and self-assured competition at the Olympic Games seem to have just taken place. In retrospect, the seventy-five years of wind and rain in China seem like yesterday. The year 2025 has silently arrived.

In 2024, China's fiber industry energetically embraced the new normal of economic development, confronted challenges head-on, and continued to move forward in the direction of progress. The security of supply and industry chains has been further strengthened, an overall recovery growth trend has been shown, the innovation-driven development strategy has been comprehensively implemented, high-quality development has been solidly promoted, and new-quality productivity has been steadily developed. The world's first "carbon dioxide capture and utilization - green glycol - functional polyester fiber" the production line has been established, and Reocoer carbon capture fiber has been highly recognized by downstream customers. The bio-based chemical fiber and raw material industry developed rapidly, with continuous breakthroughs in key technologies and an increasingly diverse range of products, entering a new track for new-quality development. The domestic production of nylon 66 monomer broke through bottlenecks, ushering in a year of expansion. The demand for high-quality nylon 66 filament in the textile and clothing industry continues to grow, and its applications in high-end sportswear and down jackets, swimsuits, yoga clothes, underwear, and professional wear, among other fields, are constantly expanding, with demand steadily released. Scientific and technological innovation unleashes vitality: "Regulation of Energy and Moisture-heat Management Function of Electro-Mechanical Transformation Fibers and Their Fabrics" won the first prize of the Natural Science Award of the China National Textile and Apparel Council Science and Technology Award; "Key Technology for Manufacturing Heat-moisture Stimuli-responsive Polyester Fibers and Comfort Intelligent Adjustment Fabrics" won the first prize of the Technical Invention Award; and "Key Technologies for the Preparation of Bulletproof and Anti-cutting UHMWPE Fibers and Their Lightweight Composite Materials and Their Industrialization", "Research and Industrialization of Engineering Technology for Direct Melt Spinning of Polyester Composite Fibers", and "Global Visual and Analyzable Intelligent Big Data Platform and Integration Technology for the Whole Polyester Fiber Industry Chain" have won the first prize of the Science and Technology Progress Award. Chinese fiber products feature high quality and abundant varieties; Chinese chemical fiber practitioners are dedicated and responsible, with skills and intelligence; China's fiber industry braves the wind and waves, always standing at the forefront.

As we welcome 2025, the year when the 14th Five - Year Plan comes to an end, Chinese chemical fiber practitioners will present a high-quality feast.

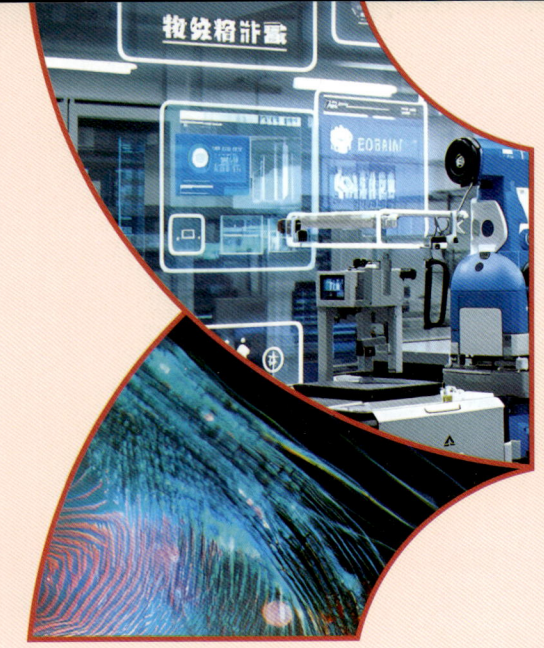

向新

　　科技引领化纤新技术、新产品、新场景大规模应用示范，打造从样品到产品，从产品到商品乃至爆品的连通全产业链研发新模式。中国纤维聚焦"首发经济""冰雪经济"，构建专业集中度高、科技融合度高、资源整合力强的时尚潮流生活场景。"峰顶见、不设限"，波司登三里屯登峰概念店发布的极地极寒系列，融合尖端科技与时尚设计，兼具巅峰性能与格调美学。通过热湿力平衡系统和极致轻量化纤维材料，达到防风、透气、轻量等多重优势，缔造出众的穿着体验。中国纤维聚力"低空经济"，开发轻量化高强高模碳纤维。无人机、新能源汽车，越山海，探空天，中国化纤人以智慧铸大国重器。一束丝中藏世界，半尺锦里绘山河。

向质

　　"人民对于美好生活的向往，就是我们的奋斗目标"。消臭纤维、防摔气囊专用锦纶66、热湿舒适性调控纤维、蓄热锁温抑菌聚酯纤维、凉感纤维、助眠纤维、纤维基传感器、可穿戴智能纤维材料……中国化纤人身体力行，超前布局面向新时尚、大健康、"银发经济"，以多元纤维铸就品质生活，助力以旧换新，为新消费提供支撑方案。中国化纤人统筹"质"与"量"——以量的积累稳住行业存量高效发展的基本盘，以质的有效提升锚定增量高质发展的新蓝图。志之所趋，无远弗届。

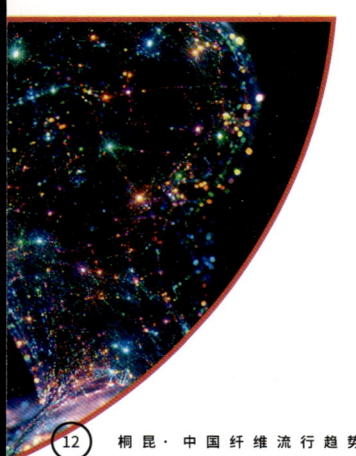

Heading towards novelty

Technology takes the lead in the large-scale application demonstration of new chemical fiber technologies, products and scenarios, creating a new research and development model that connects the entire industry chain from samples to products, from products to commodities, and even bestsellers. China's fiber industry focuses on the "debut economy" and "ice and snow economy", constructing fashionable and trendy lifestyle scenarios with high professional concentration, high technological integration, and strong resource integration capabilities. "Meet at the peak, with no limits", the polar extreme cold series launched at Bosideng's Sanlitun Peak Concept Store integrates cutting-edge technology with fashionable design, combining peak performance with aesthetic style. Through the thermal-moisture balance system and ultra-lightweight fiber materials, it achieves multiple advantages such as windproofness, breathability, and lightness, creating an exceptional wearing experience. China's fiber industry is focusing on the "low-altitude economy" and developing lightweight, high-strength, and high-modulus carbon fibers. As China's chemical fiber practitioners wisely construct the country's pillars, drones, C919s, and new energy vehicles traverse mountains, oceans, and the sky. The universe is concealed by a ball of yarn, while landscapes are painted by half a foot of brocade.

Heading towards quality

"The people's aspiration for a better life is our goal". Odor-eliminating fiber, nylon 66 fiber for anti-drop airbags, heat-moisture regulation fiber, thermal-storage, heat-locked and antibacterial polyester fiber, cool fiber, sleep-aid fiber, fiber-based sensors, wearable smart fiber material... Chinese chemical fiber practitioners earnestly practice what they advocate, planning ahead of time for new fashion, one health, and "silver economy", casting a quality life with multiple fibers, assisting in the replacement of the old with the new, and providing support programs for new consumption. Chinese chemical fiber practitioners coordinate "quality" and "quantity"— stabilizing the basic foundation of efficient development of the industry stock through quantity accumulation, and anchoring a new incremental high-quality development through effective improvement of quality. With ambition, anything is achievable.

向远

　　同球共济，人类命运共同体，对于中国，不是空洞的口号，是承诺。中国是倡导者，更是行动派。低温易染生物基呋喃聚酯纤维、碳捕集纤维、T2T废旧纺织品升级再造、超低温易定形氨纶，纺织、化纤产业链协同减污降碳，让纤维制造融合绿色低碳。可持续发展，中国纤维勇于开拓，一直在路上。秋日春朝，山明水净。

向未来

　　中国纤维工业积极开展"人工智能+"行动，培育未来产业。基于数据驱动场景应用迭代机制，使人工智能深度赋能化纤工业。聚焦生物制造高分子材料、纤维基新型储能材料、脑机接口纤维材料、未来显示用高分子材料，中国纤维拓展应用领域。面向未来，行稳致远。

　　"每个冬天的句点都是春暖花开"，年末岁尾，新篇待启。中国化纤人有一分热，发一分光，就令萤火一般，不必等候炬火，每一分光，每一分热汇聚起来便是艳阳。中国纤维，时代在延续，情怀依旧在，锚定现代化，创新再深化！"梦虽遥，追则能达；愿虽艰，持则可圆。"

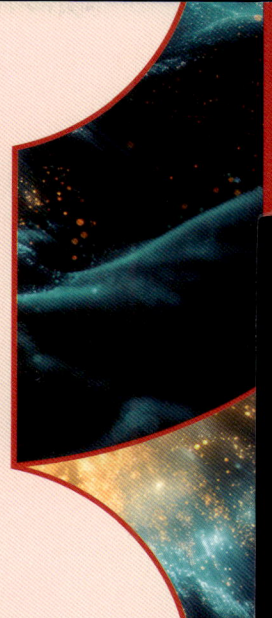

Heading towards sustainability

"Sharing a common future for mankind" and "a community with a shared future for mankind" are not just empty slogans for China. China is dedicated to becoming an advocate and even a doer. Low-temperature chromophilic bio-based furan polyester fiber, carbon capture fiber, T2T waste textile upgrading and recycling, and ultra-low temperature easy-to-set spandex are examples of how the textile chemical fiber industry chain collaborates to reduce pollution and carbon emission, integrating green and low carbon into fiber manufacturing. In terms of sustainable development, China's fiber industry dares to innovate and is constantly on the move. The water is fresh and the mountains are clear through the spring and fall.

Heading towards the future

China's fiber industry actively carries out the "AI+" action to cultivate future industries. The chemical fiber industry can be greatly empowered by AI through a data-driven scenario application iteration mechanism. China's fiber industry is extending its application fields, with a focus on bio-manufactured polymer materials, novel fiber-based energy storage materials, brain-computer interface fiber materials, and future display polymer materials. Looking to the future, it aims for stability and sustainability.

"A warm, flower-filled spring marks the end of every winter." A fresh chapter is waiting to be opened at the conclusion of the year. Every light and heat combine to form a magnificent sun as Chinese fiber practitioners do their utmost, like a firefly shining itself in the darkness of night, independent of the bigger source of light. With the times continuing, the spirit of the Chinese fiber industry endures, anchoring in modernization and deepening innovation! "Dreams and wishes may be far, but they can be fulfilled with dedicated pursuit."

PREFACE AND THEME

THE INTERPRETATION ON
CHINA FIBERS FASHION TRENDS
2025/2026

中国纤维流行趋势主题解读

质尚与致远

UPHOLDING EXCELLENCE AND PURSUING ENDURANCE

PREFACE AND THEME

质尚
Upholding Excellence

尚品质

质，是坚守的承诺，永不褪色的根基，是寻求加工技术和产品功能的最大公约数。吸湿排汗的干爽清凉，柔润弹性的舒感体验，保暖凉感的四季守候，抑菌消臭的健康保障，无熔滴阻燃的生命守望，防水透气防风的精心呵护，以质为本，以新为魂。每一根纤维都诉说着匠心，探索细分品质与场景深耕，为美好生活筑起缤纷的舞台。

Holding quality in high regard

Quality, representing an unwavering commitment, is a cornerstone that never fades away. It is the biggest factor in balancing the process technologies with product functions; It means a pleasantly dry and crisp feel while moisture is absorbed and sweat drained; It offers an experience of feeling comfort of tenderness and smoothness, and elasticity; It gives a warm or cool feel in every season; It ensures health by fighting off bacteria, eliminating foul odor; It improves safety by preventing any molten droplet, and resisting fire; It provides good care by repelling water, letting in air, and protecting against the wind. Featuring quality as its basis, with novelty at its core; every fiber tells a story about craftsmanship. Qualitative exploration and segmentation as well as the furtherance of applications will set the stage for a wonderful life.

Pushing the envelope

Pushing the envelope indicates the relentless pursuit of advanced technologies. With the large-capacity melt-direct-spinning, a high-performance "era of advancements" is ushered in. With the multi-dimensional flexible chip-spinning, the demand for custom products can be satisfied. With the elastic addition and transformation in various combinations, new styles are formed. Every time a technical breakthrough is made, it sets the bar for new techniques. Pushing the envelope signifies vigorous pursuit of product performance. Being higher, stronger, more pliable… Helps fulfill the dreams of great national craftsmen. Being lighter, finer, more flexible… Helps give free rein to the thoughts about life. Pushing the envelope symbolizes an extremely high standard of enhanced quality and efficiency. With all the operations linked with one another, the production process is carried out intensively at top speed. A manufacturing process is accurately controlled all the way with an intelligent system. The chapter about chemical fibers in all its glory is written in the process of pushing the envelope.

求极限

求极限，是工艺精进的不懈追逐；大容量熔体直纺，奏响高效的"奋进曲"；多维度柔性切片纺，迎合定制化需求；花式组合加弹变形，赋予风格新诠释。每一次技术突破，定义巅峰新边界，求极限，是产品性能的极致追求，更高、更强、更韧……支撑大国工匠的梦想，更轻、更细、更柔……编织美好生活的畅享，求极限，是质效提升的超高标准，环环相扣，紧密高速运转的生产，智能系统与制造全过程的精准控制，化纤辉煌篇章在求极限的征程中书写。

Developing the potential for expansion

Leading enterprises are advancing technological frontiers, marching into the northwest, drawing up a blueprint for Southeast Asia, securing cooperation in the Middle East. Medium-sized and small enterprises specialize in unusual and novel products, giving rapid responses, jointly making industrial arrangements that are rich in layers and firm in structure. A scientific tide is running forward. More scientific achievements have translated from what they are on bookshelves into what they are on goods shelves. Towards high speed and high precision, the trend is re-set in going flexible, digital, intelligent, and newly-ecological. Functional, differential, and high-end products appear one after another. New models and new business forms come forward in large numbers. Consumption trends, application innovation and cross-industry brands combine and work together. Fiber brands gradually rise to prominence, displaying originality that lies in costumey aesthetics. Industrial chains gain a new competitive edge.

塑动能

龙头企业引领技术前沿，挺进西北，布局东南亚，联手中东，中小企业专精特新、快反响应，共筑层次丰富、结构稳固的产业矩阵。科技潮力破浪前行，更多的科研成果从书架走向货架，以高速度、高精度为方向，重塑柔性化、数字化、智能化、新生态化，功能化、差异化、高端化产品层出不穷，新模式、新业态持续涌现，消费趋势、场景创新和品牌跨界协同，纤维品牌日渐崛起，创意表达服饰美学，赋能产业链竞争新优势。

序与主题

致远
Pursuing Endurance

「碳」索明日 致长远

寻找可持续，动植物资源利用，减少石油依赖；创新的碳捕捉技术，碧空万里；废旧衣服再利用，生生不息；生物基可降解，化作『春泥护花』原液着色技术、溶剂回收再利用，江河澄澈。绿色工厂如雨后春笋，春风拂绿，生态共建，零碳世界，未来可期。

Exploiting the source of carbon with a long-term perspective

Seeking sustainability by using animal and plant resources, the dependence on oil can be reduced. With the innovative technology for carbon capture, the sky is a cloudless blue. By recycling waste and old clothes, they can be used in endless succession. Degradable biomass changes into "soil to grow plants". With the dope-dyeing technology and solvent recycling, river water is clear and clean. Green factories spring up like mushrooms. Spring wind speeds the greening of plants, an ecological environment is jointly created. A world of zero carbon is expected to exist in the future.

数智融合　致高远

互联网+、AI+成为创新创意新范式，数智化与实体发展深度融合，向上延伸产业链，横向打通供应链和物流链，向下延伸金融与服务链，全链条数据同源、信息共享，一体化构建业务链、数据链、决策链。智能决策赋能智慧经营，智能制造引领未来制造，数智融合，竞相涌现，从高远迈向高峰。

Combining digital and intelligent applications together with high aims

Internet+ and AI+ have become the new paradigm of innovative originality. Digital and intelligent applications are closely related to the development of entities. Industrial chains are extended upwards. Supply chains are connected laterally with logistics chains. Financial and service chains are extended downwards. Data is from the same source and information shared throughout whole chains. Integrated service chains, data chains, and decision chains are formed. Intelligent decision-making enables smart operations. Intelligent manufacturing leads the way to the future. There are competitively more and more instances where digital and intelligent applications are combined together. A leap will be made from high aims to their fulfillment.

筑梦科技　致深远

国产高性能纤维以极致之道载自身之重，乘风破浪，惊艳世界。奥运健儿的科技战衣，蓝天中繁忙穿梭的无人机，轻量化新能源汽车扬帆出海，神舟家族太空接力。瞻望前路，中国纤维蓄势跃升，强科技，致鼎兴。

Achieving the dream of building a powerful country with a far-reaching effect

Domestic high-performance fibers have unique ways of carrying their own weight, braving the wind and waves, amazing the world. They feature prominently in Olympic players' scientific uniforms, in drones flying back and forth in the sky, in lightweight new-energy vehicles starting on a journey across the sea, and in the members of the Shenzhou Family who work in relays in outer space. With the future in view, China's fibers are poised to rise. A powerful country is being built, and revival staged.

性能图标
Performance Icon

 柔软 Soft

 异形截面 Specially shaped section

 尺寸稳定 Dimensional stability

 高强度 High-strength

 蓬松 Fluffy

 质量轻 Lightweight

 防切割 Cut-resistant

 循环再生 Recycling & regeneration

 抗皱 Anti-wrinkle

 挺括 Structured

 悬垂性好 Good drapability

 易打理 Ease-care

 易加工 Easy processability

 抗勾丝 Anti-snage

 耐磨 Wear resistance

 高伸长 High stretch

 使用寿命长 Long service life

 低能耗 Low energy consumption

 废旧纺织品再利用 Waste textile reuse

 耐疲劳 Fatigue resistance

 仿棉 Cotton-like

 细旦 Fine denier

 绿色环保 Green & environmental protection

 生物质 Biomass

 生物降解 Biodegradability

 生物相容性 Biocompatibility

 易上染 Easy-dyable

 色彩持久 Durable color

 原液着色 Dope dyed

 色彩丰富 Enriched colors

 染色鲜艳 Durable color

 低温定形 Low-temperature setting

 耐酸碱 Acid & alkali endurance

 抗熔滴 Anti-drip

 抗原纤化 Anti-fibrillation

 阳离子 Cationic

 除甲醛 Formaldehyde-removal

 耐腐蚀 Corrosion resistance

 耐高低温 High and low temperature resistant

 远红外 Far infrared

 抗静电 Anti-static

 阻燃 Flame retardant

 防紫外线 Anti-UV

 抗起球 Anti-pill

 亲肤 Skin friendliness

 吸湿速干 Fast dying

 凉感 Cool feeling

 保暖 Heat preservation

 隔热 Heat insulation

透湿 Moisture-penetrability

抑菌 Anti-bacteria
 防螨 Anti-mite
 抗芯吸 Anti-wicking
 耐低温 Low temperature resistant
 婴儿级纺织品 Infant textile products
 抗蠕变 Creep resistance
 水溶 Water-soluble
 氨基酸 Amino acid
 部分替代原生纤维 Virgin fiber replacement
 仿真 Imitated
 光泽好 Good luster
 导热 Heat conduction
 均匀稳定 Good stability
 吸湿发热 Absorbing moisture and emitting heat
 除臭 Deodorizing function
 驱蚊 Mosquito repellent
 防泼水 Water-repellent
 耐氯 Chlorine resistant

 耐洗涤 Washing-resistant
 耐污 Stain-resistant
 耐光 Light resistance
 高吸水性 High water absorbent
 耐高温 Heat-resistant
 温度调节 Warmth & cooling
 吸收光源 Absorption from light sourcet
 耐老化 Anti-aging
 耐腐蚀 Corrosion resistance
 低熔点 Low melting-point
 低烟 Low toxicity
 防透视 Anti-perspective
 耐辐射 Radiation resistance
 耐烧蚀 Ablation resistance
 防病毒 Antivirus
 耐化学药品 Chemical resistance
 无重金属析出 No heavy metal
 弹性持久 Durable slastic

 电绝缘 Electric insulation
 高耐(电)压 High (electricity) pressure resistant
 可塑性好 Plastic
 密度小 Low-density
 单丝纤度 Fineness monofilament
 防霉 Mildew resistance
 低温热黏合 Low-temperature thermal adhesion
 高模量 High modulus
 抗冲击性 Impact-resistance
 高抗拉强度 High tensile strength
 低应力 Low stress
 低模量 Low modulus
 分散性好 Dispersion
 可追溯性 Traceability
 效率高 High productive efficiency
 形状记忆 Shape memory
 发光 Luminescent
 透气 Breathable

纤 · 境界
Fiber · At the Limit

舒感纤维
COMFORTABLE FIBER

热湿舒适性调控聚酯纤维
Heat-humidity Comfortable Regulating Polyester Fiber

抑菌消臭高强低伸再生纤维素纤维
Anti-bacterial and Deodorizing Regenerated Cellulose Fiber with High Strength and Low Elongation

阳离子 / 原液着色聚酯混纤
Cationic/Dope-dyed Polyester Blended Fiber

超高异形仿兔毛聚酯纤维
Ultra-high Deformed Faux Rabbit Fur Polyester Fiber

超细旦抗起球聚丙烯腈纤维
Ultra-fine Denier Anti-pilling Polyacrylonitrile Fiber

柔弹纤维
THE FLEXIBLE AND ELASTIC FIBER

生物基聚酰胺 PA5X 双组分复合弹性纤维
Bio-based Polyamide PA5X Bicomponent Composite Elastic Fiber

rPET/PTT 双中空复合弹性纤维
rPET/PTT Double-hollow Composite Elastic Fiber

双组分复合聚酰胺纤维
Biocomponent Composite Polyamide Fiber

PTT 复合弹性纤维
PTT Composite Elastic Fiber

超低温易定形氨纶
Ultra-low Temperature Easy-to-set Elastane

纤 · 破界
Fiber · Beyond the Limit

抗紫外纤维
ANTI-ULTRAVIOLET FIBER

吸湿速干抗紫外聚酯纤维
Moisture-absorption and Quick-drying Anti-ultraviolet Polyester Fiber

防透抗紫外循环再利用聚酯纤维
Anti-see-through and Anti-ultraviolet Recycled Polyester Fiber

遮热抗紫外聚酰胺 6 纤维
Heat-shielding and Anti-ultraviolet Polyamide 6 Fiber

防勾丝抗紫外聚酰胺 6 纤维
Anti-snagging and Anti-ultraviolet Polyamide 6 Fiber

保暖纤维
THERMAL FIBER

高中空异形聚酯纤维
High Hollow Deformed Polyester Fiber

蓄热锁温抑菌聚酯纤维
Thermal-storage, Heat-retaining and Anti-bacteria Polyester Fiber

稀土改性蓄热聚酰胺 6 纤维
Rare Earth Modified Thermal-storage Polyamide 6 Fiber

保暖聚丙烯腈改性纤维
Thermal Polyacrylonitrile Modified Fiber

入选纤维

中国纤维流行趋势
入选纤维
CHINA FIBERS FASHION TRENDS 2025/2026
ISSUE FIBERS

纤 · 跨界
Fiber · Outside the Limit

防护用阻燃纤维
FLAME-RETARDANT FIBER FOR PROTECTION

阻燃抗熔滴聚酯纤维
Flame-retardant and Anti-melt-drop Polyester Fiber

阻燃抗熔滴原液着色聚酰胺 6 纤维
Flame-retardant and Anti-melt-drop Dope-dyed Polyamide 6 Fiber

产业用纤维
INDUSTRIAL FIBER

高模量循环再利用聚酯工业丝
High-modulus Recycled Polyester Industrial Yarn

熔纺型中强超高分子量聚乙烯纤维
Melt-spun Medium-strength Ultra-high Molecular Weight Polyethylene Fiber

原液着色高强型间位芳纶
Dope-dyed High-strength Meta-aramid

HM50E 高强高模聚丙烯腈基碳纤维
HM50E High-strength and High-modulus Polyacrylonitrile-based Carbon Fiber

纤 · 无界
Fiber · Without Limit

绿色纤维
GREEN FIBER

低温易染生物基呋喃聚酯纤维
Low Temperature Easy-to-dye Bio-based Furan Polyester Fiber

二氧化碳基乙二醇聚酯纤维
Carbon Oxide-based Glycol Polyester Fiber

黑色循环再利用再生纤维素纤维
Black Recycled Regenerated Cellulose Fiber

rPET 基化学法再生氨纶
rPET-based Chemically Regenerated Elastane

低温热黏合纤维
LOW-TEMPERATURE HEAT-BONDABLE FIBER

微细旦皮芯复合热黏合纤维
Micro-denier Sheath-Core Composite Heat-bondable Fiber

多组分复合改性聚乳酸纤维
Multi-component Composite Modified Polylactic Acid Fiber

匠心探索，非凡境界

在化纤的奇妙世界里，探索纤维的无限可能，抵达非凡境界。从原料开始，便开启粗细、刚柔、伸缩等多维探索之旅。每一根纤维，都是微观世界的匠心雕琢。多组分复合、热湿舒适调控、异味消除、超细旦异形、超仿真等，皆是品质与舒适的和谐统一，不仅赋予衣物生命与质感，让我们领略品质生活的真谛与境界，更在每一次的亲密相伴中，感受那源自细微之处的不凡与魅力。

Seeking originality to reach great heights

In the wonderful world of fibers, explore the limitless possibilities of fibers, and reach great heights. Starting from raw materials, make an exploration into multiple dimensions such as degree of thickness, degree of hardness, and degree of elasticity. Every fiber is sculpted with ingenuity in microcosm. Multicomponent-combined fibers, temperature-humidity-comfortableness regulating and controlling fibers, strange smell eliminating fibers, ultra-fine denier profiled fibers, and ultra-simulated fibers are all representative of the harmonic integration of quality and comfort. Not only do they inject life and a sense of reality into clothes so as to let us understand the true meaning and heights of quality life, but they also let us feel the uniqueness and charm of tiny details with every gentle touch.

28　舒感纤维
COMFORTABLE FIBER

44　柔弹纤维
THE FLEXIBLE AND ELASTIC FIBER

纤·境界

中国纤维流行趋势

纤·境界

FIBER AT THE LIMIT
China Fibers Fashion Trends
2025/2026

舒感纤维
COMFORTABLE FIBER

舒感纤维，恰似温柔的抚慰者，将每一寸接触柔化作极致的舒适享受。湿热致形变的热湿调控纤维，让空气在织物间自在穿梭，打造"越运动、越出汗、越透气"的应用场景。抑菌消臭再生纤维素纤维，瞬间消除异味，抑菌亲肤，给予肌肤贴心守护。阳离子搭档原液着色，展现混纤异彩效果，丰富视觉层次。仿真纤维，每一根丝都拥有独一无二的异形截面，演绎一纤一世界。超细旦聚丙烯腈纤维品质与功能全升级，优异的保暖与抗起球性，带来羊绒般轻柔细腻的穿着体验。

▲ 推荐纤维及品牌

热湿舒适性调控聚酯纤维
Heat-humidity Comfortable Regulating Polyester Fiber

抑菌消臭高强低伸再生纤维素纤维
Anti-bacterial and Deodorizing Regenerated Cellulose Fiber with High Strength and Low Elongation

阳离子 / 原液着色聚酯混纤
Cationic/Dope-dyed Polyester Blended Fiber

超高异形仿兔毛聚酯纤维
Ultra-high Deformed Faux Rabbit Fur Polyester Fiber

超细旦抗起球聚丙烯腈纤维
Ultra-fine Denier Anti-pilling Polyacrylonitrile Fiber

The comfortable fiber is akin to a gentle soother, transforming every inch of contact into an ultimate comfortable experience. The heat-humidity regulating fiber that undergoes deformation due to heat and humidity allows air to freely circulate between the fabrics, creating an application scenario where "the more you exercise and the more you sweat, the more breathable it becomes". The anti-bacterial and deodorizing regenerated cellulose fiber can instantly eliminate odors and inhibit bacteria. It is skin-friendly, providing intimate protection for the skin. The combination of cationic and dope-dyeing displays a blending fiber effect with vibrant color, enriching the visual hierarchy. The imitational fiber, each with a unique profiled section, presents a world within every fiber. The super fine denier polyacrylonitrile fiber, undergoing a comprehensive upgrade in both quality and functionality, offers excellent warmth retention and anti-pilling properties, and delivers a wearing experience as soft and delicate as cashmere.

热湿舒适性调控聚酯纤维
Heat-humidity Comfortable Regulating Polyester Fiber

推荐理由： 创新设计了湿热致形变差异的聚酯纤维，使其面料具有透气速率调节的功能，可以主动调节人体微环境、快速透湿排汗、保持体表干爽，让穿着者时刻感受舒适，打造"越运动、越出汗、越透气"的应用场景。

Reasons for recommendation
The innovatively designed polyester fiber with differential deformation in response to heat and humidity endows the fabric with the ability to actively regulate the human microenvironment by adjusting its air permeability rate. This unique feature allows for rapid moisture permeation and sweat evaporation, keeping the skin surface dry and ensuring continuous comfort for the wearer. It creates an application scenario where "the more you exercise and the more you sweat, the more breathable it becomes".

怡爽 YISUN

● 入选企业 COMPANY
中国石化仪征化纤有限责任公司
Sinopec Yizheng Chemical Fibre Co., Ltd.

制备技术
Preparative technique

聚合原料酯化后添加改性单体，依次经过预缩聚、终缩聚等步骤，分别制备低热湿刺激聚酯切片、高热湿刺激聚酯切片，然后将两种聚酯切片通过双组分熔融复合纺丝工艺制备纤维。

After esterification of polymeric raw materials, modified monomers are added, and the process proceeds through steps such as pre-polycondensation and final polycondensation to prepare low heat-humidity stimulating polyester chips and high heat-humidity stimulating polyester chips, respectively. Subsequently, these two types of polyester chips are used to produce the fiber through a two-component melt-composite spinning process.

纤维及制品特点
Features of fibers and finished products

主要规格 Main Specifications
长丝：55dtex/48f，83dtex/48f FDY/DTY
Filament: 55dtex/48f, 83dtex/48f FDY/DTY

相关标准 Relative Standards
《涤纶牵伸丝》（GB/T 8960—2015）
《涤纶低弹丝》（GB/T 14460—2015）
Polyester drawn yarns (GB/T 8960—2015)
Polyester drawn textured yarn (GB/T 14460—2015)

FDY 截面图
FDY sectional figure

DTY 截面图
DTY sectional figure

热湿舒适性调控聚酯纤维 FDY、DTY 截面图
FDY and DTY sectional figures of heat-humidity comfortable regulating polyester fiber

纤维性能与制品特点

- 纤维在不同的热湿环境下产生不同内在收缩力，实现湿热条件下自驱调控。
- 织物手感柔软，根据环境温度及湿度的变化，主动调节织物的孔隙率，达到透气、快干效果，实现人体微气候湿热管理。

Properties of fibers and features of finished products

- The fiber can generate different internal contraction forces under varying .
- The fabric features a soft touch and can actively adjust its porosity in response to changes in ambient temperature and humidity, achieving air permeability and quick-drying properties, and enabling the humidity and heat management of human microclimate.

热湿舒适性调控聚酯纤维性能指标
Performance indexes of heat-humidity comfortable regulating polyester fiber

产品规格 Specifications	断裂强度（cN/dtex） Breaking tenacity (cN/dtex)	断裂伸长率（%） Elongation at break (%)	色牢度（级） Color fastness (grade)
83dtex/48f	2.60±0.20	28.0±4.0	4.5
面料成分 Fabric composition	干态透气速率（mm/s） Dry air permeability (mm/s)	湿态透气速率（mm/s） Wet air permeability (mm/s)	
100% 本纤维 （125g 暗纹方格小提花） 100% this fiber (125g subtly patterned small jacquard with grid design)	830	902	
85% 本纤维/15% 氨纶（80g 涤氨单面提花网布） 85% this fiber/ 15% elastane (80g single-sided jacquard mesh fabric made of dacron-elastane)	2630	2830	

下游应用指导
The downstream application guidance

织造： 用于制作针织与机织面料，产品优势的体现程度与织物的组织结构设计相关，针织物能够较大程度体现出产品功能性。

染色： 建议采用分散染料高温高压染色法，浅、中色推荐使用 E 型分散染料，深色推荐使用 SE 型分散染料。

Weaving: It is used to produce knitted and woven fabrics. The degree to which product advantages are manifested is closely related to the structural design of the fabric. Therefore, knitted fabric can exhibit the functionality of the product to a greater extent.

Dyeing: It is recommended to adopt the high-temperature and high-pressure dyeing method with disperse dyes. For light and medium shades, E-type disperse dyes are recommended, while for dark shades, SE-type dispersed dyes are preferred.

热湿舒适性调控聚酯纤维下游应用实例
Examples of the downstream applications for heat-humidity comfortable regulating polyester fiber

终端领域 Terminal field	原料配比 Raw material ratio	支数 Count	主要产品及特性 Main products and properties
运动休闲 Specification	60% 热湿舒适性调控聚酯纤维/30% 涤纶/10% 氨纶 60% Heat-humidity comfortable regulating polyester fiber /30% polyester/ 10% elastane	60/1	用于高端针织类 POLO 衫，吸湿透气，柔软亲肤，不沾身 Used for high-end knitted POLO shirts, it features moisture absorption, air permeability, softness, skin-friendliness, and a non-sticking feeling
	89% 热湿舒适性调控聚酯纤维/11% 氨纶 89% heat-humidity comfortable regulating polyester fiber/11% elastane	60/1	用于运动服装，吸湿透气，柔软亲肤，不沾身 Used for sportswear, it features moisture absorption, air permeability, softness, skin-friendliness, and a non-sticking feeling
	85% 热湿舒适性调控聚酯纤维/15% 氨纶 85% heat-humidity comfortable regulating polyester fiber/15% elastane	60/1	用于高端针织类 POLO 衫及运动服装，吸湿透气，柔软亲肤，不沾身 Used for high-end knitted POLO shirts and sportswear, it features moisture absorption, air permeability, softness, skin-friendliness, and a non-sticking feeling

纤维应用
Application of fibers

| 服装用纺织品
Clothing textiles | 运动服
Sportswear | 贴身内衣
Lingerie |

| 家用纺织品
Home textiles | 窗帘
Curtain |

热湿舒适性调控聚酯纤维调节原理
Regulation principles of heat-humidity comfortable regulating polyester fiber

Q：热湿舒适性调控聚酯纤维是如何通过结构设计与分子结合，来实现对人体微环境主动调节功能的？

A： 热湿舒适性调控聚酯纤维的研发依据生态模拟，深入剖析热湿驱动器的结构原理后制成。纤维由低热湿刺激聚酯和高热湿刺激聚酯两组分复合，采用截面对称、内在结构非对称的形式，融合高聚物分子设计与纤维性能表达。高温潮湿时，单根纤维两组分之间出现变形，纤维之间更加紧密，织物孔隙打开，利于热量、湿气排出，加速汗液蒸发。低温干燥时，纤维之间更加蓬松，织物孔隙率小，实现保温保湿。

Q: How does heat-humidity comfortable regulating polyester fiber achieve active adjustment of the human microenvironment through structural design and molecular association?

A: The research and development of heat-humidity comfortable regulating polyester fiber is based on ecological simulation. The fiber is crafted after a thorough analysis of the structural principles of heat-humidity drivers. The fiber is composed of a composite of two components: low heat-humidity stimulating polyester and high heat-humidity stimulating polyester, and adopts a form of symmetrical section and asymmetrical internal structure to integrate high polymer molecular design with fiber performance expression. In conditions with high temperature and humidity, deformation occurs between the two components of a single fiber, causing the fibers to become closer to each other. Subsequently, the pores of the fabric open up, facilitate the release of heat and moisture, and accelerate the evaporation of sweat. In conditions with low temperature and humidity, the fibers become fluffier and the porosity of the fabric decreases, achieving insulation and moisture retention.

抑菌消臭高强低伸再生纤维素纤维
Anti-bacterial and Deodorizing Regenerated Cellulose Fiber with High Strength and Low Elongation

推荐理由：纤维高密度接枝消臭基团，与异味分子反应，瞬间消除异味，抑菌亲肤，给予肌肤贴心守护。

Reasons for recommendation
The fiber is densely grafted with deodorizing groups, which can react with odor molecules to instantly eliminate odors. It is anti-bacterial and skin-friendly, providing intimate protection for the skin.

● 入选企业 COMPANY
上海正家牛奶丝科技有限公司
Shanghai Zhengjia Milk Fiber Sci & Tech Co., Ltd.

制备技术
Preparative technique

采用接枝共聚技术，使用消臭基团、抑菌基团对纤维素分子链进行接枝改性，通过湿法纺丝工艺制备纤维。

The graft copolymerization technology is used to graft and modify deodorizing groups and anti-bacterial groups onto cellulose molecules, and the wet-spinning process is adopted to produce the fiber.

抑菌消臭高强低伸再生纤维素纤维制备原理

纤维及制品特点
Features of fibers and finished products

主要规格 Main Specifications
短纤：1.5dtex×38mm，6.0dtex×51mm
Staple fiber：1.5dtex×38mm，6.0dtex×51mm

相关标准 Relative Standard
《羧基化改性再生纤维素纤维（黏胶）》（Q/ZJ 31011504—2023）
Carboxylated Modified Regenerated Cellulose Fiber (Viscose) （Q/ZJ 31011504—2023）

抑菌消臭高强低伸再生纤维素纤维原貌图
Original appearance figure of anti-bacterial and deodorizing regenerated cellulose fiber with high strength and low elongation

纤维性能与制品特点
Fiber properties and product characteristics

- 快速响应、持久消臭。
- 无重金属添加、抑菌持久。
- 手感柔软、亲肤舒适。

- Rapid response and long-lasting odor elimination.
- Zero heavy metal, long-lasting anti-bacterial effect.
- Soft hand feeling, skin-friendly and comfortable.

抑菌消臭高强低伸再生纤维素纤维性能指标
Performance indexes of anti-bacterial and deodorizing regenerated cellulose fiber with high strength and low elongation

产品规格 Specifications	断裂强度 (cN/dtex) Breaking tenacity (cN/dtex)	断裂伸长率 (%) Elongation at break (%)	长度偏差率 (%) Length deviation rate (%)	倍长纤维含量 （mg/100g） Extra-long fiber content (mg/100g)	疵点含量 (%) Defect content (%)	回潮率 (%) Moisture regain (%)	碱中和值 (cm/30min) Alkali neutralization number (cm/30min)
1.5detx×38mm	2.58	14.68	-2.6	10.0	0.0	13.95	13

面料成分 Fabric composition	异味成分浓度减少率 (%) Odor component concentration reduction rate (%)			抑菌率（%） Antibacterial rate (%)
	氨气 Ammonia gas	醋酸 Acetate	异戊酸 Isovaleric acid	
30% 抑菌消臭高强低伸再生纤维素纤维/50% 莫代/20% 黏胶纤维 30% anti-bacterial and deodorizing regenerated cellulose fiber with high strength and low elongation/50% Modal/20% viscose fiber	97.9	90.3	87.5	金黄色葡萄球菌：99 大肠杆菌：96 白色念珠菌：99 Staphylococcus aureus: 99 Escherichia coli: 96 Candida albicans: 99

下游应用指导
The downstream application guidance

纺纱： 可以纯纺，也可与其他纤维进行混纺。
织造： 可纺成纱线，用于制作针织与机织面料；也可用于生产水刺、针刺、热轧等 非织造布。
染整： 建议使用活性染料，染色温度和热定形与常规产品一致，置换消臭基团中的氢氧化钠。

Spinning: It can be spun purely or blended with other fibers.
Weaving: It can be spun into yarns for knitted and woven fabrics; it can also be used in the production of spun lace, needled, calender-bonded and other non-woven fabrics.
Dyeing and finishing: It is recommended to use reactive dyes, with dyeing temperature and heat setting consistent with conventional practices, to replace the caustic alkali in deodorizing groups.

抑菌消臭高强低伸再生纤维素纤维下游应用实例
Examples of the downstream applications for anti-bacterial and deodorizing regenerated cellulose fiber with high strength and low elongation

终端领域 Terminal field	原料配比 Raw material ratio	支数 Count	主要产品及特性 Main products and properties
运动休闲 Sports and leisure clothing	50% 抑菌消臭高强低伸再生纤维素纤维/50% 黏胶 50% anti-bacterial and deodorizing regenerated cellulose fiber with high strength and low elongation/50% viscose	40/1	用于 T 恤类等，舒适、吸湿透气、消臭抑菌 Used for T-shirts, etc., it features comfort, moisture absorption, air permeability, deodorizing, and anti-bacteria
	50% 抑菌消臭高强低伸再生纤维素纤维/50% 棉 50% anti-bacterial and deodorizing regenerated cellulose fiber with high strength and low elongation/50% cotton faber	32/1	用于袜类等，舒适、吸湿透气、消臭抑菌 Used for socks, etc., it features comfort, moisture absorption, air permeability, deodorizing, and anti-bacteria

纤维应用
Application of fibers

服装用纺织品 / Clothing textiles 休闲服 Leisure wear　运动服 Sportswear　袜子 Socks

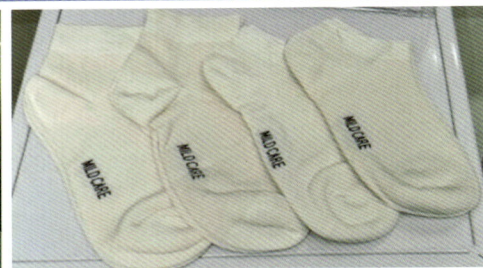

淼卡纤维制品
Products of mild care fiber

Q：抑菌消臭高强低伸再生纤维素纤维的消臭作用效果如何？
A：抑菌消臭高强低伸再生纤维素纤维能够瞬间与异味中的分子反应，短时间内消除大量异味物质。利用化学方法接枝消臭基团，消臭功能可永久维持。经多次使用和洗涤后，除异味功能依然可以保持稳定、持久。纤维呈弱酸性（pH 6.8），与人体皮肤 pH 接近，中和反应平衡酸、碱，不含重金属。

Q: What is the odor elimination effect of the anti-bacterial and deodorizing regenerated cellulose fiber with high strength and low elongation?
A: The anti-bacterial and deodorizing regenerated cellulose fiber with high strength and low elongation can instantly react with odor molecules, effectively eliminating a large number of odor substances in a short period of time. And thanks to the graft of deodorizing groups through the chemical method, the odor elimination function can be permanently maintained. The odor elimination function remains stable and long-lasting even after multiple uses and washings. In addition, the fiber exhibits a slightly acidic property (pH: 6.8), and acids and bases are balanced through a neutralization reaction, making it close to human skin. It is also free of heavy metal.

阳离子／原液着色聚酯混纤
Cationic/Dope-dyed Polyester Blended Fiber

推荐理由： 由阳离子易染聚酯纤维和原液着色聚酯纤维经加弹工艺设计而成，其面料具有丰富的纹理效果和立体美观度，同时手感柔软、易打理，兼具抗起球性。

Reasons for recommendation
It is made of cationic easy dyeing polyester fiber and dope-dyed polyester fiber through the texturing process. The fabric boasts rich texture and three-dimensional aesthetics. And it also features a soft hand feeling, easy care, and anti-pilling.

TONGKUN 桐昆

● 入选企业 COMPANY
桐昆集团股份有限公司
Tongkun Group Co., Ltd.

制备技术
Preparative technique

采用双丝道混纤生产工艺，将原液着色在线添加技术制备的黑色 POY 丝与阳离子改性聚酯 POY 丝混纤，经加弹制备纤维。

The production process involves a dual-filament blending technique, where black POY filament produced through in-line dope-dyeing addition technology and cationic modified polyester POY filament are blended. Subsequently, these blended fibers undergo a texturing process to complete the production.

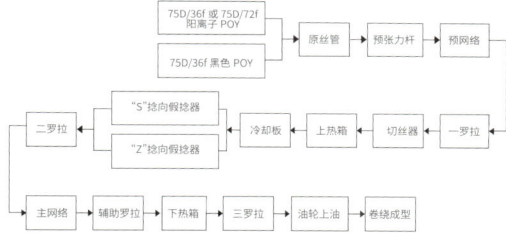

纤维及制品特点
Features of fibers and finished products

主要规格 Main Specifications
长丝：166dtex/72f，166dtex/108f，183dtex/72f，183dtex/108f
Filament: 166dtex/72f, 166dtex/108f, 183dtex/72f, 183dtex/108f

相关标准 Relative Standards
《无扭矩混纤涤纶低弹丝》（FZ/T 54103—2018）
Torque-Free combined polyester (PET) drawn textured yarns (FZ/T 54103—2018)

纤维原貌图
Original appearance figure of the fiber

纤维截面图
Cross-sectional figure of the Fiber

阳离子／原液着色聚酯混纤原貌及截面图
Original appearance figure and sectional figure of cationic/dope-dyed polyester blended fiber

纤维性能与制品特点

- 原液着色技术，色彩饱满丰富、持久鲜艳、高色牢度。
- 易上染、搭配原液着色纤维实现异彩效果。
- 面料悬垂性好，易打理、混纤设计增强面料抗起球性。

Properties of fibers and features of finished products

- Dope-dyeing technology; vibrant and rich colors, long-lasting brightness, and high color fastness.
- Easy to dye; vibrant color effect when in combination with dope-dyed fiber.
- Good drapability, easy care, and better anti-pilling properties enhanced by blended fiber design.

阳离子/原液着色聚酯混纤性能指标
Performance indexes of cationic /dope-dyed polyester blended fiber

产品规格 Specifications	断裂强度 (cN/dtex) Breaking tenacity (cN/dtex)	断裂强度变异系数 (%) Breaking strength variable coefficient (%)	断裂伸长率 (%) Elongation at break (%)	断裂伸长变异系数 (%) Variable coefficient of elongation at break (%)	沸水收缩率 (%) Boiling water shrinkage rate (%)	卷曲收缩率 (%) Crimp shrinkage (%)	含油率 (%) Oil content (%)
183dtex/72f	2.77	1.95	29.40	6.01	4.10	5	6.20

面料 (70% 阳离子/原液着色聚酯混纤/30% 全消光聚酯纤维) Fabric (70% cationic /dope-dyed polyester blended fiber/30% full-dull polyester fiber)	
耐皂洗色牢度（级） Color fastness to soaping (grade)	抗起球检测（级） Anti-pilling detection (grade)
变色 4 级，沾色 4 级 Discoloring grade 4, Staining grade 4	7200 次，4 级 7200 times, grade 4

下游应用指导
The downstream application guidance

织造：主要应用于双撑子喷气织机，经纬通用，纬线同时搭配钩编纱进行织造，可生产高密度遮光面料。

染色：建议使用阳离子染料进行染色，染浴 pH 控制在 4~5，染浅色时适当降低 pH 利于匀染，染深色时适当提高 pH 利于上染，始染温度在 70°C 左右，缓慢加热至沸腾，染色时间一般控制在 60~90min。

Weaving: It is mainly used on dual-frame air jet loom, suitable for both warp and weft. The weft can be simultaneously woven with crocheting yarn to produce high-density light-blocking fabric.

Dyeing: It is recommended to use cationic dyes for dyeing, with the pH of the dyeing bath controlled at around 4~5. For light shades, slightly lowering the pH can facilitate even dyeing, while for dark shades, slightly increasing the pH can facilitate dye up take. The initial dyeing temperature should be around 70°C , and it should be heated slowly until boiling. And the dyeing period should be generally controlled between 60~90 minutes.

阳离子 / 原液着色聚酯混纤下游应用实例
Examples of downstream applications for cationic /dope-dyed polyester blended fiber

终端应用 Terminal field	原料配比 Raw material ratio	纤维规格 Fiber specification	产品特性 Product features
家纺 Clothing textiles	100% 阳离子 / 原液着色聚酯混纤 100% cationic/dope-dyed polyester blended fiber	166dtex/72f 或 166dtex/108f 166dtex/72f or166dtex/108f	用于窗帘，挺括不易变形、独特褶皱纹理； 用于抱枕套，耐磨耐用，保持外观持久度 Used for curtains, it features stiffness and resistance to deformation, and unique pleated textures; used for pillowcases, it features resistance to abrasion, durability, and long-lasting appearance
运动 Sports products	95% 阳离子 / 原液着色聚酯混纤 /5% 氨纶 95%cationic/dope-dyed polyester blended fiber/5% elastane	166dtex/72f	用于跑步服、健身服等，有较好的弹性回复能力，适应运动时的身体变化；挺括性佳，保形性好；吸湿性好 Used for running clothes and workout clothes, etc., it features good elastic recovery, which enables it to accommodate the body's movements during exercise, good stiffness, good shape retention, and moisture absorption
休闲 Leisure products	100% 阳离子 / 原液着色聚酯混纤 100% cationic/dope-dyed polyester blended fiber	166dtex/72f 或 166dtex/108f 166dtex/72f or 166dtex/108f	用于休闲外套、裤装面料等，时尚休闲，有一定垂坠感、质感挺括、手感柔软舒适 Used for leisure outerwear, trousers, and other fashionable and casual clothing, it features good drapability, stiffness, and soft and comfortable hand feeling

纤维应用
Application of fibers

服装用纺织品 / Clothing textiles: 休闲服 Leisure wear ， 运动服 Sportswear

家用纺织品 / Home textiles: 窗帘 Curtain

阳离子 / 原液着色聚酯混纤应用制品
Products of applications for cationic/dope-dyed polyester blended fiber

Q：阳离子 / 原液着色聚酯混纤的后道织物有什么独特的优点？
A：通过将阳离子和黑色聚酯纤维加弹变形设计混纤，再经过机织机交或混纺，用不同染料染色可产生双色效果，设计的面料可具有丰富色彩与多样图案，增加了设计的灵活性和多样性，降低色织面料成本，用于制作家纺、服装面料更具时尚感和独特性。

Q: What are the unique advantages of the fabric produced by cationic/dope-dyed polyester blended fiber?
A: The cationic and black polyester fibers are textured and deformed for blended fiber, and then the shuttle loom is used for interweaving or blending. A two-tone the effect can be achieved through dyeing with different dyes. The produced fabric can exhibit rich colors and diverse patterns, providing better design flexibility and diversity while reducing the cost of yarn-dyed fabrics. When used in the production of home textiles and apparel fabrics, it offers a more fashionable and unique aesthetic.

超高异形仿兔毛聚酯纤维
Ultra-high Deformed Faux Rabbit Fur Polyester Fiber

推荐理由： 超高异形仿兔毛聚酯纤维，匠心独具，每根单丝截面各异。其织物触感温软，绒毛蓬松，逼真还原兔毛神韵，既迎合仿真皮草时尚风向，又助力可持续发展。

Reasons for recommendation
The Ultra-high deformed faux rabbit fur polyester fiber showcases ingenious craftsmanship, with each mono-filament featuring a unique section. The fabric made from such fiber has a soft touch and fluffy appearance, realistically mimicking the charm of rabbit fur. It not only caters to the fashion trend of faux fur, but also contributes to sustainable development.

● 入选企业 COMPANY
苏州龙杰特种纤维股份有限公司
Suzhou Longjie Special Fiber Co., Ltd.

制备技术
Preparative technique

切片筛选后送入干燥系统，经螺杆机熔融，由计量泵送至纺丝组件，通过超高异形喷丝板喷出，冷却成丝束，依次经上油、牵伸、网络处理后卷绕成筒。

After being chipped and screened, they are fed into the drying system, melted by a screw machine, and pumped to the spinning pack by a metering pump. Subsequently, they are extruded through ultra-high deformation spinneret plate, cooled to form tows, and undergo oiling, drawing, and web treatment before being wound into tubular.

PET 切片 → 筛选输送 → 干燥 → 熔融挤压 → 丝束冷却 → 上油 → 牵伸卷绕 → 分级包装 → 成品入库
PET pellet → screening and transportation → drying → melting and extrusion → tow cooling → oiling → drawing and winding → grading and packaging → storage of finished products

纤维及制品特点
Features of fibers and finished products

主要规格 Main Specifications
长丝：54dtex/8f FDY
Filament: 54dtex/8f FDY

相关标准 Relative Standards
《涤纶牵伸丝》（GB/T 8960—2015）
《三维卷曲涤纶牵伸丝》（FZ/T 54077—2014）
《仿生涤纶异形牵伸丝》（Q/320582LJT10—2022）
Polyester drawn yarns (GB/T 8960—2015)
Three-dimensional crimp polyester drawn yarns (FZ/T 54077—2014)
Bionic dacron profiled draw yarns (Q/320582LJT10—2022)

纤维原貌图
Original appearance figure of the fiber

纤维截面图
Cross-sectional figure of the Fiber

超高异形仿兔毛聚酯纤维原貌及截面图
Original appearance figure and cross-sectional figure of ultra-high deformed faux rabbit fur polyester fiber

纤维性能与制品特点

- 超高异形设计、每根单丝截面存在差异，更柔滑、更立体、仿真度更高。
- 织物触感柔软、保暖性优良。
- 织物耐磨、易清洁维护。

Properties of fibers and features of finished products

- Ultra-high deformation design with varying sections of all filaments; softer, more three-dimensional, and higher imitation degree.
- Soft hand feeling and excellent thermal-retention property.
- Resistance to abrasion and crease, and easy to clean and maintain.

超高异形仿兔毛聚酯纤维性能指标
Performance indexes of ultra-high deformed faux rabbit fur polyester fiber

产品规格 Specifications	断裂强度 (cN/dtex) Breaking strength (cN/dtex)	断裂强度变异系数 (%) Breaking strength variable coefficient (%)	断裂伸长率 (%) Elongation at break (%)	断裂伸长变异系数 (%) Variable coefficient of elongation at break (%)	沸水收缩率 (%) Boiling water shrinkage (%)	条干 CV (%) Yarn levelness CV (%)	含油率 (%) Oil content (%)
54dtex/8f	1.94	5.45	49.6	4.85	6.1	0.59	1.94

下游应用指导
The downstream application guidance

染整：建议使用分散性常规涤纶染料，染色温度和热定形温度与常规兔毛丝一样，将后道染色不匀率 1.5 级（灰卡级）提高到 3.5 级（灰卡级）。

Dyeing and finishing: It is recommended to use disperse conventional polyester dyes, with the dyeing temperature and heat setting temperature being the same as those for conventional rabbit hair yarn. The dyeing unevenness rate in subsequent process (gray chip, grade) is improved from grade 1.5 to grade 3.5.

超高异形仿兔毛聚酯纤维下游应用实例
Examples of downstream applications for ultra-high deformed faux rabbit fur polyester fiber

终端领域 Terminal field	原料配比 Raw material ratio	纤维规格 Fiber specification	主要产品及特性 Main products and properties
鞋材 Shoe material	50% 超高异形仿兔毛聚酯纤维/50% 纳米抑菌纤维 50% Ultra-high deformed faux rabbit fur polyester fiber/50% nano anti-bacteria fiber	54dtex/8f	用于鞋面、鞋内衬等，柔软舒适、抑菌防臭 Used for shoe uppers, shoe linings, etc., soft and comfortable, antibacterial and deodorizing
玩具 Toy			用于毛绒玩具、公仔等，造型逼真、触感柔软、抑菌 Used for plush toys, figurines, etc., with realistic shapes, soft touch, antibacterial and bacteriostatic properties
家纺 Home textiles	50% 超高异形仿兔毛聚酯纤维/50% 纳米远红外发热纤维 50% Ultra-high deformed faux rabbit fur polyester fiber/50% nano far infrared heating fiber	54dtex/8f	用于地毯、床上用品等，柔软亲肤、保暖性好 Used for carpets, bedding, etc., soft and skin friendly, with good warmth retention
高端成衣 High end ready to wear clothing			用于仿皮草服装等，仿真耐用、保暖性好 Used for imitation fur clothing, etc., it is durable and has good warmth retention

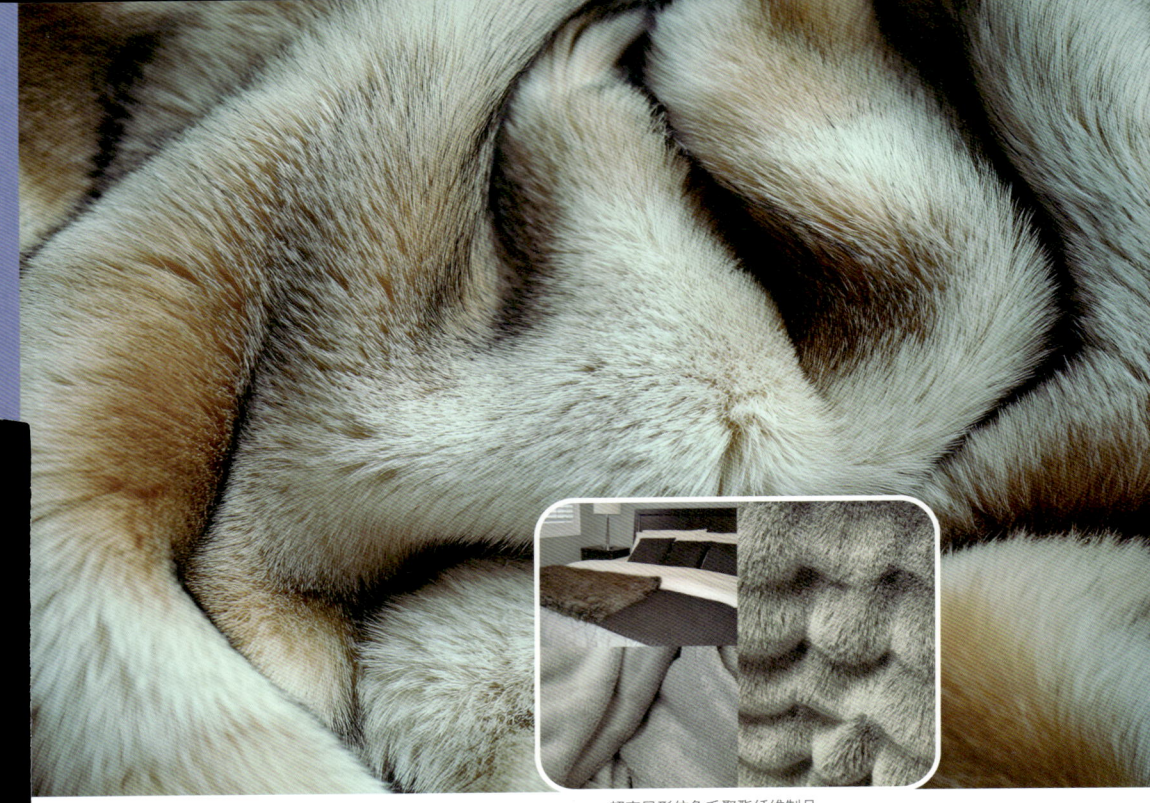

超高异形仿兔毛聚酯纤维制品
Products of ultra-high deformed faux rabbit fur polyester fiber

纤维应用
Application of fibers

| 服装用纺织品 Clothing textiles | 鞋材 Shoe material | 高端成衣 High-end ready-to-wear |

| 家用纺织品 Home textiles | 床上寝具 Bedding | 地毯 Carpet | 玩具 Toy |

Q：超高异形仿兔毛聚酯纤维制备工艺有哪些创新点？

A： 通过喷丝组件的特殊设计结合纺丝工艺参数调整，提高喷丝孔的异形程度，从而生产出每根单丝截面均不一样的超高异形纤维，异形度越高，加工后的面料手感越滑、越接近真兔毛。同时，注入吸色性好的材料，使生产出的仿兔毛纤维吸色同步，具有较好的美观度。

Q: What are the innovative aspects of the production process for Ultra-high deformed faux rabbit fur polyester fiber?

A: The combination of the special design of spinneret assembly and the adjustments to spinning process parameters enhances the deformation degree of spinneret orifices to produce an ultra-high deformed fiber with unique sections for each mono-filament. The higher the degree of deformation, the smoother the texture of the processed fabric, and the more it is to the hand feeling of real rabbit fur. In addition, the incorporation of materials with good dye absorption properties makes the produced faux rabbit fur polyester fiber exhibit synchronous dye absorption, resulting in enhanced aesthetic appeal.

超细旦抗起球聚丙烯腈纤维
Ultra-fine Denier Anti-pilling Polyacrylonitrile Fiber

推荐理由： 纤维纤细柔软，触感似羊绒般细腻亲肤，保暖出色、抗起球性佳。织物有良好的保形性，能长久维持平整，容易打理，是高端超薄保暖面料的理想选择。

Reasons for recommendation
The fiber is slender and soft with a delicate and skin-friendly touch akin to cashmere. It provides excellent thermal-retention and anti-pilling properties. The fabric has excellent shape retention, being able to maintain a smooth appearance for a long time, and is easy to handle. It is an ideal choice for high-end use of ultra-thin and thermal-retention cloth.

华绒 WALON

● 入选企业 COMPANY
吉林奇峰化纤股份有限公司
Jilin Qifeng Chemical Fiber Co., Ltd.

制备技术
Preparative technique

采用第一、第二、第三单体水相悬浮聚合工艺制备聚丙烯腈，使用高精度精密喷丝组件，经湿法纺丝工艺生产获得。

The polyacrylonitrile was copolymerized with the first, second and third monomers using an aqueous phase suspension polymerization technique, and then spun through a wet spinning process with a high-precision spinneret.

聚合 → 汽提 → 过滤 → 干燥 → 料仓 → 原液制备 → 原液过滤 → 纺丝 → 水洗 → 上油 → 烘干卷曲 → 定形 → 切断打包
polymerization → stripping → filtration → drying → storage bin → dope preparation → dope filtration → spinning → water washing → oiling → drying and curling → setting → cutting and packaging

纤维及制品特点
Features of fibers and finished products

主要规格 Main Specifications
短纤：0.67dtex×38mm
Staple fibre: 0.67dtex×38mm

相关标准 Relative Standards
《腈纶短纤维和丝束》（GB/T 16602—2008）
Acrylic staple and tow (GB/T 16602—2008)

纤维原貌图
Original appearance figure of the fiber

纤维截面图
Cross-sectional figure of the fiber

超细旦抗起球聚丙烯腈纤维原貌和截面图
Original appearance figure and cross-sectional figure of ultra-fine denier anti-pilling polyacrylonitrile fiber

纤维性能与制品特点
- 超细旦纤维，品质升级。
- 手感轻盈细腻、类似羊绒触感。
- 面料蓬松丰满、亲肤保暖、抗起毛起球。

Properties of fibers and features of finished products
- Ultra-fine denier fiber with upgraded quality.
- Light and delicate, akin to the touch of cashmere.
- Fluffy fabric, with skin-friendly, thermal-retention, and anti-pilling properties.

超细旦抗起球聚丙烯腈纤维性能指标
Performance indexes of ultra-fine denier anti-pilling polyacrylonitrile fiber

产品规格 Specifications	断裂强度 (cN/dtex) Breaking tenacity (cN/dtex)	断裂伸长 (%) Elongation at break (%)	卷曲数 (个/10cm) Number of crimps (Pc/10cm)	勾结强度 (cN/dtex) Interweaving strength (cN/dtex)	勾结伸长率 (%) Interweaving elongation (%)
0.67dtex×38mm	2.7~3.0	26~28	50~60	0.5~0.8	2~3

面料成分 Composition	抗起球（圆轨迹方法）（级） Anti-pilling (Circle locus method) (grade)
60% 超细旦抗起球聚丙烯腈纤维/40% 莫代尔 60% ultra-fine denier anti-pilling polyacrylonitrile fiber/40% Modal	4

下游应用指导
The downstream application guidance

纺纱： 可以同莫代尔、绢丝、黏胶纤维、羊绒及蛋白类差异化纤维进行组合，配比 30%~50%，生产 60 英支以上混纺纱线，建议采用赛络紧密纺。

染色： 混纺产品可单染或双染，本纤维适用于阳离子染料染色。

Spinning: It can be blended with Modal, spun silk, viscose fiber, cashmere and protein-based differentiated fiber at the ratio of 30%~50% to produce blended yarn of 60^S or above. Compact-Siro spinning is recommended.

Dyeing: The blended product can be dyed singly or doubly. This product is applicable to cationic dyes.

超细旦抗起球聚丙烯腈纤维下游应用实例
Examples of down stream applications of ultra-fine denier anti-pilling polyacrylonitrile fiber

终端应用 End-use field	原料配比 Raw material ratio	支数 Count	主要产品及特性 Main products and properties
保暖内衣 Thermal underwear	48% 超细旦抗起球聚丙烯腈纤维/43% 莫代尔/5% 氨纶/4% 绵羊毛 48% ultra-fine denier anti-pilling polyacrylonitrile fiber/43% Modal/5% elastane/4% sheep wool	60/1	用于高端保暖内衣领域，手感柔软、细腻，保暖性能优良 Used for high-end thermal-retention underwear, it features soft, delicate touch and excellent thermal-retention properties

超细旦抗起球聚丙烯腈纤维制品
Products of ultra-fine denier anti-pilling polyacrylonitrile fiber

纤维应用
Application of fibers

服装用纺织品 Clothing textiles	家居服 Home wear	婴儿服 Baby clothes	贴身内衣 Lingerie
家用纺织品 Home textiles	床上寝具 Bedding	填充物 Filler	玩具 Toy
产业用纺织品 Industrial textiles	卫生纺织品 Sanitary textile	过滤产品 Filtration product	户外用品 Outdoor product

Q&A

Q：超细旦抗起球聚丙烯腈纤维的综合优势，你了解吗？

A： 通过工艺创新和装备升级，制备的超细旦抗起球聚丙烯腈纤维截面由传统的蚕豆形变为接近圆形，更有利于下游梳理和纺纱。纤维柔软性更好、手感轻盈细腻、抗起毛起球；比表面积大，吸湿性比普通纤维高1倍等特性，赋予服装良好的穿着舒适感。

Q: Do you know about the comprehensive advantages of ultra-fine denier anti-pilling polyacrylonitrile fiber?

A: By process innovation and equipment upgrading, the section of ultra-fine denier anti-pilling polyacrylonitrile fiber has been transformed from a traditional broad-bean shape to a subrounded shape, which is more conducive to downstream combing and spinning processes. The fiber has better softness, a light and delicate touch, and anti-pilling properties. Its large specific surface area and moisture absorption capacity which is twice that of ordinary fibers impart excellent wearing comfort to clothing.

纤・境界

柔弹纤维
THE FLEXIBLE AND ELASTIC FIBER

柔弹纤维，宛如灵动舞者，适应每一次肢体的舒展与收缩。解锁触觉新机理，实现生物基聚酰胺同质异构双组分复合、生物基与循环再利用材料的8字中空双组分复合、基体弹性与卷曲弹性互融合的PTT双组分复合、超低温易定形技术应用等，创意组合演绎柔软与弹性双风格，让衣物贴合身形却不失自在，无论运动还是休憩，皆能随心而动。

推荐纤维及品牌

生物基聚酰胺 PA5X 双组分复合弹性纤维
Bio-based Polyamide PA5X Bicomponent Composite Elastic Fiber

rPET/PTT 双中空复合弹性纤维
rPET/PTT Double-hollow Composite Elastic Fiber

双组分复合聚酰胺纤维
Bicomponent Composite Polyamide Fiber

PTT 复合弹性纤维
PTT Composite Elastic Fiber

超低温易定形氨纶
Ultra-low Temperature Easy-to-set Elastane

泰纶 | YY | BIODEX | QIANXI | BANGTAI 邦泰 | EYION 伊纶

The flexible and elastic fiber, like an agile dancer, adapts to every extension and contraction of the body. It unlocks new tactile mechanisms, and realizes a series of innovative combinations, including the isomeric bicomponent composite of bio-based polyamide, the 8-shaped hollow bicomponent composite of bio-based and recycled materials, the PTT bicomponent composite integrating matrix elasticity and curling elasticity, and the application of ultra-low temperature easy-setting technology. Such combinations showcase a dual style of softness and elasticity, allowing clothing to conform to the body shape while maintaining comfort. Whether engaging in sports or resting, they move freely with you, adapting to your every move.

生物基聚酰胺 PA5X 双组分复合弹性纤维
Bio-based Polyamide PA5X Bicomponent Composite Elastic Fiber

推荐理由：生物基 PA5X 双组分复合，赋予纤维持久弹性。织物耐磨、亲肤，契合可持续发展的时尚理念。

Reasons for recommendation
The bio-based PA5X bicomponent composite endows the fiber with long-lasting elasticity. The fabric is wear-resistant and skin-friendly, and aligns with the sustainable fashion concept.

泰纶 TERRYL

● 入选企业 COMPANY
上海凯赛生物技术股份有限公司
Cathay Biotech Inc.

制备技术
Preparative technique

以生物基 PA5X 为原料，通过特殊设计并列喷丝板，双螺杆熔融纺丝工艺，经过湿热定形后，制备出具有同质异构结构的生物基聚酰胺 PA5X 双组分复合弹性纤维。

With bio-based PA5X as the raw material, the specially designed side-by-side spinneret plate and the twin-screw melt spinning process is adopted to produce the bio-based polyamide PA5X bicomponent composite elastic fiber with isomeric structure through wet-heat setting.

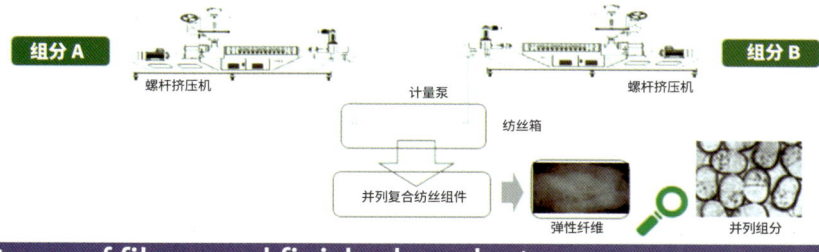

纤维
Features of fibers and finished products

主要规格 Main Specifications
长丝：78dtex/24f DTY
Filament: 78dtex/24f DTY

相关标准 Relative Standards
《锦纶 6 弹力丝》（FZ/T 54007—2019）
Polyamide 6 drawn textured yarns
(FZ/T 54007—2019)

纤维原貌图
Original appearance figure of the fiber

纤维截面图
Cross-sectional figure of the Fiber

生物基聚酰胺 PA5X 双组分复合弹性纤维原貌和截面图
Oiginal appearance figure and cross-sectional figure of bio-based polyamide PA5X bicomponent composite elastic fiber

纤维性能与制品特点

- 生物基材料、绿色环保。
- 三维螺旋卷曲结构、高弹。
- 抗疲劳、耐磨、耐久性好。
- 面料柔软蓬松、舒适性好。
- 易染色、染色均匀性佳。

Properties of fibers and features of finished products

- Bio-based raw material, green and environmentally friendly.
- Three-dimensional spiral curling structure, high elasticity.
- Resistant to fatigue and abrasion, good durability.
- Soft and fluffy fabric, high comfort.
- Easy to dye, good dyeing evenness.

生物基聚酰胺 PA5X 双组分复合弹性纤维指标
Indexes of Bio-based Polyamide PA5X Bicomponent Composite Elastic Fiber

产品规格 Specifications	断裂强度 (cN/dtex) Breaking tenacity (cN/dtex)	断裂伸长率 (%) Elongation at break (%)	弹性回复率 (%) Elastic recovery rate(%)	湿热卷曲收缩率 (%) Wet-heat curling shrinkage rate(%)	湿热卷曲稳定性 (%) Wet-heat curling stability (%)	色牢度 (级) Color fastness (grade)
78dtex/24f	3.20	36.32	90	55.04	50.77	4~5

下游应用指导
The downstream application guidance

织造：适用于机织、针织面料的织造。
预定形：在 100°C 沸水中处理 10~30min，在此过程中不能对织物施加过大的张力。
前处理：优选间歇法除油、退浆。
染色：使用酸性染料、金属络合染料等锦纶染色用染料，染色温度为 95~100°C，升温速率为 0.5~1°C /min。
后定形：定形温度 120~160°C，适当幅宽超喂，避免定形温度过高及扩幅加工造成弹性损失。

Weaving: It is suitable for the weaving of woven and knitted fabrics.
Pre-setting: Process the fabric in boiling water at 100°C for 10~30 minutes, and ensure that excessive tension is not applied to the fabric during this process.
Pre-treatment: Preferentially use batch process for oil removal and desizing.
Dyeing: Dye with dyes specifically for chinlone, Use nylon-specific dyes such as acid dyes, metal complex dyes, etc., at the dyeing temperature of 95~100°C and the heating rate of 0.5~1°C /min.
Post-setting: Adopt the setting temperature of 120~160 °C , with appropriate overfeed of the fabric width to avoid elasticity loss caused by excessively high setting temperatures or stretching processes.

纤维应用
Application of fibers

| 服装用纺织品 Clothing textiles | 休闲服 Leisure wear | 运动服 Sportswear | 羽绒服 Down jacket |

Q: 双组分复合结构给弹性纤维带来了哪些独特性能？

A： 双组分复合结构利用了两组分内在收缩特性上的差异，通过后处理使弹性纤维具有自然永久螺旋卷曲的特性，这种卷曲源自纤维的内在特性差异，是永久性的，因此能提供更稳定持久的弹性。同时，该结构还赋予纤维优异的蓬松性、弹性回复率，提升织物染色色牢度和手感，使其在服用纺织品中能够提供更好的穿着舒适性和美观性。

Q: What unique properties does the bicomponent composite structure bring to the elastic fiber?

A: The bicomponent composite structure takes advantage of the difference in intrinsic shrinkage characteristics between the two components. Through post-treatment, the elastic fiber is imparted with the characteristic of natural and permanent spiral curling. Such curling, stemming from the intrinsic difference in the properties of the fiber, is permanent and therefore provides more stable and long-lasting elasticity. At the same time, this structure also imparts excellent bulkiness and elastic recovery rate to the fiber, and enhances the color fastness and hand feeling of the fabric, enabling it to provide better wearing comfort and aesthetics in apparel textiles.

rPET/PTT 双中空复合弹性纤维
rPET/PTT Double-hollow Composite Elastic Fiber

推荐理由：循环再利用与生物基结合，低碳深绿契合可持续发展。创新的"8"字形双中空组分复合，赋予织物轻质、保暖、舒适、弹性等性能，产品保形性好。

Reasons for recommendation
The combination of recycling and bio-based material is low-carbon and environmentally friendly, fitting seamlessly into sustainable development. The innovative "8"-shaped double-hollow component composite imparts lightweight, thermal-retention, comfort, and elasticity properties, etc., to the fabric, ensuring excellent conformality of the product.

● 入选企业 COMPANY
江苏三联新材料股份有限公司
Jiangsu Sanlian New Material Co., Ltd.
坦佩罗 TEMPERO

制备技术
Preparative technique

以再生瓶片与生物基 PTT 为原料，优化出最佳 rPET/PTT 复配体系。采用不对称和多维度异形并列复合喷丝组件，经熔融复合纺丝工艺制备纤维。

With rPET and bio-based PTT as raw materials, the optimal rPET/PTT compound system has been optimized. Asymmetric and multi-dimensional deformed side-by-side composite spinneret assemblies are adopted to produce the fiber through melt composite spinning process.

再生 PET 切片 / PTT → 螺杆挤压 → 计量泵 → 纺丝组件 → 中空喷丝板 → 环吹风冷却 → 上油 → 预网络 → 第一热辊 → 第二热辊 → 主网络 → FDY

纤维及制品特点
Features of fibers and finished products

主要规格 Main Specifications
长丝：56dtex/24f，84dtex/32f，111dtex/48f FDY
Filament: 56dtex/24f, 84dtex/32f, 111dtex/48f FDY

相关标准 Relative Standards
《聚对苯二甲酸丙二醇酯/聚对苯二甲酸乙二醇酯(PTT/PET) 复合牵伸丝》(FZ/T 54094—2017)
Polytrimethylene terephthalate/polydimethylene terephthalate (PTT/PET) composite drawn yarn (FZ/T 54094—2017)

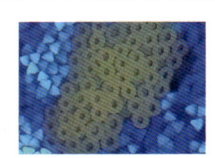

rPET/PTT 双中空复合弹性纤维长丝和截面图
Filament yarn and sectional figure of rPET/PTT double-hollow composite elastic fiber

纤维性能与制品特点

- 循环再利用与生物基结合、资源高值化利用。
- 8 字中空结构、密度低、材质轻盈。
- 弹性永久、回弹性卓越、能够快速恢复原状。
- 优异的保暖性及良好的透气性。

Properties of fibers and features of finished products

- Combination of recycling and bio-based materials.
- 8-shaped hollow structure, low density, light weight.
- Long-lasting elasticity, excellent rebound resilience, ability to recover quickly.
- Excellent thermal-retention property and good air permeability.

rPET/PTT 双中空复合弹性纤维性能指标
Performance indexes of rPET/PTT double-hollow composite elastic fiber

产品规格 Specification	断裂强度 (cN/dtex) Breaking tenacity (cN/dtex)	断断裂伸长率 (%) Elongation at break (%)	沸水收缩率 (%) Boiling water shrinkage rate (%)	干热卷曲伸长 (%) Dry-thermal curling elongation(%)	干热收缩率 (%) Dry-thermal shrinkage (%)	干热卷曲收缩 (%) Dry-thermal curling shrinkage (%)	含油率 (%) Heat retention rate (%)
84dtex/32f	3.34	32.60	8.60	72.4	6.0	42.3	1.30

面料成分 Fabric composition	保温率 (%) Heat retention rate (%)	传热系数 [W/(m²·°C)] Heat transfer coefficient [W/(m²·°C)]	克罗值 (clo) Clo value(clo)
50% rPET/PTT 双中空复合弹性纤维 /50% 常规涤纶 50% rPET/PTT double-hollow composite elastic fiber/ 50% conventional dacron	11.94	73.28	0.09

下游应用指导
The downstream application guidance

织造： 可与其他纤维进行交织，用于制作针织与机织面料。
染整： 使用分散染料，坯布染色前需预收缩、预定形，染色温度建议 125°C。

Weaving: Can be interwoven with other fibers to produce both knitted and woven fabrics.
Dyeing and finishing: Use dispersive dyes. The gray fabric needs to be pre-shrunk and pre-set before dyeing. The recommended dyeing temperature is 125°C .

纤维应用
Application of fibers

| 服装用纺织品
Clothing textiles | 休闲服
Leisure wear | 运动服
Sportswear | 羽绒服
Down jacket | 高端成衣
High-end ready-to-wear |

| 家用纺织品
Home textiles | 地毯
Carpet | 沙发布
Sofa fabric |

| 产业用纺织品
Industrial textiles | 户外用品
Outdoor product |

rPET/PTT 双中空复合弹性纤维制品
Products of applications for rPET/PTT double-hollow composite elastic fiber

Q & A

Q: 8字形中空结构设计相比单孔中空纤维、常规双组分弹性，为何更具优势？

A: 8字形中空结构的设计比单孔中空纤维，在隔热性、回弹性等方面更加优异，双中空结构承托力分布平均，加强了纤维的抱合力与保暖性能，有效提升纤维的抗弯模量。相对于传统双组分弹性纤维，8字形中空结构的纤维具有更出色的立体感和蓬松性。此外，该纤维融合了生物基材料与循环再利用材料的优势，实现了绿色、低碳、环保的完美结合，契合可持续发展趋势。

Q: Why does the 8-shaped hollow structure design have more advantages compared to single-hole hollow fiber and conventional two-component elastic fiber?

A: Compared to single-hole hollow fiber, the 8-shaped hollow structure design exhibits superior performance in terms of thermal insulation and rebound resilience. The double-hollow structure distributes the supporting force evenly, enhancing the cohesive force and thermal-retention properties of the fiber, and increasing the bending modulus of the fiber effectively. While compared to conventional two-component elastic fiber, the fiber with an 8-shaped hollow structure possesses more prominent three-dimensional effects and fluffiness. Furthermore, this fiber integrates bio-based materials with recycled materials, achieving a perfect combination of greenness, low-carbon, and environmental protection, and fitting into sustainable development.

双组分复合聚酰胺纤维
Biocomponent Composite Polyamide Fiber

推荐理由： 以生物基聚酰胺 PA56 为核心材料，碳排放量更低，环保优势突出。纤维良好的弹性与染色性，拓展弹性面料产品多样性，为高品质纺织品增值赋能。

Reasons for recommendation
With bio-based polyamide (PA56) as the core material, it has lower carbon emissions, exhibiting prominent advantages in environmental protection. Its excellent elasticity and dyeability expand the diversity of elastic fabric products, adding value to high-quality textiles.

伊纶 EYLON

● 入选企业 COMPANY
黑龙江伊品新材料有限公司
Heilongjiang Eppen New Materials Co., Ltd.

制备技术
Preparative technique

由 PA56 与 PA6 共聚生成新的高分子化合物，然后与 PA56 结合，采用并列复合喷丝组件，经双组分熔融纺丝工艺制备，通过缩率不同实现纤维弹性。

The copolymer synthesized from PA56 and PA6, which is combined with PA56 and then undergoes side-by-side composite spinneret assembly and bicomponent melt spinning processes. The elasticity of the fiber is achieved through different shrinkage rates.

纤维及制品特点
Features of fibers and finished products

主要规格 Main Specifications
长丝：78dtex/48f FDY
Filament: 78dtex/48f FDY

相关标准 Relative Standards
《聚对苯二甲酸丙二醇酯/聚对苯二甲酸乙二醇酯 (PTT/PET) 复合弹力丝》（FZ/T 54041—2011）
Polytrimethylene terephthalate/polydimethylene terephthalate (ptt/pet) co-elastic yarns (FZ/T 54041—2011)

双组分复合聚酰胺长丝及其截面图
Filament yarn and sectional figure of bicomponent composite polyamide fiber

纤维性能与制品特点
- 生物基聚酰胺56的含量提升。
- 弹性良好，纤维弹性实现面料层面的无氨弹力。
- 面料抗皱、亲肤透气、染色性优良。

Properties of fibers and features of finished products
- Increased content of bio-based polyamide 56.
- Good elasticity; the elasticity of the fiber enables ammonia-free elasticity at the fabric level.
- Anti-crease, skin-friendly, breathable fabric with good dyeability.

双组分复合聚酰胺纤维性能指标
Performance indexes of bicomponent composite polyamide fiber

产品规格 Specifications	断裂强度 (cN/dtex) Breaking tenacity (cN/dtex)	断裂伸长率 (%) Elongation at break (%)	卷曲收缩率 (%) Crimp shrinkage (%)	沸水收缩率 (%) Boiling water shrinkage (%)	色牢度 (级) Color fastness (grade)
78dtex/48f	3.18	38	32	11	4

下游应用指导
The downstream application guidance

织造：适用于针机织，需要根据产品的缩率回复率合理安排幅宽、织造密度等参数。
染色：建议使用低温染色，升温速度减慢，染色温度≤98°C。
定形：染色后成品定形温度建议165°C，视颜色深浅酌情调整温度和速度。

Weaving: Suitable for both knitting and weaving; such parameters as width and weaving density should be reasonably arranged based on the shrinkage recovery rate of the product.

Dyeing: It is recommended to use low-temperature dyeing with a slower heating rate. The dyeing temperature should be ≤98°C.

Setting: For the setting process of the finished product after dyeing, it is recommended to use the temperature of 165 °C, with adjustments to temperature and speed made as appropriate depending on the shade of the color.

双组分复合聚酰胺纤维应用实例
Examples of applications for bicomponent composite polyamide fiber

终端领域 Terminal field	原料配比 Raw material ratio	纤维规格 Fiber specifications	产品特性 Product features
高端成衣 High-end tailoring	100%	77dtex/48f	成形性好、永久弹性、吸湿排汗 Good moldability, permanent elasticity, and moisture absorption and perspiration

纤维应用
Application of fibers

| 服装用纺织品
Clothing textiles | 休闲服
Leisure wear | 运动服
Sportswear | 贴身内衣
Lingerie |

Q：从市场需求的角度分析，双组分复合聚酰胺纤维有何特点？
A：采用生物基聚酰胺 PA56 与 PA6 共聚，实现低碳环保的目的。符合单一组分的可持续设计理念。在弹性面料开发上，可以替代添加氨纶的方案，实现良好的弹性和染色性。

Q: From the perspective of market demand, what are the characteristics of the bicomponent composite polyamide fiber?
A: The copolymerization of bio-based PA56 with PA6 can achieve the goal of low carbon and environmental protection. It aligns with the sustainable design concept of a single component. For the development of elastic fabric, it serves as an alternative to adding elastane, achieving good elasticity and dyeability.

PTT 复合弹性纤维
PTT Composite Elastic Fiber

推荐理由： 融合基体弹性与卷曲弹性的全新无氨弹纤维品种。兼具卓越拉伸与回弹率，受力形变后能迅速复原。其面料柔软亲肤，舒适、轻薄，色彩表现力强。

Reasons for recommendation
A new type of ammonia-free elastic fiber that combines matrix elasticity with curling elasticity. It possesses both excellent tensile strength and rebound rate and can quickly recover after deformation under stress. The fabric is soft and skin-friendly, comfortable, lightweight, and has strong color expression.

柏黛尔 BIODEX

● 入选企业 COMPANY
上海华灏化学有限公司
HH Chemical Co., Ltd.

制备技术
Preparative technique

以含有 38% 生物基的高低黏度 PTT 聚合物为原料，采用并列型复合喷丝板组件，通过熔融纺丝工艺制备纤维。

With 38% bio-based PTT polymers of varying viscosity as the raw materials, the side-by-side composite spinneret board assembly is adopted to produce the fiber through melt spinning process.

纤维及制品特点
Features of fibers and finished products

主要规格 Main Specifications
长丝：56dtex/24f，84dtex/34f，167dtex/34f DTY
Filament: 56dtex/24f, 84dtex/34f, 167dtex/34f DTY

相关标准 Relative Standards
《聚对苯二甲酸丙二醇酯 (PTT) 弹力丝》
(FZ/T 54020—2009)
Polyptrimethylene terephthalate drawn textured yarns
(FZ/T 54020—2009)

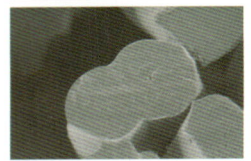

PTT 复合弹性纤维及截面图
Filament yarn and sectional figure of PTT composite elastic fiber

纤维性能与制品特点
- 生物基含量 38%，植物来源亲肤舒适。
- 优异的弹性及回复率，弹力是普通 T400 纤维的 3 倍。
- 染色性好，色彩鲜艳饱满。
- 柔软蓬松、挺括轻薄、抗污性好。

Properties of fibers and features of finished products
- 38% bio-based content, which is derived from plants, skin-friendly and comfort.
- Excellent elasticity and recovery rate, with an elasticity that is three times that of ordinary T400 fiber.
- Good dyeability, bright and vivid color.
- Soft and fluffy, stiff and lightweight, good stain-resistant property.

PTT 复合弹性纤维性能指标
Performance indexes of PTT composite elastic fiber

产品规格 Specifications	断裂强度 (cN/dtex) Breaking tenacity (cN/dtex)	断裂伸长率 (%) Elongation at break (%)	干热卷曲伸长率 (%) Dry-thermal curling elongation (%)	含油率 (%) Oil content (%)	网络度 (个/米) Network density (Pc/m)
84dtex/48f	≥ 2.1	20.5±5	117	3.0±0.3	120±5

下游应用指导
The downstream application guidance

织造： 应保持开口清晰；尽量降低上机张力的设定值以减少断头现象；适当抬高后梁高度降低上层经纱张力，以改善布面外观质量。

染整： 织物进行批量染整前，需进行染整测试，以确定温度、酸碱性介质等适合的染整条件。染色温度控制在 80°C，精练温度为 80°C，时间为 15min，使用除油剂和醋酸进行中和。

Weaving: The opening should be kept clear; the setting value of loom tension should be minimized to reduce yarn breaks; and the height of the back beam should be appropriately raised to reduce the tension of the upper warp yarns, thus improving the appearance quality of the fabric.

Dyeing and finishing: Before the fabrics being dyed and finished in bulk, dyeing and finishing tests are required to determine the suitable dyeing and finishing conditions such as temperature, acid and alkaline media, etc. The dyeing temperature should be controlled at 80°C, the refining temperature should be 80°C, and the period should be 15 minutes. Degreaser and acetate should be used for neutralization.

PTT 复合弹性纤维下游应用实例
Examples of downstream applications for PTT composite elastic fiber

终端领域 Terminal field	原料配比 Raw material ratio	规格 Specifications	产品主要特性 Main properties of the product
运动外套 Sportswear	100% PTT 复合弹性纤维 100% PTT composite elastic fiber	165dtex/72f	柔软蓬松、亲肤、有弹性 Soft and fluffy, skin-friendly, and elastic

纤维应用
Application of fibers

| 服装用纺织品
Clothing textiles | 休闲服
Leisure wear | 运动服
Sportswear |

| 家用纺织品
Home textiles | 床上寝具
Bedding |

Q & A

Q: PTT 复合弹性纤维未来会在哪些领域有所应用？

A: 随着科技的进步和纤维行业的发展，PTT 复合弹性纤维的市场需求逐步增长。该纤维因其较好的弹性、抗污性、色牢度和手感等特点，可用于各类纺织品制造，如运动服、休闲装、内衣、沙发面料等，深受消费者欢迎；因较好的耐磨性、耐热性和弹性使纤维在汽车座椅、内饰板、顶棚、地毯等领域有广阔前景；在建筑、医疗、体育休闲等领域，如建筑安全网、手术衣、绷带、运动装备等方面也有很好的应用潜力。

Q: In which fields will PTT composite elastic fiber be applied in the future?

A: With advancements in technology and the development of the fiber industry, the market demand for PTT composite elastic fiber is gradually increasing. For its good elasticity, stain-resistance, color fastness, and hand feeling, the fiber can be used in the production of various textiles such as sportswear, leisurewear, underwear, sofa fabrics, etc., which are deeply welcomed by consumers. For its good abrasion-resistance, heat-resistance, and elasticity, the fiber has broad prospects in the fields of automotive seating, interior trim panels, ceilings, carpets, etc. In addition, it also has great application potential in construction, medical, sports, and leisure fields, such as in construction safety nets, surgical gowns, bandages, sports equipment, and other aspects.

超低温易定形氨纶
Ultra-low Temperature Easy-to-set Elastane

推荐理由：可在超低温条件下定形，具有高热定形效率。能与丙纶、聚乳酸纤维等耐热性较差的纤维进行交织，拓宽氨纶应用领域。

Reasons for recommendation
It can be set at ultra-low temperature with high efficiency. It can be interwoven with fibers with poor heat resistance, such as polypropylene fiber and polylactic acid fiber, broadening the application fields of elastane.

千禧 QIANXI **安优卡 ANYOUKA** **BANGTAI 邦泰**

● 入选企业 COMPANY
华峰化学股份有限公司
Huafon Chemical Co., Ltd.
河北邦泰氨纶科技有限公司
Hebei Bangtai Spandex Technology Co., Ltd.

制备技术
Preparative technique

千禧纤维 QIANXI Fiber

干纺工艺：以聚醚多元醇、二异氰酸酯为原料，小分子二元醇为扩链剂，通过逐步聚合反应生产聚氨酯脲溶液，然后将低熔点母液与聚氨酯脲溶液混合，生产出在超低温下具有高热定形效率的聚氨酯脲纺丝液，最后经干法纺丝技术制备纤维。

Dry-spinning process: With polyether polyol and diisocyanate as raw materials, and small molecule dihydric alcohol as chain extender, stepwise polymerization is used to produce polyurethane-urea solution. Subsequently, the low-melting point mother solution is mixed with polyurethane-urea solution to produce a polyurethane-urea spinning solution with high heat-setting efficiency at ultra-low temperature. Finally, the dry-spinning technology is used to produce the fiber.

安优卡纤维 ANYOUKA Fiber

熔纺工艺：将多元醇、二异氰酸酯、扩链剂预热经灌注机后反应挤出切片，氨纶切片经熔融纺丝制备纤维。采用无溶剂的熔纺工艺，更加绿色环保。

Melt-spinning process: Polyhydric alcohols, diisocyanate, and chain extender are preheated and undergo bottler for reaction and extrusion into chips. Then, the elastane chips are processed through melt spinning to produce the fiber. The solvent-free melt spinning process is adopted, which is more environmentally friendly and green.

纤维及制品特点
Features of fibers and finished products

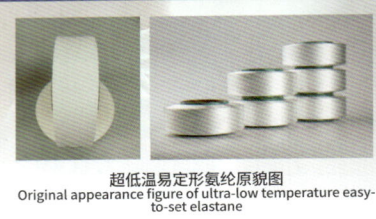

主要规格 Main Specifications
长丝：20~40旦（千禧）
20旦，30旦，40旦，70旦（安优卡）
Filament: 20~40D(QIAN XI)
20D, 30D, 40D, 70D (ANYOUKA)

超低温易定形氨纶原貌图
Original appearance figure of ultra-low temperature easy-to-set elastane

相关标准 Relative Standards
千禧纤维可参照《超低温易定形氨纶长丝》(Q/HFHX-J01003—2024)
安优卡纤维可参照《超低温定形熔纺氨纶长丝》(Q/B HBBT01—2024)

For QIANXI fiber, refer to Ultra-low temperature easy-to-set elastane filament yarns (Q/HFHX-J01003—2024)

For ANYOUKA fiber, refer to Ultra-low temperature easy-to-set elastane filament yarns (Q/B HBBT01—2024)

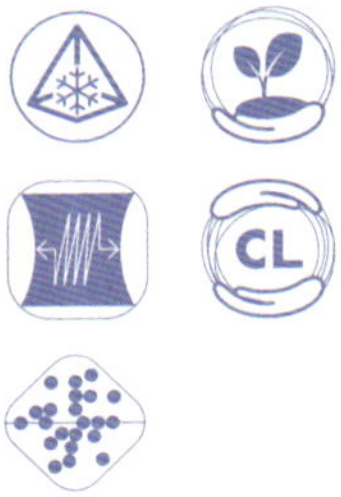

纤维性能与制品特点
- 定形温度较低，满足120~130°C的定形需求，织造工序能耗大幅降低。
- 回弹速度快，布面不易卷边、更平整美观、柔软舒适。
- 耐氯、条干更均匀。

Properties of fibers and features of finished products
- Lower setting temperature, fulfilling the setting requirements of 120~130°C; significantly energy consumption reduction in weaving process.
- Fast rebound speed, fabric edges less prone to curling, smoother and more beautiful, soft and comfortable.
- Resistant to chlorine, more uniform yarn levelness.

超低温易定形氨纶性能指标
Performance indexes of ultra-low temperature easy-to-set elastane

产品规格 Specifications	断裂强度 (cN/dtex) Breaking tenacity (cN/dtex)	断裂伸长率(%) Elongation at break (%)	300%伸长强度 (cN/dtex)(%) 300% elongation strength (cN/dtex)(%)	300%伸长弹性回复率(%) 300% elongation elastic recovery rate(%)	干热定形效率(%) Dry-heat setting efficiency(%)	湿热定形效率(%) Wet-heat setting efficiency(%)	织物缩水率(%) Fabric shrinkage rate (%)	纤维品牌 Fiber brand
20旦 20D	≥0.85	500±40	0.27±0.04	≥88.0	≥90 (140°C条件下)	≥70 (100°C条件下)	(丙纶+超低温易定形氨纶)5.0 (Polypropylene fiber + ultra-low temperature easy-to-set elastane) 5.0	千禧 QIANXI
30旦 30D	≥1.25	500±40	0.30±0.05	≥90.0	≥90 (120°C条件下)	≥92 (120°C条件下)	(聚乳酸+超低温易定形氨纶)2.0 (Polylactic acid + ultra-low temperature easy-to-set elastane) 2.0	安优卡 ANYOUKA

下游应用指导
The downstream application guidance

千禧纤维 QIANXI Fiber
定形处理工序时需考虑敏感主纱纤定形温度,以达到常规氨纶的定形效果。

During the setting process, it is necessary to consider the setting temperature for sensitive main yarn fiber to achieve the setting effect comparable to that of conventional elastane.

安优卡纤维 ANYOUKA Fiber
织造:双面 28G 大圆机的牵伸比建议 ≤ 2.6,单面 28G 大圆机的牵伸比建议 ≤ 2.7,包覆纱牵伸比建议 1.6~3.0。

定形:定形温度建议 120~130°C,定形时间 50~80s。

染色:建议染色温度不超过 110°C,染液酸碱 pH 适合范围为 3~11。

Weaving: The recommended drawing ratio for a double-sided 28G large circular knitting machine is ≤ 2.6 times, while for a single-sided 28G large circular knitting machine, it is ≤ 2.7 times. For wrap yarn, the recommended drawing ratio is 1.6~3.0 times.

Setting: The recommended setting temperature is 120~130° C, and the period is 50~80 seconds.

Dyeing: The recommended dyeing temperature is ≤ 110°C , and the suitable pH range of dyeing solution is 3~11.

超低温易定形氨纶下游应用实例
Examples of downstream applications for ultra-low temperature easy-to-set elastane

终端领域 Terminal field	原料配比 Raw material ratio	纤维规格 Fiber specifications	产品特性 Product features	纤维品牌 Fiber brand
针织面料 Knitted fabric	71% 聚乳酸纤维 /29% 超低温易定形氨纶 71% polylactic acid fiber /29% ultra-low temperature easy-to-set elastane	30 旦半消光 30D semi-dull	聚乳酸纤维专用超低温易定形氨纶 Special ultra-low temperature easy-to-set elastane for polylactic acid fiber	安优卡 ANYOUKA

纤维应用
Application of fibers

| 服装用纺织品
Clothing textiles | 运动服
Sportswear | 袜子
Socks | 泳衣
Swimsuit | 瑜伽服
Yoga clothes |

Q:超低温易定形氨纶的性能和下游应用优势体现在哪里?

A:普通氨纶定形温度在 190~205°C 之间,而丙纶、聚乳酸纤维等纤维需要在较低温度下定形。超低温易定形氨纶显著降低了热定形温度,可使定形温度为 120~130°C,染色温度为 110°C,解决了无法与丙纶、聚乳酸纤维等耐热性低的纤维共同交织的难题,可广泛应用于运动服、泳衣、紧身衣等领域。

Q: What are the performance advantages and downstream application benefits of ultra-low temperature easy-to-set elastane?

A: The setting temperature for ordinary elastane ranges between 190~205° C, whereas fibers such as polypropylene fiber and polylactic acid fiber need to be set at lower temperatures. The heat-setting temperature of ultra-low temperature easy-to-set elastane is significantly reduced that it can be set at 120~130°C and dyed at 110°C . This enables it to be interwoven with fibers that have low heat resistance, such as polypropylene fiber and polylactic acid fiber, making it widely used in fields such as sportswear, swimwear, and tights.

FIBER · BEYOND THE LIMIT

科技迭变，功能破界

科技的不断进步逐渐打破纤维的功能界限。十字形、8字形、中空、毛毛虫形截面、吸湿透气、抗紫外、防透、抑菌除臭、蓄热锁温、持续凉感……结构的多样性与功能的复合升级，为纤维材料注入新的灵魂，铸就卓越品质。多重功能守护，在冬日送来温暖，给夏日带来清凉，构筑健康屏障。让我们尽情拥抱阳光、无畏风雨、不惧严寒，领略生活的多姿与美好，畅享缤纷体验。

Advancing science and technology to break through the boundaries of functionalities

Continuous advancements in science and technology have gradually broken through the boundary of fiber's functionality. Updated structural varieties and functionalities in various combinations, e.g. fibers with cross-sections in the shapes of a cross, 8, and a caterpillar, hollow fibers, fibers that absorb moisture and let in air, fibers that protect against ultraviolet rays, fibers that prevent ventilation, fibers that fight off bacteria and eliminate foul odor, fibers that accumulate heat and keep temperature unchanged, fibers that keep giving a cool feel, breathe new life into fiber materials, delivering exceptional quality. They afford protection with multiple functionalities, provide warmth on winter days, give a cool feel on summer days, form a shield to prevent any damage to health. Let's enjoy ourselves to the utmost in the sun, brave the wind and rain, dare to be out in the cold, have a taste of a colorful and wonderful life, and go through an exhilarating experience.

62　抗紫外纤维
ANTI-ULTRAVIOLET FIBER

75　保暖纤维
THERMAL FIBER

中国纤维流行趋势

纤·破界

纤
FIBER BEYOND THE LIMIT
China Fibers Fashion Trends
2025/2026

抗紫外纤维
ANTI-ULTRAVIOLET FIBER

抗紫外纤维作为夏日服饰面料的好伴侣，营造轻松「夏」。抗紫外及多功能母粒的添加，结合十字、毛毛虫等异形截面，使抗紫外纤维与功能碰撞组合，让我们的肌肤抵挡骄阳暴晒的同时，或远离闷热不透气，或感受吸湿速干，或拥有持续凉爽，或体验服装轻薄不透，时刻迎接缤纷呈现的美好时光。

Anti-ultraviolet fiber makes the perfect companion for summer clothing fabrics, bringing you a relaxed summer. The addition of anti-ultraviolet and multifunctional master batches, combined with deformed sections such as cruciform and caterpillar, creates a unique blend of anti-ultraviolet fiber and various functionalities. This allows our skin to be protected from the intense sun while avoiding the discomfort of heat and poor air permeability, experiencing moisture-absorption and quick-drying properties, enjoying continuous coolness, or feeling the lightweight yet anti-see-through fabric. It prepares us to embrace every colorful and wonderful moment.

推荐纤维及品牌

吸湿速干抗紫外聚酯纤维
Moisture-absorption and Quick-drying Anti-ultraviolet Polyester Fiber

防透抗紫外循环再利用聚酯纤维
Anti-see-through and Anti-ultraviolet Recycled Polyester Fiber

遮热抗紫外聚酰胺 6 纤维
Heat-shielding and Anti-ultraviolet Polyamide 6 Fiber

防勾丝抗紫外聚酰胺 6 纤维
Anti-snagging and Anti-ultraviolet Polyamide 6 Fiber

天科 TIANKE 361° Different 德福伦 佳人新材料 JIAREN NEW MATERIALS 锦康纱 JIN KANG SHA Huading 华鼎股份

吸湿速干抗紫外聚酯纤维
Moisture-absorption and Quick-drying Anti-ultraviolet Polyester Fiber

推荐理由： 纤维具有抗紫外、遮热、导湿快干功能，可使肌肤远离骄阳，保持干爽感，是夏日服饰面料的好伴侣。

Reasons for recommendation
The fiber, featuring anti-ultraviolet, heat shielding, moisture-absorption and quick-drying capabilities, keeps skin protected from intense sun and maintains a dry and comfortable feeling. It is the perfect companion for summer clothing fabrics.

入选企业 COMPANY
杭州天科纺织有限公司
Hangzhou Tianke Textile Co., Ltd.
三六一度（中国）有限公司
361°(China) Co., Ltd.

制备技术
Preparative technique

将一定比例的抗紫外功能母粒与聚酯切片共混，通过异形喷丝板，经熔融纺丝工艺制备纤维。

A certain proportion of anti-ultraviolet functional master batches are blended with polyester pellets, and then processed through a deformed spinneret plate to produce the fiber through the melt spinning technique.

纤维及制品特点
Features of fibers and finished products

主要规格 Main Specifications
长丝：50dtex/48f DTY
Filament: 50dtex/48f DTY

相关标准 Relative Standards
《涤纶低弹丝》（GB/T 14460—2015）
Polyester draw textured yarns
(GB/T 14460—2015)

纤维原貌图
Original appearance figure of the fiber

纤维截面图
Cross-section figure of the fiber

吸湿速干抗紫外聚酯纤维原貌和截面图
Original appearance figure and cross-sectional figure of moisture-absorption and quick-drying anti-ultraviolet polyester fiber

纤维性能与制品特点

- 十字异形截面设计，使汗水经过芯吸、传输、扩散的过程，迅速迁移至织物表面并散发出去，达到导湿速干效果。
- 抗紫外性能 UPF50+，T(UVA)4.44%。

Properties of fibers and features of finished products

- Cruciform section design, which allows sweat to be quickly transported to the fabric surface and evaporated in the process of wicking, transporting, and diffusing, and achieves the effect of moisture-absorption and quick-drying.
- Anti-ultraviolet performance UPF50+, T(UVA) 4.44%.

吸湿速干抗紫外聚酯纤维性能指标
Performance indexes of moisture-absorption and quick-drying anti-ultraviolet polyester fiber

产品规格 Specifications	断裂强度 (cN/dtex) Breaking strength (cN/dtex)	断裂伸长率 (%) Elongation at break (%)	卷曲收缩率 (%) Curling shrinkage rate(%)	卷曲稳定性 (%) Curling stability(%)	沸水收缩率 (%) Boiling water shrinkage rate (%)
50dtex/48f	3.82	23.98	12.05	78.30	3.05

面料检测 (100% 本纤维)
Fabric testing (100% this fiber)

抗紫外性 Anti-ultraviolet performance	遮热率 (%) Heat-shielding rate (%)	抗起球 (圆规迹法, 级) Anti-pilling (Circular locus method, grade)	芯吸高度 (mm) Wicking height(mm)	吸水率 (%) Water absorption (%)	滴水扩散时间 (s) Drip diffusion time (s)	干燥速率 (g/h) Drying rate (g/h)
UPF：79 T(UVA)：4.44% T(UVB)：0.77%	34.0	3	>200	282	<1.0	≥ 0.20

下游应用指导
The downstream application guidance

织造：可直接用于织造针织面料或机织面料。
染整：参考常规聚酯纤维。

Weaving: It can be directly used for weaving knitted fabrics or woven fabrics.
Dyeing and finishing: Refer to conventional polyester fibers.

纤维应用
Application of fibers

服装用纺织品 Clothing textiles	专业运动服 Professional sportswear	T恤 T-shirt
产业用纺织品 Industrial textiles	户外用品 Outdoor products	

Q：纤维及织物抗紫外功能的原理及影响因素主要有哪些？

A： 抗紫外纤维是一种能够有效防止紫外线透过的纤维材料，其原理是通过添加具有反射和散射紫外线功能的添加剂，有效阻隔紫外线抵达人体皮肤，进而起到防晒的作用。纤维的截面形状和织物结构会影响其抗紫外性能，表面越光滑、表面积越大的纤维抗紫外效果越好。此外，孔隙率低、厚而密的织物有更好的抗紫外效果。

Q: What are the main principles and influencing factors of the anti-ultraviolet function in fibers and fabrics?

A: Anti-ultraviolet fiber is a type of fiber material that can effectively prevent the penetration of ultraviolet rays. Its principle involves the addition of additives that have the function of reflecting and scattering ultraviolet rays, effectively blocking ultraviolet rays from reaching human skin and serving as a sunscreen. The section shape of the fiber and the structure of the fabric will affect their anti-ultraviolet performance. Fibers with smoother surfaces and larger surface areas tend to have better anti-ultraviolet performance. Fabrics with low porosity and that are thick and dense have better anti-ultraviolet performance.

防透抗紫外循环再利用聚酯纤维
Anti-see-through and Anti-ultraviolet Recycled Polyester Fiber

推荐理由：循环再利用聚酯纤维功能化，抗紫外和舒适性统一，在夏季白色服装轻薄不透的应用场景中非常实用。

Reasons for recommendation
The functionalized recycled polyester fiber, combining anti-ultraviolet property and comfort, is highly practical for lightweight and anti-see-through white summer clothing application scenarios.

入选企业 COMPANY
上海德福伦新材料科技有限公司
Shanghai Different Advanced Material Co., Ltd.
浙江佳人新材料有限公司
Zhejiang Jiaren New Materials Co., Ltd.

制备技术
Preparative technique

将高分散性抗紫外功能母粒与采用物理或化学法制备的再生聚酯切片共混，通过异形喷丝板，经熔融纺丝工艺制备纤维。

The highly-dispersive anti-ultraviolet functional master batches are blended with the recycled polyester pellets prepared through physical or chemical methods, and then processed through a deformed spinneret plate to produce the fiber through the melt spinning technique.

纤维及制品特点
Features of fibers and finished products

主要规格 Main Specifications
短纤（物理法再生）：1.11dtex×38mm
长丝（化学法再生）：84dtex/36f，84dtex/72f，111dtex/36f，111dtex/96f，111dtex/144f，167dtex/48f，167dtex/96f，167dtex/144f，167dtex/288f，333dtex/96f DTY
Staple (Regenerated by physical method)：1.11dtex×38mm
Filament (Regenerated by chemical method)：84dtex/36f，84dtex/72f，111dtex/36f，111dtex/96f，111dtex/144f，167dtex/48f，167dtex/96f，167dtex/144f，167dtex/288f，333dtex/96f DTY

相关标准 Relative Standards
《再生涤纶短纤维》（FZ/T 52010—2014）
《循环再利用涤纶低弹丝》（FZ/T 54047—2020）
Recycled polyester staple fiber (FZ/T 52010—2014)
Recycled poly (ethylene terephthalate) drawn textured yarns (FZ/T 54047—2020)

纤维原貌图
Original appearance figure of the fiber

纤维截面图
Cross-section figure of the fiber

防透抗紫外循环再利用聚酯纤维原貌和截面图
Original appearance figure and cross-section figure of anti-see-through and anti-ultraviolet recycled polyester fiber

纤维性能与制品特点

- 循环再利用、绿色环保。
- 抗紫外、防透性能优异。
- 棉柔手感、蓬松性和透气性。

Properties of fibers and features of finished products

- Recycling, green and environmentally friendly.
- Excellent anti-ultraviolet and anti-see-through performance.
- Cotton-like softness, fluffiness, and air permeability.

防透抗紫外循环再利用聚酯纤维性能指标
Performance indexes of anti-see-through and anti-ultraviolet recycled polyester fiber

产品规格 Specifications	断裂强度 (cN/dtex) Breaking strength (cN/dtex)	断断裂伸长率 (%) Elongation at break (%)	卷曲数 (个/25mm) Curl Amount (Pc/25mm)	卷曲收缩率 (%) Curling shrinkage rate(%)	线密度偏差率 (%) Thread density deviation rate (%)	长度偏差率 (%) Length deviation rate (%)	疵点含量 (mg/100mg) Defect content (mg/100mg)	干热收缩率 (%) Dry-thermal shrinkage (%)
1.11dtex×38mm	5.1	21.7	12	12.0	2.3	−2.4	2.4	7.1
84dtex/72f	3.68	20.93	—	12.52	2.50	—	—	—

面料检测 (100% 本纤维) Fabric testing (100% this fiber)			
抗紫外性 Anti-ultraviolet performance	防透级别（级） Anti-see-through grade (grade)	防透指数 Anti-see-through index	耐光黄变色牢度（级） Color fastness to light yellowing (grade)
UPF : 1300 UVA : 0.60% UVB : 0.05%	5	99.6	4
UPF : 1300 UVA : 0.60% UVB : 0.05%	5	96.5	4

下游应用指导
The downstream application guidance

短纤的应用指导 Guide on the applications of staple fiber

纺纱：采用短纤维纺纱，推荐纺纱支数 20~60 英支。

织造：采用短纤维混纺时，推荐纤维含量≥ 30%。

Spinning: When using staple fiber for spinning, it is recommended to use yarn 20~60^S.

Weaving: When blending with staple fibers, it is recommended that the fiber content is ≥ 30%.

长丝的应用指导 Guide on the applications of filament yarn

前定形：预定形温度 160~170°C，适当加大超喂量，幅宽适当收窄。

前处理：入缸除油尽量干净，尽快进入下一工序，避免浮油沾附布面形成色花；缸内做前处理，务必添加缸中柔软剂，防止擦伤。

染色：同涤纶常规染色工艺，水流速度适当减缓。如遇含氨纶面料，必须采用和缓的温度处理，且需防止分散染料沾污氨纶组分造成牢度降低现象。

后整理：后定形温度建议 160~170°C。

Pre-setting: The pre-setting temperature should be 160~170°C , with an appropriate increase in overfeed and a slight narrowing of fabric width.

Pre-treatment: De-oil as clean as possible before putting it into the vat, and enter the next process as soon as possible to avoid oil slick sticking to the fabric surface to form a dyeing defect; for pre-treatment in the vat, add vat softener to prevent fabric scraping.

Dyeing: Follow the conventional dyeing process for dacron, with an appropriate reduction in water flow rate; for fabrics containing elastane, the gentle temperature treatment must be adopted, and it is necessary to prevent dispersed dyes from staining the elastane component, which may lead to reduced fastness.

Post-finishing: The recommended temperature for post-setting is 160~170°C .

FIBER · BEYOND THE LIMIT

防锈抗紫外线循环再利用聚酯纤维下游应用实例
Examples of downstream applications for anti-see-through and anti-ultraviolet recycled polyester fiber

终端领域 Terminal field	原料配比 Raw material ratio	纤维规格 Fiber specification	产品特性 Properties of the product
机织面料 Woven fabric	42% 锦纶 /31% 防透抗紫外循环再利用聚酯纤维 / 15% 黏胶纤维 /12% 氨纶 42% chinlon /31% anti-see-through and anti-ultraviolet recycled polyester fiber/15% viscose fiber /12% elastane	全消光 1.11dtex×38mm Full-dull 1.11dtex×38mm	四面弹力、防透抗皱、超柔手感、适当凉感 Four-way elasticity, anti-see-through and anti-wrinkle, super-soft hand feeling, and appropriate cool feeling
	100% 防透抗紫外循环再利用聚酯纤维 100% anti-see-through and anti-ultraviolet recycled polyester fiber	全消光 1.11dtex×38mm Full-dull 1.11dtex×38mm	抗紫外、吸湿速干、防透抗皱 Anti-ultraviolet, moisture-absorption and quick-drying, anti-see-through and anti-wrinkle
针织面料 Knitted fabric	87% 防透抗紫外循环再利用聚酯纤维 /13% 氨纶 87% anti-see-through and anti-ultraviolet recycled polyester fiber /13% elastane	半消光 84dtex/72f Semi-dull 84dtex/72f	防透视、防紫外、吸湿排汗 Anti-see-through, anti-ultraviolet, moisture absorption and perspiration

纤维应用
Application of fibers

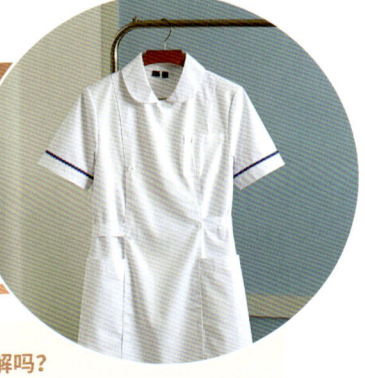

| 服装用纺织品
Clothing textiles | 白色泳衣
Swimsuit | 白色衬衣
Shirt | 白色裤装
White pants | 护士服
Nurse uniform |

| 家用纺织品
Home textiles | 窗帘
Curtain |

Q：防透抗紫外循环再利用聚酯纤维的竞争优势，你了解吗？

A：解决了功能粉体在纤维中均匀分散的技术难题，实现了功能粉体的高比例添加，在提升功能的同时满足了织造服用要求的物化性能。由于纤维本身具备抗紫外及防透视性能，面料无须涂层处理即可达到优于一般涂层面料的效果，同时具有优异的耐水洗色牢度。以循环再利用聚酯为原料生产高品质的差别化纤维，契合可持续发展理念。

Q: Do you know the competitive advantages of anti-see-through and anti-ultraviolet recycled polyester fiber?

A: It solves the technical challenge of evenly dispersing functional powders in fibers, and realizes the addition of a high proportion of functional powders. This not only enhances functionality but also meets the physical and chemical properties required for textile weaving and apparel applications. Given the inherent anti-ultraviolet and anti-see-through properties of the fiber, the fabric can achieve effects superior to those of commonly coated fabrics without the need for coating treatment. Additionally, it possesses excellent washability. The production of high-quality differentiated fibers with recycled polyester as raw material aligns with the concept of sustainable development.

遮热抗紫外聚酰胺 6 纤维
Heat-shielding and Anti-ultraviolet Polyamide 6 Fiber

推荐理由：纤维实现多种功能的叠加，兼具遮热、抗紫外、凉感和透气等性能，在保护皮肤免受紫外线伤害的同时，可有效解决夏季防晒、闷热等问题。

Reasons for recommendation
The fiber achieves the multi-functional integration, possessing heat-shielding, anti-ultraviolet, thermoregulating, and moisture permeability properties, etc. It can effectively protect the skin from ultraviolet injury while addressing issues such as sun protection and stuffiness in summer.

锦康纱 JIN KANG SHA

● 入选企业 COMPANY
福建永荣锦江股份有限公司
Fujian Eversun Jinjiang Co., Ltd.

制备技术
Preparative technique

将具有遮热、抗紫外、凉感的复合纳米级功能母粒与聚酰胺 6 切片共混，结合特殊截面喷丝板，经熔融纺丝制备纤维。

The composite nano-functional master batches with heat-shielding, anti-ultraviolet and thermoregulating properties are blended with polyamide 6 chips, and the spinneret plate with a profiled cross-section is used to produce the fiber through melt spinning.

纤维及制品特点
Features of fibers and finished products

主要规格 Main Specifications
长丝：22dtex/24f，44dtex/34f，77dtex/48f FDY，DTY
Filament: 22dtex/24f, 44dtex/34f, 77dtex/48f FDY, DTY

相关标准 Relative Standards
《锦纶 6 弹力丝》（FZ/T 54007—2019）
《锦纶牵伸丝》（GB/T 16603—2017）

Polyamide 6 drawn textured yarns (FZ/T 54007—2019)
Polyamide drawn yarn (GB/T 16603—2017)

纤维原貌图
Original appearance figure of the fiber

纤维截面图
Cross-section figure of the fiber

遮热抗紫外聚酰胺 6 纤维原貌和截面图
Original appearance figure and cross-sectional figure of heat-shielding and anti-ultraviolet polyamide 6 fiber

纤维性能与制品特点

- 抗紫外性能优异，热量阻隔性良好。
- 接触凉感系数可达到 0.3。
- 轻质、耐磨、透湿性能较好。

Properties of fibers and features of finished products

- Excellent anti-ultraviolet and heat insulation performance.
- Thermoregulating coefficient on contact 0.3.
- Lightweight, and good anti-abrasion and moisture-penetrability performance.

遮热抗紫外聚酰胺 6 纤维性能指标
Performance indexes of heat-shielding and anti-ultraviolet polyamide 6 fiber

产品规格 Specifications	断裂强度 (cN/dtex) Breaking tenacity (cN/dtex)	断裂伸长率 (%) Elongation at break (%)	卷曲数（个/25mm） Number of crimps (Pc/25mm)	卷曲收缩率 (%) Curling shrinkage (%)	卷曲稳定度 (%) Curling stability (%)	热收缩率 (%) Thermal shrinkage (%)	染色性（级） Dyeing performance (grade)
77dtex/48f	4.10	5.87	2	2.32	46.50	4.72	4.5

面料检测 (91% 遮热抗紫外凉感聚酰胺 6 纤维 /9% 氨纶) Fabric testing (91% heat-shielding and anti-ultraviolet polyamide 6 fiber/9% elastane)			
抗紫外性 Anti-ultraviolet performance	遮热率 (%) Heat-shielding rate (%)	接触凉感系数 [J/(cm²·s)] Thermoregulating coefficient on contact [J/(cm²·s)]	透湿性 [g/(m²·24h)] Moisture penetrability [g/(m²·24h)]
UPF：131 T(UVA)：0.80% T(UVB)：0.75%	50.7	0.30	1.04×10^4

下游应用指导
The downstream application guidance

织造：设计合适的布面组织结构，建议纤维使用占比 60% 以上，以确保功能的稳定性。

染整：建议坯布水洗温度设置在 80~90 ℃，染色 pH 控制在 5~6，定形布面温度在 192~200℃。

Design an appropriate fabric weaving structure: It is recommended that the fiber content accounts for more than 60% to ensure the stability of its functions.

Dyeing and finishing: It is recommended to set the washing temperature of the gray fabric at 80~90°C, control the dyeing pH within the range of 5~6, and set the fabric surface setting temperature at 192~200°C.

遮热抗紫外聚酰胺 6 纤维下游应用实例
Examples of downstream applications for heat-shielding and anti-ultraviolet polyamide 6 fiber

终端领域 Terminal field	原料配比 Raw material ratio	纤维规格 Fiber specification	产品特性 Properties of the product
经编面料 Warp knitting fabric	87% 遮热抗紫外聚酰胺 6 纤维 /13% 氨纶 87% Heat-shielding and anti-ultraviolet polyamide 6 fiber/13% elastane	22dtex/16f	四面弹力、凉感 Four-way elasticity, cool feeling
机织面料 Woven fabric	80% 遮热抗紫外聚酰胺 6 纤维 /20% 氨纶 80% heat-shielding and anti-ultraviolet polyamide 6 fiber/20% elastane	44dtex/34f	四面弹力、保形抗皱、适当凉感、超柔贴肤 Four-way elasticity, conformality and anti-wrinkle, appropriate thermoregulating, super-soft against skin

纤维应用
Application of fibers

| 服装用纺织品 Clothing textiles | 运动服 Sportswear | 瑜伽服 Yoga clothes | 鲨鱼裤 Shark pants | 防晒服 Sun-protective clothing |

| 家用纺织品 Home textiles | 汽车内部遮挡布 Car interior cover cloth |

Q&A

Q： 该纤维属于多功能复合纤维，它的功能原理是什么？

A： 该纤维的复合功能源于添加剂、异形截面及材料本身的性能。遮热、抗紫外、凉感源于添加的功能母粒，它能够反射阻隔近红外线及紫外线，有效降低了因吸收近红外线和紫外线而产生的热量；透湿、排汗源于特殊设计的纤维截面，它能够加速汗水排散，进而起到降低体温效果。

Q: The fiber belongs to multifunctional composite fibers. What are the function principles of the fiber?

A: The composite functions of this fiber originate from the additives, its profiled section, and the properties of the materials themselves. The heat-shielding, anti-ultraviolet and thermoregulating properties are derived from the added functional master batches, which can reflect and block near-infrared and ultraviolet rays, effectively reducing the heat generated by the absorption of near-infrared and ultraviolet rays. The moisture permeability and moisture-wicking performance are derived from the specially designed fiber section, which can enhance capillary action for rapid moisture transport, aiding in lowering body temperature.

防勾丝抗紫外聚酰胺 6 纤维
Anti-snagging and Anti-ultraviolet Polyamide 6 Fiber

推荐理由： 抗紫外、抗起毛起球、防勾丝、高耐磨，其面料手感柔糯细腻、耐磨、不变形，可为消费者户外着装提供更佳选择。

Reasons for recommendation
With anti-ultraviolet, anti-pilling, anti-snagging and high abrasion resistance properties, the fabric boasts a soft and delicate touch, durability, and shape retention. It is an excellent choice for consumers' outdoor wear.

华鼎锦纶 Huading

● 入选企业 COMPANY
义乌华鼎锦纶股份有限公司
Yiwu Huading Nylon Co., Ltd.

制备技术
Preparative technique

将抗紫外母粒与聚酰胺 6 切片共混，结合特殊截面设计的喷丝板，经熔融纺丝及特殊高牵伸工艺制备纤维。

The anti-ultraviolet master batches are blended with the polyamide 6 chips, and the spinneret plate with a special cross-section is used to produce the fiber through melt spinning and special high-drawing processes.

纤维及制品特点
Features of fibers and finished products

主要规格 Main Specifications
长丝：78dtex/48f，33dtex/24f FDY
22dtex/12f，44dtex/34f DTY
Filament: 78dtex/48f, 33dtex/24f FDY
22dtex/12f, 44dtex/34f DTY

相关标准 Relative Standards
《锦纶 6 弹力丝》（FZ/T 54007—2019）
《锦纶牵伸丝》（GB/T 16603—2017）
Polyamide 6 drawn textured yarns (FZ/T 54007—2019)
Polyamide drawn yarn (GB/T 16603—2017)

纤维原貌图
Original appearance figure of the fiber

纤维截面图
Cross-section figure of the fiber

防勾丝抗紫外聚酰胺 6 纤维原貌和截面图
Original appearance figuress and cross-sectional figure of anti-snagging and anti-ultraviolet polyamide 6 fiber

纤维性能与制品特点

- 高效抗紫外，异形沟槽截面设计可以吸收与多向反射光线，无惧紫外线。
- 抗起球、防勾丝、耐磨性俱佳。
- 总纤度细、强度高、抗弯刚度小；微管芯吸，兼具吸排、透湿、速干性。
- 织物轻薄柔软、手感爽滑、悬垂性好。

Properties of fibers and features of finished products

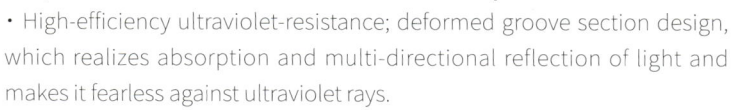

- High-efficiency ultraviolet-resistance; deformed groove section design, which realizes absorption and multi-directional reflection of light and makes it fearless against ultraviolet rays.
- Excellent anti-pilling, anti-snagging and abrasion resistance performance.
- Fine total denier, high strength, low flexural rigidity; microtubule wicking: absorption and perspiration, moisture permeability, and quick-drying.
- Lightweight and soft fabric, smooth hand feeling and good drapability.

防勾丝抗紫外聚酰胺 6 纤维性能指标
Performance indexes of anti-snagging and anti-ultraviolet polyamide 6 fiber

产品规格 Specifications	断裂强度 (cN/dtex) Breaking tenacity (cN/dtex)	断裂伸长率 (%) Elongation at break (%)	断裂强度变异系数 (%) Variable coefficient of break tenacity(%)	断裂伸长率变异系数 (%) Variable coefficient of elongation at break (%)	卷曲稳定度 (%) Curling stability (%)	沸水缩率 (%) Boiling water shrinkage (%)	染色均匀度 (灰卡，级) Dyeing uniformity (gray chip, grade)
44dtex/34f	4.85	40.7	3.07	4.96	61.7	11.30	4~5

面料检测 (88% 本纤维 /12% 氨纶)
Fabric testing (88% this fiber/12% elastane)

抗紫外性 Anti-ultraviolet performance	起毛起球 (圆规迹法，级) Pilling (Circular locus method, grade)	织物勾丝测试 Fabric snagging test	耐磨性能 (次) Abrasion resistance property (times)	吸湿速干性 Moisture absorption and moisture-wicking performance
UPF:1592.34 T(UVA):0.35% T(UVB):0.05%	4~5	经向、纬向 4~5 级 Wrap, weft, Grade 4~5	> 60000	浸湿时间洗前≥ 3 级，洗后≥ 3 级 Soaking time before washing ≥ Grade 3, after washing ≥ Grade 3 吸水速率洗前≥ 3 级，洗后≥ 3 级 Water absorption before washing ≥ Grade 3, after washing ≥ Grade 3

下游应用指导
The downstream application guidance

织造： 直接用于制作机织或针织面料。
染色： 同锦纶常规染色工艺，水流速度适当减缓。
定形： 定形温度建议＜ 200°C，否则面料弹力降低或失去弹性。

Weaving: It can be directly used in woven or knitted fabrics.
Dyeing: Same as the conventional dyeing process of chinlone, with water flow rate being slowed down appropriately.
Setting: The setting temperature is recommended to be ＜ 200°C , otherwise the elasticity of the fabric will be reduced or lost.

防勾丝抗紫外聚酰胺 6 纤维制品
Products of anti-snagging and anti-ultraviolet polyamide 6 fiber

纤维应用
Application of fibers

| 服装用纺织品 Clothing textiles | 运动服 Sportswear | 防晒服 Sun-protective clothing | 登山服 Climbing clothes |

Q: 防勾丝抗紫外聚酰胺 6 纤维与普通抗紫外纤维有什么不同？

A： 防勾丝抗紫外聚酰胺 6 纤维在生产中采用低温高牵伸工艺，在高牵伸过程中，纤维的分子间作用力因被拉伸而增强，纤维的强度也因此提高。该技术主要通过提高单丝断裂强度来避免单丝断裂引起的起毛起球，同时提高产品的防勾丝、耐磨性能。适当降低定形温度可以使长丝避免因为温度过高而发生卷曲的趋势，避免纤维表面的纤维头端增多而相互纠缠，降低起毛起球。此外，采用了特殊的异形截面设计，提高了纤维的比表面积，增强了对紫外线的吸收与反射能力，其沟槽芯吸效果还能改善纤维的吸湿透气性能。

Q: What are the differences between anti-snagging and anti-ultraviolet polyamide 6 fiber and ordinary anti-ultraviolet fiber?

A: The production of anti-snagging and anti-ultraviolet polyamide 6 fiber adopts the low-temperature high-drawing process. During the high-drawing process, the intermolecular forces within the fiber are stretched and strengthened, resulting in increased fiber strength. This technology primarily aims to prevent pilling caused by mono-filament breakage by enhancing the breaking strength of mono-filament, while simultaneously improving the product's anti-snagging and abrasion resistance performance. In addition, appropriately lowering the setting temperature can prevent the filament from curling due to excessive heat, thus avoiding an increase in fiber ends on the fiber surface that may intertwine and cause pilling. Furthermore, the adoption of a special profiled cross-section design increases the specific surface area of the fiber, enhancing its ability to absorb and reflect ultraviolet rays. And the grooved wicking effect improves the fiber's moisture absorption and moisture permeability performance.

保暖纤维
THERMAL FIBER

保暖纤维,把寒风"拒之身外",在秋冬季节里带来温暖如春的呵护。创意五角高中空截面使织物更轻、更暖、更柔软。稀土、植物萃取成分、纳米硅硼化合物、纳米陶瓷等元素添加,实现纤维光能到热能的快速转化及远红外升温,微纳米层叠多孔结构将聚热锁温双倍效应发挥极致。聚丙烯腈纤维改性技术助力织物直达航天级保暖水平。

推荐纤维及品牌

高中空异形聚酯纤维
High Hollow Deformed Polyester Fiber

蓄热锁温抑菌聚酯纤维
Thermal-storage, Heat-retaining and Anti-bacteria Polyester Fiber

稀土改性蓄热聚酰胺 6 纤维
Rare Earth Modified Thermal-storage Polyamide 6 Fiber

保暖聚丙烯腈改性纤维
Thermal Polyacrylonitrile Modified Fiber

春盛 CHUNSHENG　　AIREPAI+热湃　　White-flame 白焰　　ANSINGH 安芯纤维

纤·破界

Thermal fibers keep out the cold wind and bring warmth and care in the fall and winter. An innovative pentagonal ultra-hollow cross-section makes the fabric softer, warmer, and lighter. Rare earths, plant extracts, nano-silicon-boron compounds, nano-ceramics, and other components are added to achieve far-infrared warming and the quick conversion of fiber light energy to heat energy. The micro and nano-layered porous structure also has the dual effect of retaining heat and promoting heat polymerization. The fabric is able to achieve the aircraft's level of warmth thanks to polyacrylonitrile fiber modification technology.

High Hollow Deformed Polyester Fiber
高中空异形聚酯纤维

推荐理由： 创新设计的五角形中空截面改变了纤维承力状态、光反射途径及水在纤维表面的走向，进而赋予织物轻薄、保暖、丰满、柔软、干爽等特征，可广泛用于保暖内衣、贴身内衣、户外运动等领域。

Reasons for recommendation
The novel pentagonal hollow cross-sectional design alters the load-bearing state of the fiber, the pathway for light reflection, and the direction of water on the fiber's surface, giving the fabric its light, warm, plump, soft, dry, and other characteristics. The fiber has many applications in the fields of outdoor sports, skin-fitting underwear, and thermal underwear.

● 入选企业 COMPANY
苏州春盛环保纤维有限公司
Suzhou Chunsheng Environmental Protection Fiber Co., Ltd.

制备技术
Preparative technique

聚酯切片结合五角中空特殊截面设计，经熔融纺丝工艺制备纤维。

The polyester pellets are combined with the special pentagonal hollow cross-sectional design, and prepared by melt spinning process.

纤维及制品特点
Features of fibers and finished products

主要规格 Main Specifications
长丝：55.6dtex/12f FDY
Filament: 55.6dtex/12f FDY

相关标准 Relative Standards
《涤纶牵伸丝》（GB/T 8960—2015）
Polyester drawn yarns (GB/T 8960—2015)

纤维原貌图
Original appearance figure of the fiber

纤维截面图
Cross-section figure of the fiber

高中空异形聚酯纤维原貌和截面图
Original appearance figure and cross-section figure of high hollow deformed polyester fiber

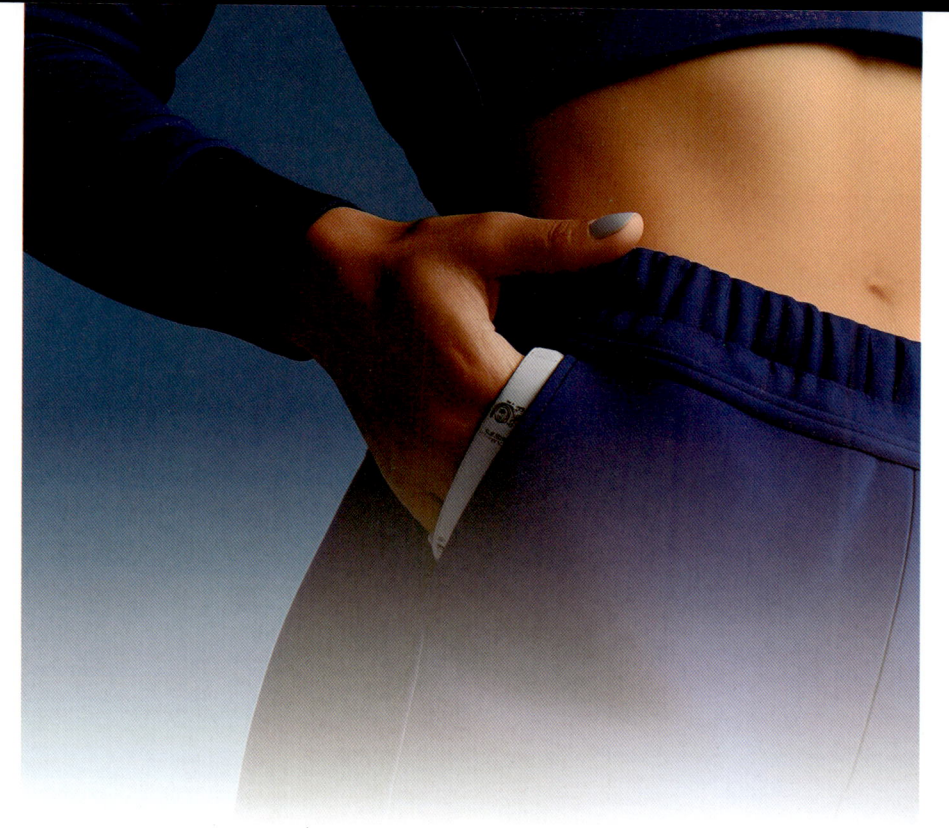

纤维性能与制品特点

- 五角中空异形、32.3% 的高中空度（常规中空纤维 20%~25%）、不易被压扁。
- 密度小、质轻、保暖性强。
- 面料丰满蓬松柔软、干爽舒适、易染色。

Properties of fibers and features of finished products

- Pentagonal hollow profiled, 32.3% high hollowness (conventional hollow fiber: 20%~25%), not easy to be flattened.
- Low density, lightweight, and strong warmth.
- The fabric is plump, fluffy, soft, dry, comfortable and easy to dye.

高中空异形聚酯纤维性能指标
Performance indexes of high hollow deformed polyester fiber

产品规格 Specifications	断裂强度 (cN/ dtex) Breaking strength (cN/ dtex)	断裂伸长率 (%) Elongation at break (%)	中空度 (%) Hollowness (%)	网络度 (N/m) Network density (N/m)	含油率 (%) Oil content (%)	沸水缩率 (%) Boiling water shrinkage (%)
55.6dtex/12f	3.29	26.1	32.3	18	1.15	8

下游应用指导
The downstream application guidance

织造： 织造过程张力要控制好，不宜过大，否则影响单丝圆整性。
染色： 吸色性好，染色时温度比正常稍低。
存储： 织物堆放不易过高，防止重压影响中空度。

Weaving: In order to avoid affecting the roundness of the mono-filament, tension should be properly managed during the fabric manufacturing process.
Dyeing: Good color absorption, with a slightly lower dying temperature than regular fibers.
Storing: Fabrics should not be stacked too high to prevent heavy pressure affects the degree of hollowness.

纤维应用
Application of fibers

| 服装用纺织品 Clothing textiles | 休闲服 Leisure wear | 运动服 Sportswear | 贴身内衣 Lingerie |

| 家用纺织品 Home textiles | 毛毯 Blanket |

Q: 五角中空异形的特殊截面为纤维带来哪些优势？

A: 五角中空异形纤维可以增大织物的摩擦系数，改善织物蜡状手感；在光泽方面，五角中空异形纤维对光线形成反射分散，起到消光作用；由于纤维比表面积大，上色速度快，且织物表观覆盖性增强，不易透视。

Q: What advantages does the special pentagonal hollow deformed cross section bring to the fiber?

A: Pentagonal hollow profiled fiber can increase the coefficient of friction of the fabric, and improve the waxy feel of the fabric. In terms of luster, the pentagonal hollow profiled design has a dispersive reflection and extinction effect on the light; the fiber's large specific surface area allows it to color quickly and enhances the fabric's apparent covering, making it difficult to see through.

蓄热锁温抑菌聚酯纤维
Thermal-storage, Heat-retaining and Anti-bacteria Polyester Fiber

推荐理由： 纤维吸收光能提升温度，并通过远红外反射将人体热量续存，植物萃取羰基活性组分及硅硼纳米化合物的添加为纤维带来抑菌功效，集抗寒、聚热、锁温、抑菌于一体的新型纤维，可满足消费者秋冬季高效保暖且抑菌的着装诉求。

Reasons for recommendation
The fibers absorb light energy to increase temperature and retain body heat through far-infrared reflection. The addition of carbonyl active components extracted from plants and silicon-boron nano compounds endows the fibers with antibacterial properties. This new type of fiber, which integrates cold resistance, heat collection, temperature locking, and antibacterial functions, can meet consumers' demands for efficient warmth retention and antibacterial properties in autumn and winter clothing.

AIREPAI⁺热湃 热湃 AIREPAI   **White-flame 白焰** 白焰 White-flame

● 入选企业 COMPANY
山东稀有科技发展有限公司
Shandong Rare Technology Development Co., Ltd.
江苏康溢臣生命科技有限公司
Jiangsu KECens Life Science&Tenchnology Co., Ltd.

制备技术
Preparative technique

热湃纤维： 将多孔蓄热纳米粉体、植物萃取羰基活性组分、聚合物粉体按比例进行共混制备光蓄热功能母粒，再与聚酯切片经熔融纺丝工艺制备纤维。

白焰纤维： 硅硼纳米化合物和纳米陶瓷复配制备功能母粒，与聚酯切片经熔融纺丝工艺制备纤维。

AIREPAI Fiber: The porous thermal-storage nanopowder, plant-extracted carbonyl active component, and polymer powder are blended proportionally to prepare light heat storage functional masterbatches, which are then mixed with polyester chips to prepare the fibers through melt spinning technique.

White-flame Fiber: Silicon-boron nanocompounds and nanoceramics are compounded to prepare functional masterbatches, which are then mixed with polyester chips to prepare the fibers through melt spinning technique.

纤维原貌图(热湃)
Original appearance figure of the fiber (airepai)

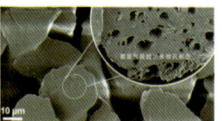

纤维截面图(热湃)
Cross-section figure of the fiber (airepai)

热湃纤维原貌和截面图
Original appearance and cross-section figure of airepai fiber

纤维原貌图（白焰）
Original appearance figure of the fiber (white-flame)

纤维电镜图（白焰）
The fiber under electron microscope (white-flame)

白焰纤维原貌和电镜图
Original appearance and under electron microscope figure of white-flame fiber

纤维及制品特点
Features of fibers and finished products

主要规格 Main Specifications
热湃纤维 AIREPAI Fiber
短纤：1.33dtex×38mm，1.67dtex×38mm，2.22dtex×51mm，5.56dtex×51mm
长丝：56dtex/48f，84dtex/72f，111dtex/96f，167dtex/144f DTY
Staple: 1.33dtex×38mm, 1.67dtex×38mm, 2.22dtex×51mm, 5.56dtex×51mm
Filament: 56dtex/48f, 84dtex/72f, 111dtex/96f, 167dtex/144f DTY

白焰纤维 White-flame Fiber
短纤：1.67dtex×38mm，3.3dtex×64mm
长丝：56dtex/72f，84dtex/72f，111dtex/96f，167dtex/144f DTY
Staple: 1.67dtex×38mm, 3.3dtex×64mm
Filament: 56dtex/72f, 84dtex/72f, 111dtex/96f, 167dtex/144f DTY

相关标准 Relative Standards
《涤纶短纤维》（GB/T 14464—2017）
《涤纶低弹丝》（GB/T 14460—2015）
Polyester staple fiber (GB/T 14464—2017)
Polyester drawn textured yarn (GB/T 14460—2015)

纤维性能与制品特点
Properties of fibers and features of finished products

热湃纤维 AIREPAI Fiber
• 吸光发热蓄热、人体远红外发热蓄热。
• 植物萃取活性成分为纤维带来持久抑菌功效。
• 纤维内部呈现纳米层叠孔腔结构，利于锁温保温，且与同材质对比轻12%以上。
• Light absorption, heat generation and storage, body far-infrared heat generation and storage.
• Plant-extracted active components bring lasting anti-bacterial effect to the fiber.
• The interior of the fiber presents a nano-layered pore structure, which is conducive to heat preservation, and the fiber is more than 12% lighter than that with the same material.

白焰纤维 White-flame Fiber
• 吸光发热蓄热、人体远红外发热蓄热。
• 硅硼化合物的添加为纤维带来持久抑菌功效。
• 不含重金属，安全性能通过婴幼儿A类标准。
• Light absorption, heat generation and storage, body far-infrared heat generation and storage.
• Silicon-boron compounds are added to provide long-lasting anti-bacterial effect to the fiber.
• No heavy metals, with safety performance satisfying the Class A standard for infants.

蓄热锁温抑菌聚酯纤维性能指标
Performance indexes of the thermal-storage, heat-retaining and anti-bacteria polyester fiber

热湃纤维产品规格 AIREPAI Fiber Specifications	断裂强度 (cN/dtex) Breaking tenacity (cN/dtex)	断裂伸长率 (%) Elongation at break (%)	回潮率 (%) Moisture regain (%)	干热收缩率 (%) Dry thermal shrinkage (%)	含油率 (%) Oil content (%)
1.33dtex×38mm	4.50	24.80	0.38	6.70	2.40

面料检测 (50% 热湃纤维 /50% 聚酯纤维)
Fabric testing (50% AIREPAI Fiber / 50% polyester fiber)

光蓄热性能 (400±10)W/m² Light thermal storage performance (400±10)W/m²	远红外发射率 Far-infrared emissivity	远红外辐射升温值 (°C) Far-infrared radiation temperature rise value (°C)	克罗值 (clo) Clo value (clo)	热传系数 [(m²·K)/W] Heat transfer coefficient [W·(m²·K)]	热阻 [(m²·K)/W] Thermal resistance [W·(m²·K)]	抑菌率 (%) Antibacterial rate (%)
最大升温值 8.7°C, 平均升温 6.7°C Maximum temperature rise: 8.7°C, average temperature rise: 6.7°C	0.89	3.80	0.486	13.30	0.075	金黄色葡萄球菌 :99 大肠杆菌 :88 白色念珠菌 :96 Staphylococcus aureus: 99 Escherichia coli: 88 Candida albicans: 96

白焰纤维产品规格 White-flame Fiber Specification	断裂强度 (cN/dtex) Breaking tenacity (cN/dtex)	断裂伸长率 (%) Elongation at break (%)	断裂强度变异系数 (%) Variable coefficient of break tenacity (%)	伸度变异系数 (%) Coefficient of variation of elongation (%)	卷曲收缩率 (%) Curling shrinkage rate (%)	沸水收缩率 (%) Boiling water shrinkage (%)	含油率 (%) Oil content (%)
84dtex/72f	4.12	22.1	1.77	7.46	10.50	3.50	2.60

面料 (84% 本纤维 /16% 氨纶) / 含 20% 该纤维的絮片 / 面料 (60% 莱赛尔 /40% 涤纶)
Fabric (84% this fiber/16% elastane) / Wadding containing 20% of the fiber / Fabric (60% Lyocell/40% dacron)

吸光发热性能 20 分钟升温值 (500W 射灯照射 20min, °C) Light-absorbing and heat-generating performance: temperature rise in 20 minutes (°C after being exposed to 500W spotlight for 20 minutes)	吸光发热性能 20 分钟温差 (500W 射灯照射 20min, °C) Light-absorbing and heat-generating performance: temperature difference after 20 minutes (°C after being exposed to 500W spotlight for 20 minutes)	红外透射率 (%) Infrared transmittance (%)	热传系数 [W/(m²·K)] Heat transfer coefficient [W/(m²·K)]	热阻 [(m²·K)/W] Thermal resistance [(m²·K)/W]	抑菌率 (%) Antibacterial Rate (%)
68.79	27.56	0.069	1.51	0.662	金黄色葡萄球菌：99 大肠杆菌：99 白色念珠菌：91 Staphylococcus aureus: 99 Escherichia coli: 99 Candida albicans: 91

蓄热锁温抑菌聚酯纤维下游应用实例
Examples of downstream applications of thermal-storage, heat-retaining and anti-bacteria polyester fiber

终端领域 Terminal field	原料配比 Raw material ratio	纤维规格 Fiber specification	产品特性 Properties of the product
保暖内衣和内搭服装 (针织双面面料 220g/m²) Thermal underwear and inner wear (220g/m² knitted double-sided fabric)	34.5% 棉 /34.5% 热湃纤维 /25% 腈纶 /6% 氨纶 34.5% cotton/34.5% AIREPAI Fiber/25% acrylon/6% elastane	1.33dtex×38mm	轻薄但保暖效果出色，保温率 37.7%，克罗值 0.514clo Lightweight yet quite thermal, with a warmth retention rate of 37.7% and a Clo value of 0.514 clo
运动、休闲、户外、商务外装 (摇粒绒面料 315g/m²) Sports, leisure, outdoor, business exterior (315g/m² fleece fabric)	60% 聚酯纤维 /40% 热湃纤维 60% polyester fiber/40% AIREPAI Fiber	82.5dtex/72f	面料蓬松度好保暖效果好，保温率 52.7%，克罗值 0.791clo Fluffy fabric and quite thermal, with a warmth retention rate of 52.7% and a Clo value of 0.791 clo
棉服、棉被、防寒装备 (中棉絮片 200g/m²) Cotton clothing, cotton quilts, and cold protection equipment (200g/m² medium wadding)	60% 聚酯纤维 /40% 热湃纤维 60% polyester fiber/40% AIREPAI Fiber	1.67dtex×51mm	絮片非常蓬松轻盈，保温率 83%，克罗值 5.41clo，数据对比接近鸭绒 Fluffy and lightweight wadding, with a warmth retention rate of 83% and a Clo value of 5.41 clo, equivalent to duck's down
针织面料 Knitted fabric	63% 白焰纤维 /37% 棉 63% White-flame Fiber/37% cotton	167dtex/144f	吸收热能、舒适包容、柔软保暖 Absorbing heat energy, comfortable and inclusive, soft and warm

纤·破界

FIBER · BEYOND THE LIMIT

下游应用指导
The downstream application guidance

织造： 短纤可与羊毛纤维、羊绒纤维、腈纶、纤维素纤维、棉纤维等混纺织造机织或针织面料，也可以与各种纤维混合制作填充棉、絮片、非织造布等填充物。长丝可以直接用于生产针织和机织面料，也可以直接应用于无缝织造产品。

染整： 建议使用低温分散染料，染色温度≤120℃，热定形温度≤190℃。

Weaving: Staple fibers can be blended with wool, cashmere, acrylon, cellulose fibers, cotton and other materials to weave woven or knitted fabrics. They can also be mixed with various fibers to make fillers such as filling cotton, wadding, and non-woven fabrics. Filaments can be directly used to produce knitted and woven fabrics, as well as in seamless woven products.

Dyeing and finishing: Low-temperature disperse dye is recommended, with the dyeing temperature ≤ 120 °C , and the heat-setting temperature ≤ 190 °C .

纤维应用
Application of fibers

| 服装用纺织品
Clothing textiles | 围巾
Scarf | 防寒服
Insulated coat | 保暖内衣
Thermal underwear |

| 家用纺织品
Home textiles | 填充物
Filler |

| 产业用纺织品
Industrial textiles | 户外用品
Outdoor product |

Q：热湃纤维的保暖原理及应用是什么？
A： 植物萃取羰基活性组分的添加使纤维实现高效吸光发热、远红外辐射升温、抑菌功效。多孔蓄热纳米粉体的添加使纤维呈现丰富的纳米微孔形态，实现远红外辐射和保暖锁温；纤维具备在全波段光热转化、蓄热锁温双倍保暖以及天然抑菌性，在应对极寒气候时，具有较强的抗寒保温优势，目前已在部分军需领域得到应用。

Q: What′s the thermal insulation principle and application of AIREPAI Fiber?
A: The addition of carbonyl active components extracted from plants enables the fiber to have efficient light absorption and heat generation, far-infrared radiation temperature rise, and antibacterial efficacy. The addition of porous thermal-storage nanopowder endows the fiber with rich nanometer microporous morphology, facilitating far-infrared radiation and heat retaining; the fiber possesses the light-thermal conversion ability in the whole band, the dual effect of thermal-storage and heat-retaining, as well as natural bacteriostatic properties. In extremely cold climates, it demonstrates significant cold resistance and heat preservation advantages and has currently been applied in some military supply fields.

Q：白焰纤维中添加的硅硼纳米化合物和纳米陶瓷改性材料，分别起到什么作用呢？
A： 通过材料的开发，设计多层级结构的硅硼纳米化合物，对可见光和红外光有非常强的吸收能力，进而提高材料的光能转化率。同时将纳米陶瓷改性材料添加到纤维中，制成颜色接近白色的纤维，可以保持人体热量不散失，自动循环散发热能反射到身体最需要的部位，让体温可保持在平衡的最佳温度，实现了发热功能的突破。

Q: What are the roles of silicon-boron nanocompounds and nanoceramic modified materials added to the White-flame Fiber?
A: The multi-layer structured silicon-boron nanocompounds designed through the development of materials that have strong visible and infrared light absorption capabilities, improving the light energy conversion rate of the material; nanoceramic modified materials are added to the fiber to make the fiber with a color close to white, which can keep the heat of the human body from being lost, automatically circulate the heat and reflect it to the most needed parts of the body, so that the body temperature can be maintained at the optimal balanced temperature, achieving a breakthrough in heating function.

稀土改性蓄热聚酰胺 6 纤维
Rare Earth Modified Thermal-storage Polyamide 6 Fiber

推荐理由：突破蓄能发热纤维颜色局限性，解决了细旦可纺、光蓄热升温效果好与白色纤维不兼具的问题。

Reasons for recommendation
Overcoming the color restrictions of heat-generating and energy-storage fibers, obtaining fine-denier spinnability, producing good temperature-rising and photo-thermal storage effects, and integrating with the whiteness of the fibers.

● 入选企业 COMPANY
镧明材料技术（上海）有限公司
RM Nano Material Technology (Shanghai) Co., Ltd.

制备技术
Preparative technique

稀土功能粉体通过复配不同比例的母粒，制备稀土复合功能母粒。然后与聚酰胺 6 切片共混，经熔融纺丝工艺制备成纤维。
Rare earth functional powders are blended in varying proportions to prepare rare earth composite functional master batches, which are blended with polyamide 6 chips and prepared into the fiber by melt spinning process.

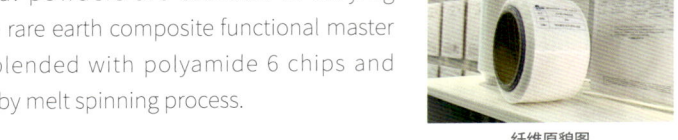

纤维原貌图
Original appearance figure of the fiber

纤维电镜图
Electron microscope image of the fiber

稀土改性蓄热聚酰胺 6 纤维原貌和电镜图
Original appearance figure and electron microscope image of rare earth modified thermal-storage polyamide 6 fiber

纤维及制品特点
Features of fibers and finished products

主要规格 Main Specifications
长丝：22dtex/24f，22dtex/17f，22dtex/8f DTY
Filament: 22dtex/24f, 22dtex/17f, 22dtex/8f DTY

相关标准 Relative Standards
《锦纶 6 弹力丝》（FZ/T 54007—2019）
Polyamide 6 drawn textured yarns (FZ/T 54007—2019)

纤维性能与制品特点

- 纤维细旦化、功能化、稀土添加改性。
- 光源发热蓄热，远红外发热，升温值高。
- 高效持久抑菌，对金黄色葡萄球菌、大肠杆菌以及白色念珠菌的抑菌率大于 85%。
- 织物具有吸湿透气、抗皱、耐磨性。

Properties of fibers and features of finished products

- Fine denier and functional fiber, with rare earth added for modification.
- light source heat generation and storage, far-infrared heat generation, high-temperature rise value.
- highly efficient and long-lasting anti-bacterial properties, with an anti-bacterial rate of more than 85% for staphylococcus aureus, escherichia coli and candida albicans.
- The fabric is moisture-absorbing, breathable, anti-wrinkle and abrasion resistant.

稀土改性蓄热聚酰胺 6 纤维性能指标
Performance indexes of rare earth modified thermal-storage polyamide 6 fiber

产品规格 Specifications	干断裂强度 (cN/ dtex) Dry fracture strength (cN/ dtex)	断裂伸长率 (%) Elongation at break (%)	断裂强度变异系数 (%) Variable coefficient of break tenacity(%)	伸度变异系数 (%) Coefficient of variation of elongation (%)	沸水收缩率 (%) Boiling water shrinkage(%)
22dtex/24f	4.34	45.09	3.50	5.10	11.39

面料检测 (43% 本纤维 /57% 常规聚酰胺 6 纤维) Fabric testing (43% this fiber /57% conventional polyamide 6 fiber)		面料检测 (96% 本纤维 /4% 其他纤维) Fabric testing (96% this fiber /4% other fibers)				
吸光发热性 (500W 射灯照射 20min，°C) Light-absorbing and heat-generating performance (°C after being exposed to 500W spotlight for 20 minutes)		光蓄热性能 (400 ± 10) W/m² Light thermal storage performance (400±10) W/m²	远红外辐射升温值 (°C) Far-infrared radiation temperature rise value (°C)	远红外发射率 (%) Far-infrared emissivity	抑菌率 (%) Antibacteria rate (%)
20min 升温值：57.80 Temperature rise in 20 minutes: 57.80	20min 温差：13.00 Temperature difference in 20 minutes: 13.00	最大升温值 13.2°C, 平均升温 7.4°C Maximum temperature rise: 13.2°C, average temperature rise: 7.4°C	2.3	0.94	金黄色葡萄球菌 :98 大肠杆菌 : 96 白色念珠菌 :90 Staphylococcus aureus: 98 Escherichia coli: 96 Candida albicans: 90

稀土改性蓄热聚酰胺 6 纤维下游应用实例
Examples of downstream applications of rare earth modified thermal-storage polyamide 6 fiber

面料类型 Types of Fabric	代表规格 Specifications	特性 Properties
外套里布、面料（机织为主） Jacket lining, fabrics (weaving-based)	50% 常规聚酰胺 6 纤维 /50% 稀土改性蓄热聚酰胺 6 纤维 50% conventional polyamide 6 fibers/50% rare-earth modified thermal-storage polyamide 6 fibers	用于羽绒服里布或羽绒服外套面料、冲锋衣里布、风衣里布等，柔软舒适，减少摩擦，红外发热，高效锁住人体温度，AAA 抗菌 It is used in down jacket lining or down jacket, winter jacket lining, windbreaker lining, etc. In addition to being softer and more comfortable, it has minimal friction and infrared heating, effectively maintains body temperature, and is AAA anti-bacterial.
贴身面料（机织或针织） Close-fitting fabrics (woven or knitted)	70% 稀土改性蓄热聚酰胺 6 纤维 /30% 氨纶 70% rare earth modified thermal-storage polyamide 6 fiber/30% elastane	用于家居服、贴身内衣、瑜伽服等。柔软亲肤，红外发热，高效锁住人体温度，AAA 抗菌，附带人体保健功能 Used in household clothing, intimate apparel, yoga wear, etc. Soft and skin-friendly, infrared heating, efficiently maintaining body temperature, AAA antibacterial, with human health care function.
	40% 莫代尔 /40% 稀土改性蓄热聚酰胺 6 纤维 /20% 氨纶 40% modal/40% rare earth modified thermal-storage polyamide 6/20% elastane	
户外用品 Outdoor supplies	55% 常规聚酰胺 6 纤维 / 45% 稀土改性蓄热聚酰胺 6 纤维 55% conventional polyamide 6 fibers/ 45% rare-earth modified thermal-storage polyamide 6 fibers	用于户外帐篷、睡袋等，轻便易携带，使用寿命长，可同时发挥红外发热与吸光蓄热作用，AAA 抗菌 Usable in outdoor tents, sleeping bags, etc., lightweight and easy to carry, long service life, having the dual effect of infrared heat-generation and light-absorbing heat storage, AAA anti-bacterial.

稀土改性蓄热聚酰胺 6 纤维蓄热原理
Thermal-storage principle of rare earth modified thermal-storage polyamide 6 fiber

下游应用指导
The downstream application guidance

织造： 可与其他纤维交织、包覆等组合使用。
染色： 参考常规聚酰胺 6 纤维。

Weaving: Can be interwoven or wrapped with other fibers.
Dyeing: Referring to conventional polyamide 6 fiber.

纤维应用
Application of fibers

服装用纺织品 Clothing textiles	羽绒服 Down jacket	裤装 White pants	发热内衣 Thermal underwear	商务衬衫 Business Shirt

Q & A

Q：稀土蓄热升温的原理是什么?
A： 由于稀土粒子与光辐射的共振效应，可以高效吸收近红外光线，具有很好的光蓄热性能，达到外部升温的效果。同时，稀土粒子可以吸收人体辐射出的远红外线，并将远红外线高效返回人体，纤维与人体形成热循环效应，防止人体热量流失。皮肤吸收的远红外线可以加速细胞中水分子的运动，实现人体内部加热的效应。

Q: What is the principle of rare earth thermal storage and temperature rise?
A: Due to the resonance effect between rare earth particles and light radiation, rare-earth particles can efficiently absorb near-infrared light, and have superior photo-thermal storage performance to achieve the effect of external warming. Meanwhile, rare earth particles can absorb the far-infrared radiation emitted by the human body and efficiently reflect it back. Thus, the fiber and the human body form a thermal cycle effect to prevent the loss of human heat. The absorption of far-infrared rays by the skin can accelerate the movement of water molecules in the cells, allowing internal heating of the human body.

保暖聚丙烯腈改性纤维
Thermal Polyacrylonitrile Modified Fiber

推荐理由：纤维兼具吸湿发热、远红外发热、抑菌等功能，极低的热导率赋予制品优异的保暖性。

Reasons for recommendation
The fiber has antibacterial, far-infrared, heat-generating, and moisture-absorbing properties. Because of its incredibly low thermal conductivity, its products are exceptionally warm.

安芯纤维 ANSINGH

● 入选企业 COMPANY
佛山市安芯纤维科技有限公司
Foshan Anxin Fiber Technology Co., Ltd.

制备技术
Preparative technique

将腈纶短纤均匀填充到反应釜中，通过添加配方助剂，在高温下发生酸转型反应，经清洗、开松、烘干、打包等工序制备纤维。

Acrylon staple fibers are evenly packed into a reactor, where the acid transformation reaction is triggered by the addition of specially produced additives at a high temperature. And then the modified fibers are cleaned, loosened, dried, and packed.

纤维及制品特点
Features of fibers and finished products

主要规格 Main Specifications
短纤：1.33dtex×38mm，1.67dtex×38mm
Staple: 1.33dtex×38mm, 1.67dtex×38mm

相关标准 Relative Standards
《腈纶短纤维和丝束》(GB/T 16602—2008)
Acrylic staple and tow (GB/T 16602—2008)

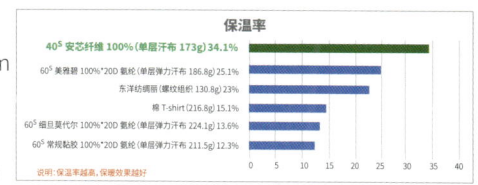

纤维原貌图
Original appearance figure of the fiber

纤维电镜图
Electron microscope image of the fiber

保暖聚丙烯腈改性纤维原貌和电镜图
Original appearance figure and electron microscope image of thermal polyacrylonitrile modified fiber

保暖聚丙烯腈改性纤维制品保温率
Thermal insulation rate of thermal polyacrylonitrile modified fiber products

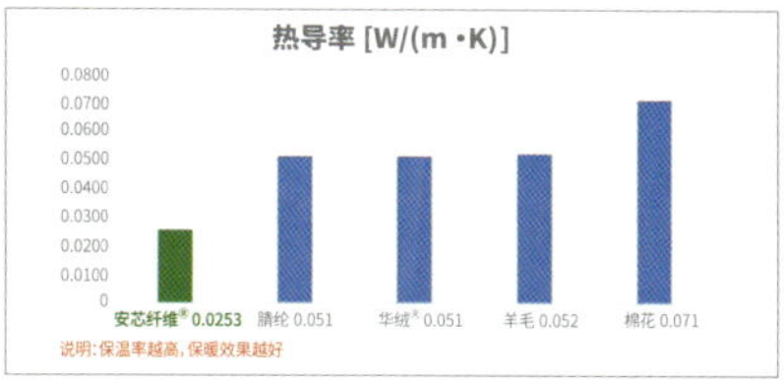

保暖聚丙烯腈改性纤维等热导率
Equivalent thermal conductivity of thermal polyacrylonitrile modified fiber

纤维性能与制品特点

- 同时具备吸湿发热和远红外发热特性，导热率低接近空气 0.0253W/（m·K），保暖性优异。
- 回潮率指标突出、抗静电性优异，抗起毛起球性优异。
- 持久高效抑菌。
- 符合《婴幼儿及儿童纺织产品安全技术规范》中 A 类产品标准，适于制作母婴类产品。

Properties of fibers and features of finished products

- Moisture absorption and heat generation and far-infrared heat generation, low thermal conductivity close to air [0.0253W/(m·K)], and excellent thermal protection property.
- Outstanding moisture regain rate, excellent anti-static properties, and anti-pilling.
- Long lasting and efficient anti-bacteria properties.
- Conforms to the standard for Class A products in the *Technical Specification for the Safety of Textile Products for Infants and Children*, and is fully applicable to maternal and infant products.

保暖聚丙烯腈改性纤维性能指标
Performance indexes of thermal polyacrylonitrile modified fiber

产品规格 Specifications	断裂强度（cN/dtex） Breaking tenacity (cN/dtex)	断裂伸长率（%） Elongation at break (%)	回潮率（%） Moisture regain (%)	超长率（%） Elongation at break (%)
1.67dtex×38mm	2.02	36.06	11.41	0.20

面料检测（100% 本纤维）
Fabric testing (100% this fiber)

导热率 [W/(m·K)] Thermal conductivity [W/(m·K)]	吸湿发热最高升温值（℃） Maximum temperature rise value after moisture-absorbing and heat-generating (℃)	远红外辐射温升值（℃） Far-infrared radiation temperature rise value (℃)	远红外发射率 Far-infrared emissivity	远红外辐射升温值（℃） Far-infrared radiation temperature rise value (℃)	抑菌率（水洗 150 次，%） Antibacterial rate (after 150 times of washing,%)	抗起球性（级） Anti-pilling (grade)	静电半衰期 HDT Static half-life HDT
0.0253	最高升温值 :5.6 30min 内平均升温值 :3.1 Maximum temperature rise: 5.6 Average temperature rise within 30 minutes: 3.1	3.8	0.92	2.1	大肠杆菌 :97 金黄色葡萄球菌 :99 白色念珠菌 :98 Escherichia coli: 97 Staphylococcus aureus:99 Candida albicans:98	4~5	< 10

下游应用指导
The downstream application guidance

织造：可与羊毛纤维、羊绒纤维、腈纶、黏胶纤维、棉纤维、涤纶纤维、锦纶等混纺纱线，直接用于织造机织或针织面料，也可以与各种纤维混合制作填充絮片、非织造布等填充物。

染色：建议采用酸性染料染色。

后整理：后定形温度建议在 160 ℃以下。

Weaving: It can be blended with wool, cashmere, acrylon, viscose fiber, cotton, dacron, chinlone and other yarns, directly used for weaving woven or knitted fabrics, and can also be blended with a variety of fibers to produce filler wadding, nonwovens and other fillers.

Dyeing: Acid dyes are recommended.

Post-finishing: The post-setting temperature is recommended to be below 160 ℃.

纤维应用
Application of fibers

服装用纺织品 Clothing textiles	家居服 Home wear	贴身内衣 Lingerie	袜子 Socks	鞋材 Shoe materials
家用纺织品 Home textiles	填充物 Filler			
产业用纺织品 Industrial textiles	户外用品 Outdoor products	睡袋 Sleeping bag		

保暖聚丙烯腈改性纤维下游应用实例
Examples of downstream applications of thermal polyacrylonitrile modified fiber

终端领域 Terminal field	原料配比 Raw material ratio	纤维规格 Fiber specification	产品特性 Properties of the product
帽子围巾 Hats and scarfs	50% 膨体腈纶 /50% 保暖聚丙烯腈改性纤维 50% expanded acrylon/50% thermal polyacrylonitrile modified fiber	1.33dtex×38mm	抑菌、吸湿发热、远红外发热、抗静电、抗起毛起球、保暖 Anti-bacteria, moisture absorption, heat-generation, far-infrared health care, anti-static, anti-pilling and thermal
鞋材 Shoe materials	50% 涤纶 /50% 保暖聚丙烯腈改性纤维 50% dacron/50% thermal polyacrylonitrile modified fiber		
袜子 Socks	70% 天竹纤维 /30% 保暖聚丙烯腈改性纤维 70% crude bamboo fiber/30% thermal polyacrylonitrile modified fiber		
保暖内衣 Thermal underwear	60% 腈纶 /40% 保暖聚丙烯腈改性纤维 60% acrylic/40% thermal polyacrylonitrile modified fiber		
毛巾 Towels	70% 棉 /30% 保暖聚丙烯腈改性纤维 70% cotton/30% thermal polyacrylonitrile modified fiber		
服装外套 Jackets	夏季：70% 莱赛尔 /30% 保暖聚丙烯腈改性纤维 Summer: 70% lyocell/30% thermal polyacrylonitrile modified fiber 春秋冬：60% 莱赛尔 /40% 保暖聚丙烯腈改性纤维 Spring, Autumn and Winter: 60% lyocell/40% thermal polyacrylonitrile modified fiber		

Q: 保暖聚丙烯腈改性纤维的抑菌原理是什么？

A：保暖聚丙烯腈改性纤维通过在纤维分子链中接枝上多种有机官能团从而实现多种功能，其中抑菌官能团是通过分子合成嵌入纤维链段，在纤维表面形成一种电荷环境，该环境会破坏细菌繁殖，大多数菌落无法停留选择逃逸，同时抑菌官能团的 N 端与细菌或病毒的细胞膜接触，嵌入扰乱细菌的包膜或病毒结构，达到接触式杀菌效果。

Q: What is the antibacterial principle of thermal polyacrylonitrile modified fiber?

A: Thermal polyacrylonitrile modified fiber achieves various functions by grafting a variety of organic functional groups in the fiber molecular chain, in which the antibacterial functional group is embedded in the fiber chain through molecular synthesis, forming a charged environment on the fiber surface, which will destroy the reproduction of bacteria, so that most of the colonies can't stay and escape. Meanwhile, the N-terminal end of this organic group is in contact with the cell membranes of bacteria/viruses, which embedded in and disturbed the cell membrane structure of the bacteria/viruses, realizing the contact sterilization effect.

FIBER · OUTSIDE THE LIMIT

极限挑战，应用跨界

纤维跨越传统的界限，在极端环境的挑战下，耐得住高温的炙烤，扛得住强力的拉扯，经得起循环往复的磨炼，为拓展应用领域开辟新的赛道。阻燃防护纤维打造坚强护盾，筑起生命防火墙，呵护生命安全。产业用纤维助力竞技体育，为桥梁加固，为飞机添翼，为汽车减重，为建筑铸魂。从时尚的工业设计到先进的医疗设备，从高效的交通工具到智能的电子产品，纤维无处不在，尽显人类的智慧和创造力。

Challenging the limit to achieve cross-industry applications

Fibers have gone beyond the established limit, able to withstand the intense heat in a high temperature in the face of a challenge from the extreme environment, to endure being pulled with great force, to stand up to repeated tests, opening up new vistas for the expansion of applications. Fire-retardant protective fibers form a defensive shield, serving as a firewall to protect life, improving life safety. Fibers for industrial use give impetus to competitive sports, enable bridges to be reinforced, aircraft to have wings added, vehicles to have weight reduced, and buildings to come to life. From fashionable industrial designs to advanced medical equipment, and from high-efficiency means of transportation to intelligent electronic products, fibers are everywhere, and serve various purposes, fully exhibiting human wisdom and creativity.

92　防护用阻燃纤维
FLAME-RETARDANT FIBER FOR PROTECTION

99　产业用纤维
INDUSTRIAL FIBER

中国纤维流行趋势

纤·跨界

纤·跨界
FIBER
OUTSIDE THE LIMIT
China Fibers Fashion Trends
2025/2026

防护用阻燃纤维
FLAME-RETARDANT FIBER FOR PROTECTION

防护用阻燃纤维默默守护家中点滴温馨，打造一面无形护盾。突破无卤阻燃与聚酯原位聚合技术，协同出色的抗熔滴功能，使聚酯纤维阻燃高效持久，降低火灾中火焰蔓延速度。复合磷硅系阻燃与原液着色技术融合，使阻燃聚酰胺6纤维集色彩鲜艳、无熔滴、环保属性于一体，为家居、特种工装等领域架起生命防火墙，呵护生命的温度。

推荐纤维及品牌

阻燃抗熔滴聚酯纤维
Flame-retardant and Anti-melt-drop Polyester Fiber

阻燃抗熔滴原液着色聚酰胺6纤维
Flame-retardant and Anti-melt-drop Dope-dyed Polyamide 6 Fiber

HENGYI　CESALON®

Flame-retardant fiber for protection softly protects every drop of warmth in your home, maintaining even the smallest amount of warmth and creating an undetectable barrier. The development of halogen-free flame retardant and polyester in-situ polymerization technology, together with superior anti-drip properties, make polyester fiber flame-retardant efficient and long-lasting, reducing the rate of flame spread in a fire. The combination of dope-dyed technology and composite phosphate-silicon flame retardant gives the flame-retardant polyamide 6 fiber its vibrant colors, no melting droplets, and environmental protection qualities, creating a life firewall for homes, specialized tools, and other areas to preserve life's temperature.

阻燃抗熔滴聚酯纤维
Flame-retardant and Anti-melt-drop Polyester Fiber

推荐理由： 通过共聚改性获得稳定的阻燃及高抗熔滴性能，制品离火自熄，可显著降低火灾时火焰的蔓延速度，有效减少火灾对人体的二次伤害。

Reasons for recommendation
With stable flame-retardant and high anti-melt-drop properties obtained through the copolymerization modification, the products are self-extinguishing from the fire, which can significantly reduce the rate of flame spreading during a fire, and effectively reducing the secondary damage to the human body during a fire.

● 入选企业 COMPANY
浙江恒逸石化研究院有限公司
Zhejiang HENGYI Petrochemical Research Institute Co., Ltd.

制备技术
Preparative technique

在酯化工序加入阻燃剂及抗熔滴剂，经缩聚、切粒得到阻燃抗熔滴聚酯切片，再通过熔融纺丝工艺制备纤维。

Flame-retardant and anti-melt-drop agents are introduced during the esterification process, and flame-retardant and anti-melt-drop polyester pellets are created through polycondensation and pelletizing, before the fibers are prepared using the melt spinning technique.

纤维及制品特点
Features of fibers and finished products

主要规格 Main Specifications
长丝：83dtex/36f，83dtex/48f，83dtex/72f，111dtex/48f，167dtex/48f，333dtex/96f DTY

Filament: 83dtex/36f, 83dtex/48f, 83dtex/72f, 111dtex/48f, 167dtex/48f, 333dtex/96f DTY

相关标准 Relative Standards
《阻燃抗熔滴涤纶预取向丝》（Q/HYYJ 034—2024）
《阻燃抗熔滴涤纶低弹丝》（Q/HYYJ 033—2024）

Flame-retardant and anti-melt-drop pre-oriented dacron yarns (Q/HYYJ 034—2024)
Flame-retardant and anti-melt-drop low-elasticity dacron yarns (Q/HYYJ 033—2024)

纤维原貌图
Original appearance figure of the fiber

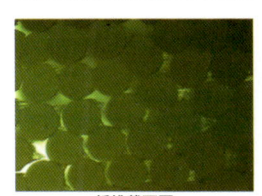

纤维截面图
Cross-section figure of the fiber

阻燃抗熔滴聚酯纤维原貌和截面图
Original appearance figure and cross-section figure of flame-retardant and anti-melt-drop polyester fiber

FIBER · OUTSIDE THE LIMIT

纤维性能与制品特点

- 良好的阻燃性能，属于无卤磷系阻燃，极限氧指数大于 30%，燃烧时无滴落物。
- 共聚阻燃，阻燃效果持久，耐洗涤。

Properties of fibers and features of finished products

- Good flame-retardant (non-halogen phosphorus flame-retardant) performance, with the limiting oxygen index >30%, no droplets during combustion.
- Co-polymerized flame-retardant, long lasting flame-retardant effect, washable.

阻燃抗熔滴聚酯纤维性能指标
Performance indexes of flame-retardant and anti-melt-drop polyester fiber

产品规格 Specifications	断裂强度 (cN/dtex) Breaking strength (cN/dtex)	断裂伸长率 (%) Elongation at break (%)	面料成分 (100% 本纤维) Fabric composition (100% this fiber)			
			极限氧指数 (%) Limiting oxygen index (%)	阴燃、续燃时间 (s) Smoldering and sustained combustion duration (s)	损毁长度 (mm) Damage length (mm)	燃烧时有无滴落物 Burning with or without dripping
167dtex/48f	2.77	21.50	经向:32.30 纬向:32.30 Wrap: 32.30 Weft: 32.30	经向:0 纬向:0 Wrap: 0 Weft: 0	经向:96 纬向:101 Wrap: 96 Weft: 101	无 None

下游应用指导
The downstream application guidance

织造：可与其他阻燃纤维交织，用于制作针织和机织面料。
染整：建议染色温度 120~125°C，热定形温度 130~150°C。

Weaving: Can be blended with other flame-retardant fibers for knitted and woven fabrics.
Dyeing and finishing: The suggested dyeing temperature is 120~125°C , and the heat setting temperature is 130~150°C .

阻燃抗熔滴聚酯纤维下游应用实例
Examples of downstream applications of flame-retardant and anti-melt-drop polyester fiber

面料类型 Types of Fabric	原料配比 Raw material ratio	纤维规格 Fiber specification	产品特性 Properties of the product
家纺 Home textiles	100% 阻燃抗熔滴聚酯纤维或与其他阻燃纤维混织 100% flame-retardant and anti-melt-drop polyester fiber or blended with other flame-retardant fibers	333dtex/96f DTY 83dtex/72f DTY	用于窗帘的底纱和面纱织造，其织物垂悬性好，手感柔软 Used in the weaving of bottom and top yarns for curtains, with good drape and soft hand-feel fabrics
汽车内饰 Automotive interiors	100% 阻燃抗熔滴聚酯纤维或与其他阻燃纤维混织 100% flame-retardant and anti-melt-drop polyester fiber or blended with other flame-retardant fibers	83dtex/48f FDY 83dtex/36f DTY	用于汽车内饰的底纱和面纱织造，其织物持久耐用，触感舒适 Used in the weaving of bottom and top yarns for automotive interiors with long-lasting, durable and comfortable fabrics

阻燃抗熔滴聚酯纤维制品
Products of applications of flame-retardant and anti-melt-drop polyester fiber

纤维应用
Application of fibers

| 家用纺织品 / Home textiles | 窗帘 Curtain　　沙发布 Sofa fabric |

| 产业用纺织品 / Industrial textiles | 汽车内饰 Automotive interior |

Q：相较常规阻燃聚酯纤维，阻燃抗熔滴聚酯纤维的优势体现在哪里？
A： 常规阻燃聚酯纤维的阻燃机理之一是通过纤维熔融产生熔滴消耗热量，从而减缓织物燃烧速度，但高温熔滴会对人体造成严重危害，而阻燃抗熔滴聚酯纤维加入了特殊研发的协效抗燃滴剂后，进一步加强了纤维的阻燃效果及耐久性，大大减少二次伤害的发生，有效保证了人体安全。其制备的面料触感柔软舒适，可广泛应用在家用及产业用纺织品领域。

Q: What are the advantages of flame-retardant and anti-melt-drop polyester fibers over conventional flame-retardant polyester fibers?
A: One of the flame-retardant mechanisms of conventional flame-retardant polyester fibers is to consume heat by melting droplets generated by the melting of fibers, thus slowing down the burning speed of fabrics. However, high-temperature melt droplets will cause serious harm to the human body. While flame-retardant and anti-melt-drop polyester fibers combined with specially developed synergistic anti-melt-drop agents, which can further strengthen the flame-retardant effect and the durability of the fibers, greatly reducing the occurrence of secondary injuries, and effectively ensuring the safety of the human body. The fabrics are soft and comfortable, and can be widely used in automotive interiors, curtain fabrics and home textiles.

阻燃抗熔滴原液着色聚酰胺 6 纤维
Flame-retardant and Anti-melt-drop Dope-dyed Polyamide 6 Fiber

推荐理由：纤维耐磨性好，具有优异的阻燃抗熔滴特性，原液着色技术符合绿色环保的趋势，为家纺、航空、工装辅料等应用场景中面料的阻燃需求提供有力支持。

Reasons for recommendation
The fiber has good abrasion resistance and excellent flame-retardant and anti-melt-drop properties. The dope-dyed technology is in line with the trend of environmental protection, and provides favorable support for the flame-retardant needs of fabrics in home textiles, aviation, and workwear accessories.

恒申新材 H-tech　　CESALON®　　安凸阻燃 CESALON

● 入选企业 COMPANY
广东恒申美达新材料股份公司
Guangdong Highsun Meida New Materials Co., Ltd.
上海安凸塑料添加剂有限公司
Shanghai ANTU Masterbatch Co., Ltd.

制备技术
Preparative technique

将"有机—无机杂化的无卤素协同阻燃体系"的复合磷硅系阻燃剂、颜料与特定聚合物按一定比例通过共混改性技术制备阻燃切片，后经熔融纺丝工艺及多级牵伸处理技术制备纤维。
The composite phosphorus-silicon flame retardant and pigment of the "organic-inorganic hybrid halogen-free synergistic flame retardant system" and specific polymers are blended and modified in a certain ratio to prepare flame-retardant chips, which are then used to prepare the fiber by melt spinning and multi-stage drafting processing technology.

纤维及制品特点
Features of fibers and finished products

主要规格 Main Specifications
长丝：78dtex/24f，156dtex/48f，280dtex/48f，470dtex/96f FDY
Filament: 78dtex/24f, 156dtex/48f, 280dtex/48f, 470dtex/96f FDY

相关标准 Relative Standards
《有色锦纶 6 牵伸丝》(FZ/T 54114—2019)
《中、高强锦纶 6 牵伸丝》(FZ/T 54128—2020)
Spun-dyed polyamide 6 yarns (FZ/T 54114—2019)
Medium or high tenacity polyamide 6 drawn yarns (FZ/T 54128—2020)

纤维原貌图
Original appearance figure of the fiber

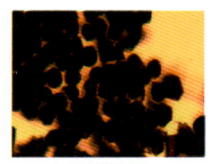

纤维截面图
Cross-section figure of the fiber

阻燃抗熔滴原液着色聚酰胺 6 纤维原貌图和纤维截面图
Original appearance figure and cross-section figure of flame-retardant and anti-melt-drop dope-dyed polyamide 6 fiber

纤维性能与制品特点

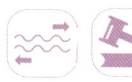

- 原液着色，可生产黑色或其他色彩，绿色环保。
- 阻燃性能优良，燃烧时无滴落。
- 强度高，面料耐磨性较好。

Properties of fibers and features of finished products

- Dope-dyed, allowing black or other colors, which is green and environmentally friendly.
- Excellent flame-retardant properties, no droplets during burning.
- High strength, good abrasion resistance of fabrics.

阻燃抗熔滴原液着色聚酰胺 6 纤维性能指标
Performance indexes of flame-retardant and anti-melt-drop dope-dyed polyamide 6 fiber

产品规格 Specifications	断裂强度 (cN/ dtex) Breaking tenacity (cN/ dtex)	断裂强度 变异系数（%） Variable coefficient of break tenacity (%)	断裂伸长率（%） Elongation at break (%)	断裂伸长率 变异系数（%） Variable coefficient of elongation at break (%)	沸水收缩率（%） Boiling water shrinkage (%)	色牢度（级） Color fastness (grade)
280dtex/48f	5.60	1.70	24.20	5.50	14.40	4

面料成分 (100% 本纤维) Fabric composition (100% this fiber)					
极限氧指数（%） Limiting oxygen index (%)	阴燃时间 (s) Smoldering duration (s)	续燃时间 Sustained combustion duration (s)	损毁长度 (mm) Damage length (mm)	燃烧时有无滴落物 Burning with or without dripping
经向 :33.50 纬向 :32.30 Wrap: 33.50 Weft: 32.30	经向 :0 纬向 :0 Wrap: 0 Weft: 0	经向 :11.70 纬向 :8 Wrap: 11.70 Weft: 8	经向 :92 纬向 :86 Wrap: 92 Weft: 86	无 None

下游应用指导
The downstream application guidance

织造： 可与其他阻燃纤维混织，用于制作针织和机织面料。
Weaving: Can be blended with other flame-retardant fibers for knitted and woven fabrics.

阻燃抗熔滴原液着色聚酰胺 6 纤维制品及应用实例
Examples of applications of flame-retardant and anti-melt-drop dope-dyed polyamide 6 fiber products

纤维应用
Application of fibers

| 家用纺织品
Home textiles | 窗帘
Curtain | 地毯
Carpet | 沙发布
Sofa fabric |

Q & A

Q：阻燃抗熔滴原液着色聚酰胺 6 纤维在民用与产业用领域应用十分广泛，如遇到火灾情况，它又发挥了哪些重要作用呢？

A：作为一种耐磨兼具阻燃特性的纤维材料，其在绳索、飞机、高铁内饰、军事装备及个人防护等领域发挥着重要的阻燃功能与防护作用。由于采用先进的无卤、无硫研发设计及高温微交联协效体系，其织物在燃烧时实现了缓熔不滴，极大减少了火灾对人体可能造成的烫伤及其他二次伤害，且能有效减缓火灾势态。

Q: Flame-retardant and anti-melt-drop dope-dyed polyamide 6 fibers are widely applied in civil and industrial applications, and what important role does it play in case of fire?

A: As a wear-resistant fiber material with flame-retardant properties, it plays an important flame-retardant role and protective role in the fields of ropes, aircraft interiors, high-speed railroad interiors, military equipment and personal protection. Thanks to the adoption of advanced halogen-free, sulfur-free R & D design and high-temperature micro-crosslinking synergistic system, the fabric achieves slow melting without dripping when burning, greatly reducing the risk of burns and other secondary injuries caused by fire to the human body, and effectively slowing down the fire.

产业用纤维
INDUSTRIAL FIBER

产业用纤维,千锤百炼铸就一条波澜壮阔的鼎新之路。100%再生聚酯工业丝,强度高、拉伸形变小,为车用橡胶骨架制品提供绿色环保材料新选择;兼具凉感与中强度的熔纺型超高分子量聚乙烯纤维在冰感床品及防护用品中大放异彩;拥有丰富色彩、高强度的间位芳纶,实现自我颠覆;强度和模量出色的碳纤维,在航空航天、军事装备等领域扮演核心角色。

推荐纤维及品牌

高模量循环再利用聚酯工业丝
High-modulus Recycled Polyester Industrial Yarn

熔纺型中强超高分子量聚乙烯纤维
Melt-spun Medium-strength Ultra-high Molecular Weight Polyethylene Fiber

原液着色高强型间位芳纶
Dope-dyed High-strength Meta-aramid

HM50E 高强高模聚丙烯腈基碳纤维
HM50E High-strength and High-modulus Polyacrylonitrile-based Carbon Fiber

尤夫股份　九州星际　泰和新材　恒海股份

After a great deal of hammering and training, industrial fibers cast a stunning new path. With its excellent strength and minimal tensile deformation, 100% recycled polyester industrial yarn offers a new option for eco-friendly and sustainable materials for automotive rubber frame products. Melt-spun ultra-high molecular weight polyethylene fibers, which combine coolness and medium strength, make a big splash in ice-feeling bedding and protective products. Meta-aramid, which has rich colors and high-strength, achieves self-subversion. Carbon fibers with outstanding strength and modulus play a central role in fields such as aerospace and military equipment.

纤·跨界

高模量循环再利用聚酯工业丝
High-modulus Recycled Polyester Industrial Yarn

推荐理由： 采用 100% 再生聚酯原料，纤维强度高、尺寸稳定性好，为轮胎帘子布、胶管线等车用橡胶骨架制品以及绳索、骨架材料等提供可持续纤维原料支持。

Reasons for recommendation
Made from 100% recycled polyester material, the fiber has high strength and good dimensional stability, providing sustainable fiber raw material support for automotive rubber frame products such as builder fabrics and coil hoses, as well as ropes and frame materials.

入选企业 COMPANY
浙江尤夫高新纤维股份有限公司
Zhejiang Unifull Industrial Fiber Co., Ltd.

制备技术
Preparative technique

以再生聚酯切片为原料，采用固相增黏技术，通过高取向纺丝技术、低牵伸后处理工艺制备纤维。

The fiber is prepared by high-oriented spinning technology and low-draw post-treatment process using recycled polyester chips from solid state polycondensation technology.

纤维及制品特点
Features of fibers and finished products

主要规格 Main Specifications
长丝：1100dtex/320f，1440dtex/384f，1670dtex/480f
Filament: 1100dtex/320f, 1440dtex/384f, 1670dtex/480f

相关标准 Relative Standards
《涤纶工业长丝》（GB/T 16604—2017）
《绿色设计产品评价技术规范 再生涤纶》（FZ/T 07015—2021）
Polyester filament for industry (GB/T 16604—2017)
Technical specification for eco-design product assessment-recycled polyester (FZ/T 07015—2021)

纤维原貌图
Original appearance figure of the fiber

纤维截面图
Cross-section figure of the fiber

高模量循环再利用聚酯工业丝原貌和截面图
Original appearance figure and cross-section figure of high-modulus recycled polyester industrial yarn

纤维性能与制品特点
- 采用 100% 再生聚酯原料，绿色环保。
- 强度高、模量高、承受外力拉伸性形变小，品质媲美原生纤维。
- 尺寸稳定性良好、耐化学性好，耐磨性好。

Properties of fibers and features of finished products
- Made from 100% recycled polyester, and is green and environmentally friendly.
- high strength, high modulus, low tensile deformation under external force, comparable original quality.
- Good dimensional stability, chemical resistance, and abrasion resistance.

高模量循环再利用聚酯工业丝性能指标
Performance indexes of high-modulus recycled polyester industrial yarn

产品规格 Specifications	断裂强度 (cN/dtex) Breaking tenacity (cN/dtex)	断裂伸长率 (%) Elongation at break (%)	初始模量 (cN/dtex) Initial modulus (cN/dtex)	定负荷伸长 (%) Constant load elongation(%)	干热收缩 (%) Dry thermal shrinkage (%)	热老化后强力保持率 (180°C 24h, %) Strength retention after thermal aging (180°C 24h, %)
1100dtex/320f	≥ 6.80	12.00±2.00	110	5.20±0.80	3.00±0.50	≥ 90

下游应用指导
The downstream application guidance

合捻： 可以两股或多股捻成帘线，也可与其他纤维进行混捻成胶管线、线绳等。

织造： 主要采用平纹组织按一定经密排列织造，制成帘子布、白坯布；也可以用于织带及其他面料的开发。

浸胶： 通过特定的浸胶处理，以一定的热拉伸定形工艺制成帘子布，可与橡胶进行硫化黏合。

Co-twisting: Two or more of its strands can be twisted into cords, and it can also be mixed with other fibers into coil hoses, ropes, among others.

Weaving: The fiber is mainly arranged by a certain warp density in a plain structure to make cord fabrics and gray cloth; it can also be used for the development of webbing and other cloth covers.

Impregnation: It can be made into cord fabrics by specific impregnation treatment and certain thermal stretching and setting process, and can be vulcanized and bonded with rubber.

高模量循环再利用聚酯工业丝下游应用实例
Examples of downstream applications of high-modulus recycled polyester industrial yarn

终端领域 Types of Fabric	原料配比 Raw material ratio	纤维规格 Fiber specification	主要产品及特性 Main products and properties
帘子布 Cord fabrics	99% 经纱：高模量循环再利用聚酯工业丝 / 1% 纬纱：包芯纱 99% warp: high-modulus recycled polyester industrial yarn/ 1% weft: Core-spun yarn	1100dtex/320f 1650dtex/384f 1650dtex/480f	用于轮胎帘子布，强度高、延伸率低、尺寸稳定性好 Used in tire cord fabrics, with high strength, low elongation, and good dimensional stability
胶管线 Coil hoses	100% 高模量循环再利用聚酯工业丝 100% high-modulus recycled polyester industrial yarn	470dtex/160f 550dtex/160f	用于汽车用橡胶制品，强度高、黏合力高、耐疲劳度好 For automotive rubber products with high strength, high adhesion and good fatigue resistance

FIBER · OUTSIDE THE LIMIT

高模量循环再利用聚酯工业丝应用实例
Examples of applications of high-modulus recycled polyester industrial yarn

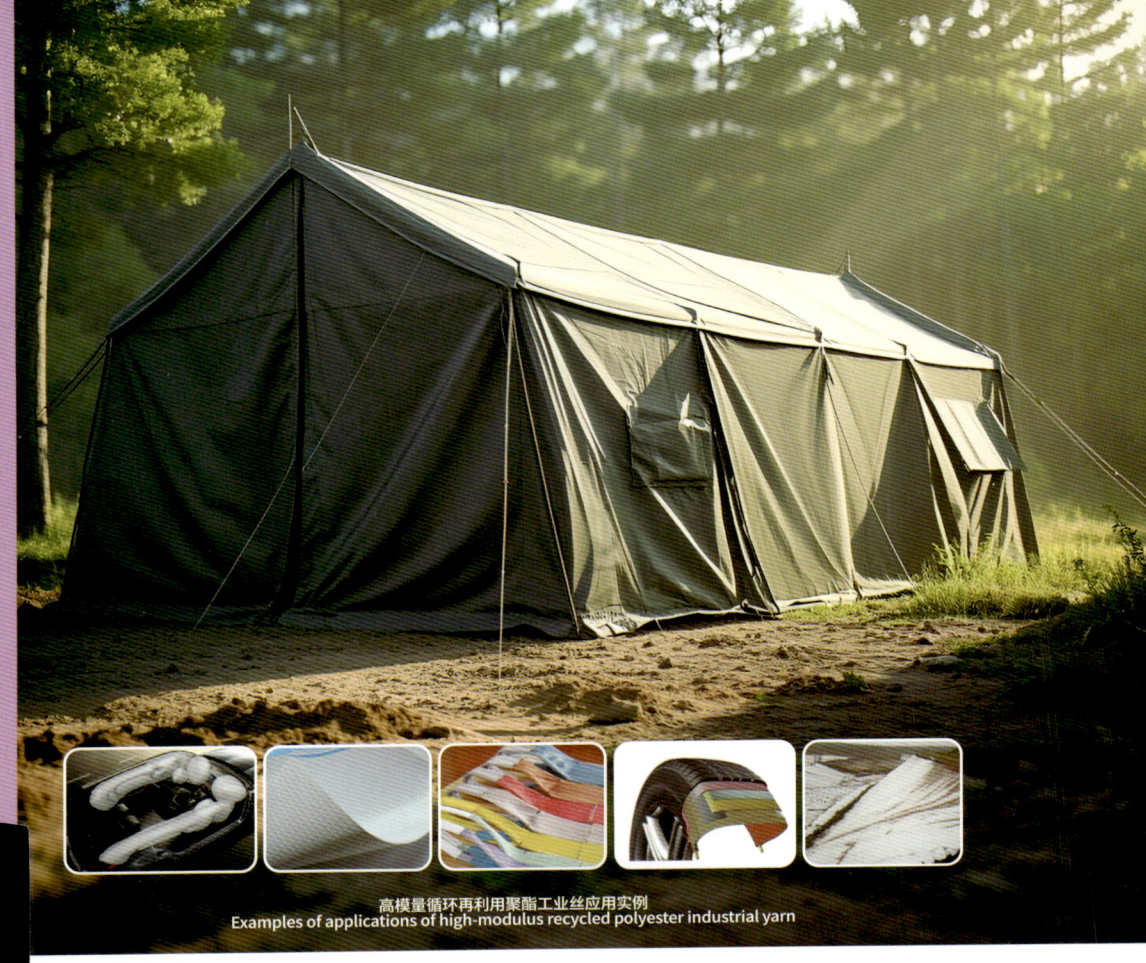

纤维应用
Application of fibers

产业用纺织品
Industrial textiles

汽车内饰　　　户外用品　　　橡胶制品
Automotive interior　Outdoor products　Rubber product

Q & A

Q: 高模量循环再利用聚酯工业丝在汽车行业的应用具体有哪些？
A： 随着人们对环保的要求日益提升，在汽车行业，高模量循环再利用聚酯工业丝主要应用于汽车安全带、安全气囊、车顶内衬、座椅套等汽车安全件及内饰，采用再生聚酯为原料有助于汽车制造商实现可持续发展的目标。

Q: What are the specific applications of high-modulus recycled polyester industrial yarn in the automotive industry?
A: With increasing demand for environmental protection, high-modulus recycled polyester industrial yarn is mainly used in automotive seat belts, airbags, inside roof lining, seat covers and other automotive safety parts and interior in the automotive industry. Using recycled polyester as a raw material can assist automobile manufacturers in achieving the goal of sustainable development.

桐昆·中国纤维流行趋势报告 2025/2026　TONGKUN · CHINA FIBERS FASHION TRENDS REPORT 2025/2026

熔纺型中强超高分子量聚乙烯纤维
Melt-spun Medium-strength Ultra-high Molecular Weight Polyethylene Fiber

推荐理由： 首次采用熔融纺丝工艺，生产流程短、效率高，节能环保。纤维优异的凉感可用于制造差别化家纺产品，良好的抗穿刺与耐切割性可在防护品的应用上大放异彩。

Reasons for recommendation
The melt spinning process is adopted for the first time to prepare medium-strength ultra-high molecular weight polyethylene fiber, with short production flow, high efficiency, energy saving and environmental protection. With its excellent coolness, the fiber can be used to manufacture differentiated home textile products. Its good puncture resistance and cut resistance can shine in the application in protective goods.

● 入选企业 COMPANY
九州星际科技有限公司
Xingi Technology Co., Ltd.

制备技术
Preparative technique

以聚乙烯为原料加热熔融后，通过控制一定的纺丝速度和温度，经熔融挤出、冷却固化、超倍拉伸等工序制备中强度的超高分子量聚乙烯纤维。

The medium-strength ultra-high molecular weight polyethylene fiber is prepared through melt extrusion of polyethylene by controlling spinning speed and temperature, cooling and solidifying, and super-stretching.

纤维及制品特点
Features of fibers and finished products

主要规格 Main Specifications
长丝： 385dtex/120f，440dtex/120f，880dtex/240f，1760dtex/480f
Filament: 385dtex/120f, 440dtex/120f, 880dtex/240f, 1760dtex/480f

相关标准 Relative Standards
《超高分子量聚乙烯纤维》（GB/T 29554—2013）
Ultra high molecular weight polyethylene fiber (GB/T 29554—2013)

熔纺型中强超高分子量聚乙烯纤维原貌图
The original appearance figure of melt-spun medium-strength ultra-high molecular weight polyethylene fiber

纤维性能与制品特点

- 具有良好的耐切割性能。
- 具有较高强度，符合用于民用领域所需要的强度级别。
- 触摸体感冰凉，具有优异的凉感性能。
- 良好的耐化学腐蚀性。

Properties of fibers and features of finished products

- Good cut-resistant performance.
- Higher strength, which is in line with the strength level required for civil applications.
- Cool hand-feel, with excellent coolness properties.
- Good chemical resistance.

熔纺型中强超高分子量聚乙烯纤维性能指标
Performance indexes of melt-spun medium-strength ultra-high molecular weight polyethylene fiber

产品规格 Specifications	断裂强度 (cN/dtex) Breaking tenacity (cN/dtex)	断裂伸长率 (%) Elongation at break (%)	初始模量 (cN/dtex) Initial modulus (cN/dtex)	织物防切割级别（级） Cut resistance grade of fabrics (grade)	织物耐撕裂（级） Tear resistance of fabrics (grade)	织物抗穿刺（级） Puncture resistance of fabrics (grade)	凉感系数值 (W/cm²) Coolness coefficient value (W/cm²) 面料 100% 本纤维 Fabrics (100% this fiber) 测试条件：温度：20±2°C 相对湿度：65%+4% RH Testing Conditions: TEMP: 20±2°C Relative humidity: 65%+4% RH
440dtex/120f	12	6.50	≤ 420	IV	IV	IV	0.355

下游应用指导
The downstream application guidance

染色：建议低温染色或采用冷染工艺，控制温度不超过 120°C，优选 80~100°C，染液需保持中性至弱酸性以保护纤维强度和光泽。
织造：适当降低机织速度，以减少震动对纤维的损伤，织机辊速建议优选控制在 250~400r/min。织造过程中建议通过提升车间湿度或增加静电消除装置以解决静电问题。
后整理：采用低温烘干和热定形，定形温度优选 60~80°C。在后整理中增加抗静电整理剂消除表面静电，保证纤维材料的高强度、轻量化的性质。

Dyeing: Low temperature dyeing or cold dyeing is advised, with the temperature kept at or below 120° C, ideally between 80~100° C; the dyeing solution should be kept neutral to weak acidic to protect the fiber strength and luster.
Weaving: Reduce the weaving speed appropriately to lessen vibration damage to the fiber; ideally, the loom roller speed should be kept between 250~400 r/min. It is advised to boost the workshop's humidity levels or install a static electricity elimination equipment to address the issue of static electricity during the weaving process.
After-finishing: Low temperature drying and heat setting (preferably 60~80 °C). The high strength and lightweight nature of the fiber are ensured by adding an anti-static finishing agent in the after-finishing to remove surface static electricity.

纤维应用
Application of fibers

- **服装用纺织品 Clothing textiles**: 防切割手套 Cut Resistant gloves
- **家用纺织 Home textiles**: 床上寝具 Bedding
- **产业用纺织 Industrial textiles**: 渔网 Fishing net, 绳缆 Rope

Q：除了在产业用领域的应用，熔纺型中强超高分子量聚乙烯纤维是如何向民用领域发展的？

A：作为一款中等强度的超高分子量聚乙烯纤维，不同于常规的湿法与干法纺丝工艺，该纤维采用熔融纺丝法制备，具有设备投资少、生产成本低、节能环保等优势。由于在某些应用场合并不需要特别高强的产品，这正是该产品向民用领域发展的契机。其强度、耐磨、耐切割等性能完全可以满足增强、防护装备等民用产品的需求，例如用来制作防割手套、增强材料、绳索等，还可以利用该纤维的凉感制作冰丝席、运动鞋等产品。

Q: How melt-spun medium-strength ultra-high molecular weight polyethylene fiber has developed into civilian uses in addition to industrial ones?

A: This medium-strength, ultra-high molecular weight polyethylene fiber is made by melt spinning, which has the advantages of inexpensive equipment investment, low production costs, energy conservation, and environmental preservation. This method differs from the traditional wet and dry spinning process. There is a chance for this product to be used in the civilian sector because some applications do not call for products with very high strength. The fiber's coolness can be utilized to make ice silk mats, sports shoes, and other items, and its strength, abrasion resistance, and cut resistance, among other qualities, can completely satisfy the needs of protective gear, enhancing gear, and other civilian products, such as cut-resistant gloves, reinforcing materials, and ropes.

原液着色高强型间位芳纶
Dope-dyed High-strength Meta-aramid

推荐理由： 纤维本质阻燃、强度高、耐腐蚀、耐高温，原液着色技术加深了产品的绿色环保属性，拓展了其在电力作业、防火救援等场景中的应用。

Reasons for recommendation
The fiber is constitutionally flame-retardant, strong, corrosion resistant and high temperature resistant. The dope-dyed process enhances the product's ecological and environmental protection features and broadens its use in scenarios like electric power operation and fire rescue, among others.

入选企业 COMPANY
泰和新材集团股份有限公司
泰美达® Tametar®
Tayho Advanced Materials Group Co., Ltd.

制备技术
Preparative technique

以间苯二甲酰氯、间苯二胺及第三单体为原料，采用低温溶液聚合与原液着色在线添加，突破纤维交联关键技术，实现分子链微交联结构的构建，经湿法纺丝工艺制备纤维。

Using isophthaloyl dichloride, m-phenylenediamine, and the third monomer as raw materials, we use low-temperature solution polymerization and on-line dope-dyed to break through the key technology of fiber cross-linking, realize the construction of a micro-cross-linking structure of the molecular chain, and prepare the fiber by wet spinning.

纤维及制品特点
Features of fibers and finished products

主要规格 Main Specifications

短纤：1.67dtex×51mm，1.82dtex×51mm，2.22dtex×51mm
长丝：220dtex/100f，440dtex/200f，1320dtex/600f
Staple: 1.67dtex×51mm, 1.82dtex×51mm, 2.22dtex×51mm
Filament: 220dtex/100f, 440dtex/200f, 1320dtex/600f

相关标准 Relative Standards

《间位芳纶短纤维》(GB/T 31889—2015)
《原液着色间位芳纶短纤维》(Q/0601 THX010—2019)
Meta-aramid staple fiber (GB/T 31889—2015)
Staple fibers of dope-dyed meta-aramid (Q/0601 THX010—2019)

纤维原貌图（短纤）
Original appearance figure of the fiber(staple)

纤维原貌图（长丝）
Original appearance figure of the fiber (filament)

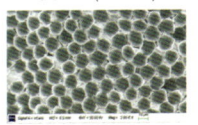

纤维截面图
Cross-section figure of the fiber

原液着色高强型间位芳纶原貌和截面图
Original appearance figure and cross-section figure of dope-dyed high-strength meta-aramid

纤维性能与制品特点
- 原液着色、纤维色彩丰富、色牢度高，绿色环保。
- 高强度、耐腐蚀、耐高温。
- 纤维本质阻燃，其面料阴燃、续燃时间小于或等于 2s，燃烧过程中无熔滴。

Properties of fibers and features of finished products
- Dope-dyed, colorful fiber with high color fastness, green and environmentally friendly.
- High strength, corrosion resistance, high temperature resistance.
- The fiber is constitutionally flame retardant. The smoldering and sustained combustion duration of its fabric is less than or equal to 2s, without melt drop in the combustion process.

原液着色高强型间位芳纶性能指标
Performance indexes of dope-dyed high-strength meta-aramid

产品规格 Specifications	断裂强度 (cN/dtex) Breaking tenacity (cN/dtex)	断裂伸长率 (%) Elongation at break (%)	初始模量 (cN/dtex) Initial modulus (cN/dtex)	干热收缩率 (%) 测试条件：180℃, 30min Dry thermal shrinkage (%) Testing conditions:180℃, 30min	色牢度（级） Color fastness (grade)
1.82dtex×51mm	5.29	38.70	91.88	0.10	6

面料成分 (93% 本纤维 /5% 对位芳纶 /2% 导电纤维) Fabric composition (93% this fiber/5% para-aramid/2% conductive fibers)			
极限氧指数 Limiting oxygen index	阴燃、续燃时间 (s) Smoldering and sustained combustion duration (s)		燃烧时有无滴落物 Burning with or without dripping
31.90	≤ 2		无 None

原液着色高强型间位芳纶下游应用实例
Examples of downstream applications of performance indexes of dope-dyed high-strength meta-aramid

面料类型 Types of Fabric	原料配比 Raw material ratio	纤维规格 Fiber specification	支数 Count	产品特性 Properties of the product
消防用防护面料 Protective fabrics for firefighting	93% 原液着色高强型间位芳纶 / 5% 对位芳纶 /2% 抗静电纤维 93% dope-dyed high-strength meta-aramid/5% para-aramid/2% antistatic fibers	1.67dtex×51mm 2.22dtex×51mm	32/1 35/2 40/2	用于消防领域，阻燃、强力高、色牢度高 Used in fire-fighting field, with flame retardance, high strength and high color fastness.
产业用防护面料 Industrial protective fabrics	88% 原液着色高强型间位芳纶 / 10% 阻燃黏胶纤维 /2% 抗静电纤维 88% dope-dyed high-strength meta-aramid/ 10% flame-retardant viscose fibers/ 2% antistatic fibers	1.67dtex×51mm 2.22dtex×51mm	32/1 35/2 40/2	用于石油、石化产业用工人防护领域，阻燃、强力高、舒适、色牢度高 Used in petroleum and petrochemical industry for worker protection, with flame retardance, high strength, comfort and high color fastness.
抢险防护面料 Emergency protective fabrics	98% 原液着色高强型间位芳纶 / 2% 抗静电纤维 98% dope-dyed high-strength meta-aramid/ 2% antistatic fibers	1.67dtex×51mm 2.22dtex×51mm	32/1 35/2 40/2	用于抢险救援领域，阻燃、强力高、色牢度高 Used in emergency rescues, with flame retardance, high strength and high color fastness.
航空套管 Aviation casing	100% 原液着色高强型间位芳纶长丝 100% dope-dyed high-strength meta-aramid filaments	220dtex/100f 440dtex/200f 1320dtex/600f	—	用于航空航天防护套管，阻燃、易覆合、强力高、色牢度高 Used in aerospace protective casing, with flame retardance, easy laminating, high strength and high color fastness.
家纺用品 Home textiles	60% 原液着色高强型间位芳纶 / 38% 阻燃黏胶纤维 /2% 抗静电纤维 60% dope-dyed high-strength meta-aramid/ 38% flame-retardant viscose fibers/ 2% antistatic fibers	1.67dtex×51mm 2.22dtex×51mm	50/1 60/1	用于家居床单、被罩，阻燃、舒适、色牢度高 Used for home bed sheets and quilt covers, with flame retardance, comfort and high color fastness.

纤 · 跨界

下游应用指导
The downstream application guidance

纺纱：短纤可纯纺，也可与其他纤维进行任何比例的混纺。
织造：长丝用于制作针织或机织面料；也可加工成捻线，用于编织制造。
染整：使用阳离子染料，染色温度和热定形温度≥130℃。

Spinning: Staple fibers can be spun purely or blended with other fibers in any ratio.
Weaving: Filaments are used for knitted or woven fabrics; they can also be processed into twisted yarns for weaving.
Dyeing and finishing: Positive ion dyes are used, with the dyeing and heat-setting temperature ≥ 130 °C.

纤维应用
Application of fibers

家用纺织品 Clothing textiles	窗帘 Curtain			
产业用纺织品 Industrial textiles	军用纺织品 Military textile	消防用品 Fire supplie	航空航天防护套管 Aerospace	防护工装 Protective gear

Q&A

Q： 间位芳纶产品不断迭代升级，原液着色高强型间位芳纶的优势体现在哪里？
A： 该纤维不仅强度有所提高，而且解决了间位芳纶不易染色的问题，产品色彩丰富、色牢度高，进一步拓展了其在防护服装、阻燃服等领域的应用。此外，原液着色技术应用还避免了染色工艺带来的污染与排放，达到了绿色生产的要求，符合中国经济"生态优先，绿色发展"趋势。

Q: Upgrades to meta-aramids are ongoing. What are the advantages of dope-dyed high-strength meta-aramids?
A: The fiber not only has enhanced strength, but also addresses the problem that meta-aramids are not easy to dye. The product is rich in color, and has high color fastness, further expanding its application in protective apparel, flame-retardant clothing, among others. In addition, the application of dyed technology also avoids the pollution and emission brought about by the post-dyeing process, which meets the requirements of green production and is in line with the trend of "ecology first and green development" of China's economy.

HM50E 高强高模聚丙烯腈基碳纤维
HM50E High-strength and High-modulus Polyacrylonitrile-based Carbon Fiber

推荐理由： 兼具高强度与高模量的碳纤维在航空航天、军事装备等关键战略性领域扮演着核心角色，为进一步实现轻量化、高性能应用提供解决方案。

Reasons for recommendation
The carbon fiber with both high strength and high modulus plays an important role in key strategic areas such as aerospace and military equipment, providing solutions for further lightweight and high-performance applications.

入选企业 COMPANY
江苏恒神股份有限公司
Jiangsu Hengshen Co., Ltd.

制备技术
Preparative technique

以聚丙烯腈为原料，采用干喷湿法纺丝工艺得到碳纤维原丝，再经预氧化、低温碳化、高温碳化、石墨化、表面处理上浆等工序制备 HM50E 高强高模聚丙烯腈基碳纤维。

The carbon precursor fiber is made from the polyacrylonitrile through the dry-jet wet spinning technology, and then experienced the process of pre-oxidation, low-temperature carbonization, high-temperature carbonization, graphitization, surface treatment, and sizing procedures to prepare the HM50E high-strength and high-modulus polyacrylonitrile-based carbon fiber.

纤维及制品特点
Features of fibers and finished products

主要规格 Main Specifications
丝束规格：12K
Filament: 12K

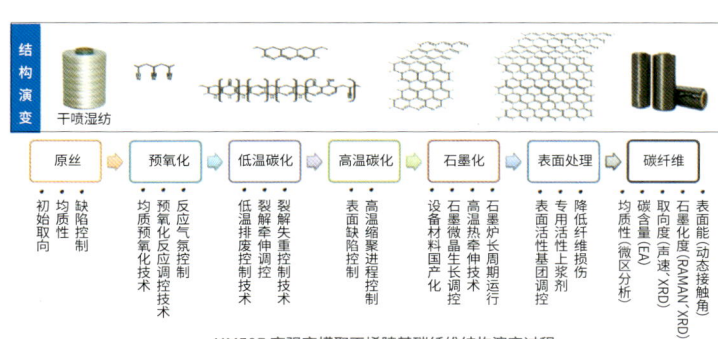

HM50E 高强高模聚丙烯腈基碳纤维结构演变过程
Structural evolution of HM50E high-strength and high-modulus polyacrylonitrile-based carbon fiber

纤维原貌图（短纤）
Original appearance figure of the fiber(staple)

纤维截面图
Cross-section figure of the fiber

HM50E 高强高模聚丙烯腈基碳纤维原貌和截面图
Original appearance figure and cross-section figure of HM50E high-strength and high-modulus polyacrylonitrile-based carbon fiber

相关标准 Relative Standards

《聚丙烯腈基碳纤维》（GB/T 26752—2020）
PAN-based carbon fiber (GB/T 26752—2020)

纤维性能与制品特点

- 高模量，模量比 T800 级碳纤维高 30%。
- 强度与 T800 级碳纤维基本一致，优异的强度更有利于轻量化。
- 可在 -180℃保持性能稳定，在惰性气氛下，高温 1000℃下性能基本不变。
- 具有良好的耐腐蚀性，对大多数酸、碱和有机溶剂具有很好的耐受性。

Properties of fibers and features of finished products

- High modulus, 30% higher modulus than T800 grade carbon fiber.
- Its strength is basically the same as T800 grade carbon fiber, with excellent strength that is more conducive to light weight.
- At -180° C, it can continue to function steadily, and at 1000° C, it can continue to function almost unmodified in an inert atmosphere.
- good corrosion resistance, good resistance to most acids, alkalis and organic solvents.

HM50E 高强高模聚丙烯腈基碳纤维性能指标
Performance indexes of hm50e high-strength and high-modulus polyacrylonitrile-based carbon fiber

产品规格 Specifications	拉伸强度 (MPa) Tensile strength (MPa)	拉伸强度变异系数 (%) Coefficient of variation of tensile strength (%)	拉伸模量 (GPa) Tensile modulus (GPa)	拉伸模量变异系数 (%) Coefficient of variation of tensile modulus (%)	断裂伸长率 (%) Elongation at break (%)	断裂伸长变异系数 (%) Variable coefficient of elongation at break (%)	体密度 (g/cm³) Bulk density (g/cm³)
12K	≥5700	≤5	370~400	≤3	≥1.50	≤5	1.77±0.03

下游应用指导
The downstream application guidance

织造： 可用于经编织物，也可用于预浸料、缠绕制件等。
后整理： 制造过程中注意纤维展纱程度，树脂适配程度，树脂浸润程度。

Weaving: It can be used for warp knitting fabrics, and can also be used for prepreg and winding parts.
After-finishing: Attention should be paid to the degree of fiber spreading, resin suitability and resin infiltration during the manufacturing process.

纤维应用
Application of fibers

产业用纺织品 | 航空航天 | 发动机壳体 | 无人机
Industrial textiles | Aerospace | Engine shell | UAV

缠绕制件
Winding parts

经编织物
Warp knitting fabrics

预浸料
Prepreg

HM50E 高强高模聚丙烯腈基碳纤维制品
HM50E high-strength and high-modulus polyacrylonitrile-based carbon fiber products

Q&A

Q：随着研发的不断迭代更新，HM50E 高强高模聚丙烯腈基碳纤维都有哪些同步升级呢？

A： HM50E 高强高模聚丙烯腈基碳纤维相较于同级别高强度碳纤维，模量提高了近 30%。HM50E 碳纤维可同步实现高拉伸强度、高弹性模量等，可以满足新一代重大复合材料对碳纤维材料性能均衡化提高的要求，也是支撑第三代先进复合材料的理想材料，未来市场应用广阔。

Q: As research and development continues to be iterative and updated, what are the synchronous improvements of HM50E high-strength and high-modulus polyacrylonitrile-based carbon fiber?

A: HM50E high-strength and high-modulus polyacrylonitrile-based carbon fiber has a modulus increase of nearly 30% compared to similar high-strength carbon fibers. In addition to meeting the demands of the new generation of major composite materials for better balanced performance of carbon fiber materials, HM50E carbon fiber can simultaneously achieve high tensile strength and high modulus of elasticity. It is also the perfect material to support the third generation of advanced composite materials, which has a wide range of potential applications in the future market.

万物共生，无界交融

纤维在天地中探寻与自然的和合共生。曾经被遗忘的资源，在创新的魔法下重焕生机。原料绿色、后道加工低碳，勾勒循环闭环，模糊产品生命界限。废旧纺织品、废弃塑料瓶华丽"逆袭"，改写填埋焚烧的命运，打破报废即终点的旧规，让原料边界归于循环浪潮，奠定纤维的绿色基因。技术创新雕琢纤维生命历程，促进加工流程从粗放高碳向精细低碳跃进，开启纤维全生命周期及应用之旅的节能减排新篇章。

Enabling all things of creation to blend them with each other without limit

Fibers are meant to harmoniously coexist with nature in the world. Resources that were once forgotten have a new lease of life like magic thanks to innovation. Green materials and low-carbon downstream manufacturing present an overview of a circulatory closed loop, where the boundary of product service life is blurred. Waste and old textiles, as well as rejected plastic bottles gorgeously "turn over a new leaf", avoiding the fate that would have seen them landfilled or burnt, breaking away from the old convention of treating the discarded as useless, allowing the tide of recycling to have an impact on the boundary of raw materials, laying the foundation for fibers that are green products in nature. Technical innovation creates the life cycle of fibers, facilities the transition of process flow from being extensive and high-carbon to being intensive and low-carbon, and opens a new chapter about energy-saving and emission reduction in the entire life cycle of fibers.

114 绿色纤维
GREEN FIBER

127 低温热黏合纤维
LOW-TEMPERATURE HEAT-BONDABLE FIBER

中国纤维流行趋势

纤·无界

FIBER WITHOUT LIMIT
China Fibers Fashion Trends
2025/2026

纤·无界

绿色纤维
GREEN FIBER

绿色纤维凝聚着锁住碳排放、转化环境压力的科技伟力，重塑绿色价值，打造循环经济。低温易染兼具高生物基含量的新型生物基纤维，更上一层楼，创造低碳深绿属性。二氧化碳废气『逆』袭，特殊精妙的工序将气体分子驯服重组，化碳为『丝』。循环再利用纤维打破产品报废即终点的旧规，纺织旧品再利用，消费后的增量转变为可利用的存量，纤维原料边界消融于循环浪潮。

📖 推荐纤维及品牌

低温易染生物基呋喃聚酯纤维
Low Temperature Easy-to-dye Bio-based Furan Polyester Fiber

二氧化碳基乙二醇聚酯纤维
Carbon Oxide-based Glycol Polyester Fiber

黑色循环再利用再生纤维素纤维
Black Recycled Regenerated Cellulose Fiber

rPET 基化学法再生氨纶
rPET-based Chemically Regenerated Elastane

TONGKUN 桐昆　**reocoer 芮控**
PangCell 邦丝　**AOSHEN**

Green fiber transforms environmental pressure, locks carbon emissions, reshapes green value, and creates a circular economy by combining scientific and technical strength. With its high bio-based content and ease of dyeing at low temperatures, the new bio-based fiber goes above and beyond to produce deep green and low-carbon qualities. By employing a unique, nuanced mechanism to tame and restructure the gas molecules, carbon dioxide waste gas flips the roles and transforms carbon into yarns. Reusing outdated textile items, converting post-consumer recycled materials into usable stock, and dissolving the fiber raw material border in the cycle wave are all examples of how recycling fiber breaks the old norm that product scrap is the end.

低温易染生物基呋喃聚酯纤维
Low Temperature Easy-to-dye Bio-based Furan Polyester Fiber

推荐理由： 纤维部分原料源于生物基材料，纤维本身具有低温易染特点，该纤维可降低石油资源依赖及染整工序能耗消耗，是具有低碳深绿属性的新型生物基聚酯纤维。

Reasons for recommendation
Part of the raw material of the fiber is derived from bio-based materials, and the fiber itself has the characteristics of easy-to-dye at low-temperature. The fiber can reduce the dependence on petroleum resources and the energy consumption of dyeing and finishing processes, and it is a new type of bio-based polyester fiber with the attribute of low-carbon and deep-green.

● 入选企业 COMPANY
浙江桐昆新材料研究院有限公司
Tongkun Institute for Advanced Materials Co., Ltd.

制备技术
Preparative technique

以生物基 2,5-呋喃二甲酸和乙二醇为原料，同时添加改性单体，经聚合得到呋喃聚酯切片，再通过熔融纺丝、加弹等工艺制备纤维。

The fiber is prepared by melt spinning and elasticizing furan polyester chips, which are obtained by polymerization of bio-based 2,5-furandicarboxylic acid and ethylene glycol as raw materials and 1,4-cyclohexanedimethanol as a copolymerization monomer.

纤维及制品特点
Features of fibers and finished products

主要规格 Main Specifications
长丝：56dtex/48f，84dtex/72f，135dtex/72f，167dtex/96f，167dtex/144f DTY
Filament: 56dtex/48f, 84dtex/72f, 135dtex/72f, 167dtex/96f, 167dtex/144f DTY

相关标准 Relative Standards
《涤纶低弹丝》（GB/T 14460—2015）
Polyester drawn textured yarns (GB/T 14460—2015)

纤维原貌图
Original appearance figure of the fiber

纤维截面图
Cross-section figure of the fiber

低温易染生物基呋喃聚酯纤维原貌和截面图
Original appearance figure and cross-section figure of low temperature easy-to-dye bio-based furan polyester fiber

纤维性能与制品特点

- 以生物基呋喃二甲酸为原料生产,生物基含量超过 60%。
- 天然抑菌,洗涤 150 次后织物仍具有较高的抑菌效果。
- 具有在常压、100°C条件下低温易染的优点,纤维上染率高。

Properties of fibers and features of finished products

- Produced from bio-based furandicarboxylic acid, with more than 60% bio-based content.
- High anti-bacteria effect after 150 times of washing.
- It has the advantages of easy dyeing at low temperature under normal pressure and 100°C, and has high dyeing rate.

低温易染生物基呋喃聚酯纤维性能指标
Performance indexes of low temperature easy-to-dye bio-based furan polyester fiber

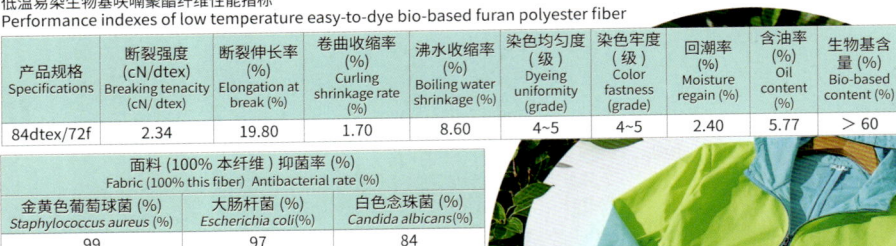

产品规格 Specifications	断裂强度 (cN/dtex) Breaking tenacity (cN/dtex)	断裂伸长率 (%) Elongation at break (%)	卷曲收缩率 (%) Curling shrinkage rate	沸水收缩率 (%) Boiling water shrinkage (%)	染色均匀度 (级) Dyeing uniformity (grade)	染色牢度 (级) Color fastness (grade)	回潮率 (%) Moisture regain (%)	含油率 (%) Oil content (%)	生物基含量 (%) Bio-based content (%)
84dtex/72f	2.34	19.80	1.70	8.60	4~5	4~5	2.40	5.77	>60

面料 (100% 本纤维) 抑菌率 (%) Fabric (100% this fiber) Antibacterial rate (%)		
金黄色葡萄球菌 (%) Staphylococcus aureus (%)	大肠杆菌 (%) Escherichia coli (%)	白色念珠菌 (%) Candida albicans (%)
99	97	84

下游应用指导
The downstream application guidance

织造:可与棉纤维、锦纶、低温氨纶等进行交织,可在针织面料上进行开发应用。

染整:对面料进行定形等后处理时,建议热处理温度≤140°C;建议使用分散染料染色,染色温度≤110°C。

Weaving: It can be interwoven with cotton, nylon, and low-temperature elastane, and can be applied to knitted fabrics.

Dyeing and finishing: For the post-processing of fabrics such as setting, it is recommended that the heat treatment temperature should be ≤140°C; It is recommended that disperse dyes should be used, and the dyeing temperature should be ≤110°C.

低温易染生物基呋喃聚酯纤维下游应用实例
Examples of downstream applications of low temperature easy-to-dye bio-based furan polyester fiber

面料类型 Terminal field	原料配比 Raw material ratio	纤维规格 Fiber specifications	产品特性 Properties of the product
PEF 双面珠地布 PEF double-sided pique	36% 低温易染生物基呋喃聚酯纤维 /64% 棉纤维 36% low temperature easy-to-dye bio-based furan polyester fiber/64% cotton	84dtex/72f	布面软滑,手感好;可应用于春夏秋季节,做男女童装休闲产品,如T恤、卫衣等 Soft and smooth fabric with good hand-feel, It can be used in spring, summer and fall seasons to make men's, women's and children's casual products, such as T-shirts, sweatshirts, among others
PEF 网眼珠地布 PEF mesh pique	100% 低温易染生物基呋喃聚酯纤维 100% low temperature easy-to-dye bio-based furan polyester fiber	84dtex/72f	面料丝滑垂坠,柔顺亲肤,吸湿性好;可应用于春夏季节,做男女童装休闲、运动类产品,如T恤 The fabric is silky and drapey, soft and skin-friendly, with good moisture absorption, It can be used in spring and summer seasons to make men's, women's and children's casual and sports products, such as T-shirts

低温易染生物基呋喃聚酯纤维应用实例
Examples of applications of low temperature easy-to-dye bio-based furan polyester fiber

纤维应用
Application of fibers

服装用纺织品
Clothing textiles

休闲服　　运动服　　衬衣
Leisure wear　Sportswear　Shirt

Q & A

Q：低温易染生物基呋喃聚酯纤维从生产端到应用端都体现了哪些环保优势与应用特点呢？

A： 纤维原料来源于绿色生物基材料，可以大幅减少对石油资源的消耗，从而降低二氧化碳排放。其加工温度较常规聚酯纤维低10~20℃，可减少生产加工过程中使用的能耗，低温易染的特点也可减少下游在染整阶段的能耗。除了抑菌外，其纤维模量相对低，回潮率也较普通聚酯纤维好，制成的面料亲肤柔软，手感顺滑。

Q: What are the environmental advantages and application characteristics of low temperature easy-to-dye bio-based furan polyester fiber from the production end to the application end?

A: The raw material of the fiber comes from green bio-based materials, which can significantly reduce the consumption of petroleum resources, thus reducing carbon dioxide emissions. Its processing temperature is 10~20°C lower than conventional polyester fiber, which can reduce energy consumption in the production and processing process. Its low-temperature dyeability can also reduce the downstream energy consumption in the dyeing and finishing stage. Along with being antibacterial, it also has a relatively low fiber modulus, retains moisture better than regular polyester fibers, and produces a smooth, soft, and skin-friendly fabric.

纤·无界

二氧化碳基乙二醇聚酯纤维
Carbon Oxide-based Glycol Polyester Fiber

推荐理由： 利用二氧化碳为原料开发纤维，生产过程中有效减少碳排放，相较原生涤纶纱线，碳排放下降28.4%，且品质达到原生标准，产品全程可追溯。

Reasons for recommendation
The fiber is developed from carbon dioxide raw material, which efficiently reduces carbon emissions in the manufacturing process. When compared to virgin dacron yarns, its carbon emissions were reduced by 28.4%, while its quality met the virgin norm and could be traced throughout the process.

reocoer 芮控

● 入选企业 COMPANY
江苏国望高科纤维有限公司
Jiangsu Guowang Hi-Tech Fiber Co., Ltd.

制备技术
Preparative technique

将工厂排放的二氧化碳经捕捉、液化、提纯、加氢等工序制成二氧化碳基乙二醇，再将该乙二醇与对苯二甲酸聚合成聚酯切片，最终经熔融纺丝制成纤维。

Carbon dioxide emitted from plants is captured, liquefied, purified and hydrogenated to make carbon dioxide-based glycol, which is then polymerized with terephthalic acid to form polyester pellets, and finally melt-spun to make the fiber.

纤维及制品特点
Features of fibers and finished products

主要规格 Main Specifications
长丝：33dtex/72f，55dtex/48f，66dtex/72f，84dtex/72f，148dtex/72f，165dtex/72f POY、DTY、FDY
Filament: 33dtex/72f, 55dtex/48f, 66dtex/72f, 84dtex/72f, 148dtex/72f, 165dtex/72f POY, DTY, FDY

二氧化碳基乙二醇聚酯纤维原貌图
The original appearance figure of carbon oxide-based glycol polyester fiber

相关标准 Relative Standards

《纤维级聚酯切片（PET）》（GB/T 14189—2015）
《涤纶低弹丝》（GB/T 14460—2015）
《涤纶牵伸丝》（GB/T 8960—2015）
《涤纶预取向丝》（FZ/T 54003—2023）

Fiber grade polyester chip (PET) (GB/T 14189—2015)
Polyester drawn textured yarn (GB/T 14460—2015)
Polyester drawn yarn (GB/T 8960—2015)
Polyester partially oriented yarn (FZ/T 54003—2023)

纤维性能与制品特点

- 具备可再生性与环保性，持续助力减少碳排放。
- 品质达到原生纤维标准。
- 面料舒适柔软、亲肤透气，且具有一定的棉感。

Properties of fibers and features of finished products

- Renewable and environmentally friendly, continuing to help reduce carbon emissions.
- Comparable to virgin fibers in terms of quality.
- The fabric is comfortable and soft, skin-friendly and breathable, with a cotton-like feel.

二氧化碳基乙二醇聚酯纤维性能指标
Performance indexes of carbon oxide-based glycol polyester fiber

产品规格 Specifications	断裂强度 (cN/dtex) Breaking tenacity (cN/dtex)	断裂强力变异系数 (%) Variable coefficient of break strength(%)	断裂伸长率 (%) Elongation at break (%)	断裂伸长率变异系数 (%) Variable coefficient of elongation at break (%)	卷曲收缩率 (%) Curling shrinkage rate(%)	卷曲收缩率变异系数 (%) Coefficient of variation of crimp shrinkage (%)	卷曲稳定度 (%) Curling stability (%)	沸水收缩率 (%) Boiling water shrinkage (%)	网络度（个/m） Network density (Pc/m)	含油率 (%) Oil content (%)
84dtex/72f	4.08	1.90	21.60	5.70	10.50	4.20	79.40	4.0	122	2.5

下游应用指导
The downstream application guidance

织造、染色、后整理： 参考常规聚酯纤维工艺即可。
Weaving, dyeing and post-finishing: Prefer to the processes of conventional polyester fibers.

二氧化碳基乙二醇聚酯纤维下游应用实例
Examples of downstream applications of carbon oxide-based glycol polyester fiber

面料类型 Terminal field	原料配比 Raw material ratio	纤维规格 Fiber specifications	产品特性 Properties of the product
服装用纺织品 Textiles for apparel	100% 二氧化碳基乙二醇聚酯纤维 100% carbon oxide-based glycol polyester fiber	经纱：66dtex/72f 消光 DTY 纬纱：55dtex/48f 消光 SSY Warp: 66dtex/72f dull DTY Weft: 55dtex/48f dull SSY	用于制作成衣，运动服，户外服等，高价值环保属性，柔软舒适、富有弹性与棉感功能 It can be utilized to create ready-to-wear, sportswear, outdoor clothes, and other products with strong environmental protection features, as well as soft and comfortable, elastic, and cotton-like functions
	二氧化碳基乙二醇聚酯纤 / 30 旦氨纶 Carbon Oxide-based Glycol Polyester Fiber/30D elastane	经纱、纬纱：148dtex/72f Warp and weft: 148dtex/72f	用于制作成衣，运动服，户外服等，具有柔软舒适，富有弹性与棉感功能 It can be utilized to create ready-to-wear, sportswear, outdoor clothes, and other products, with soft and comfortable, elastic, and cotton-like functions

二氧化碳基乙二醇聚酯纤维制品
Products of applications of carbon oxide-based glycol polyester fiber

纤维应用
Application of fibers

| 服装用纺织品 Clothing textiles | 休闲服 Leisure wear | 运动服 Sportswear | 衬衣 Shirt | 专业运动服 Professional sportswear |

| 产业用纺织品 Industrial textiles | 户外用品 Outdoor products |

Q：为什么说二氧化碳基乙二醇聚酯纤维的成功开发对助力生态环保有重大的意义？

A：二氧化碳是造成全球气候变暖的重要因素之一，因此，采取各种措施减少二氧化碳的排放已成为人们的共识与行动。二氧化碳基乙二醇聚酯纤维的推出，让工业"废气"重获新生。生产3万吨二氧化碳基乙二醇聚酯纤维约等于每年从环境中捕获并封存近1万吨的二氧化碳，其环境效益相当于约100万棵树一年对二氧化碳的吸收量，等同于为地球"新添"了约1.5万亩的绿色森林，在为消费者提供对环境影响较低的可持续产品的同时，有效促进碳循环经济。

Q: Why is the successful development of carbon oxide-based glycol polyester fibers of great significance in contributing to ecological protection?

A: Since carbon dioxide is one of the main causes of global warming, reducing carbon dioxide emissions through a variety of techniques has become widely accepted. The introduction of carbon oxide-based glycol polyester fiber has revitalized industrial "waste gas." As a result of producing 30,000 tons of carbon dioxide-based glycol polyester fiber, approximately 10,000 tons of carbon dioxide are captured and sequestered from the environment annually, which is equivalent to the amount of carbon dioxide absorbed by one million trees annually and the addition of roughly 15,000 mu of green forest to the earth. This effectively promotes the circular carbon economy while offering consumers environmentally friendly products.

黑色循环再利用再生纤维素纤维
Black Recycled Regenerated Cellulose Fiber

推荐理由： 以部分或全部回收再利用废旧棉或纤维素制品制取浆粕，减少森林资源的砍伐量，叠加原液着色技术，实现绿色升级。

Reasons for recommendation
The amount of deforestation of forest resources can be decreased by recycling and reusing waste cotton or cellulose products to make pulp, either fully or partially. Green upgrading is accomplished when dope-dyed technology is included.

● 入选企业 COMPANY
唐山三友集团兴达化纤有限公司
Tangshan Sanyou Group Xingda Chemical Fiber Co., Ltd.

唐丝 TangCell

制备技术
Preparative technique

以回收浆粕为原料，在线添加色浆，经湿法纺丝工艺制得黑色循环再利用再生纤维素纤维产品。

Recycled pulp is wet spun with color paste added to create the black recycled regenerated cellulose fiber product.

纤维及制品特点
Features of fibers and finished products

主要规格 Main Specifications
短纤：1.33dtex×38mm，1.67dtex×38mm
Staple: 1.33dtex×38mm, 1.67dtex×38mm

相关标准 Relative Standards
《黏胶短纤维》（GB/T 14463—2008）
Viscose staple fiber (GB/T 14463—2008)

黑色循环再利用再生纤维素纤维原貌图
The original appearance figure of black recycled regenerated cellulose fiber

黑色循环再利用再生纤维素纤维性能指标
Performance indexes of black recycled regenerated cellulose fiber

产品规格 Specifications	干断裂强度 (cN/dtex) Dry breaking strength (cN/dtex)	湿断裂强度 (cN/dtex) Wet breaking strength (cN/dtex)	干断裂伸长率 (%) Dry elongation at break (%)	湿模量 (cN/dtex) Wet modulus (cN/dtex)	色牢度 （级） Color fastness (grade)
1.33dtex×38mm	2.3	1.2	21.4	0.3	4

纤·无界

纤维性能与制品特点

- 以部分或全部回收再利用材料制取的浆粕为原料，绿色环保。
- 原液着色，省去了后续的染色环节，降低了生产成本。
- 示踪溯源技术，做到从产品到终端品牌整体产业链的透明。
- 可生物降解，源于自然，归于自然。
- 面料手感柔软，亲肤透气。

Properties of fibers and features of finished products

- The pulp made from partially or completely recycled materials is used as raw material, which is green and environmentally friendly.
- The dope-dyed technique eliminates the subsequent dyeing process and reduces the production cost.
- The traceability technology makes the whole industry chain transparent from products to end brands.
- Biodegradable, coming from nature and returning to it.
- Soft, skin-friendly and breathable fabrics.

下游应用指导
The downstream application guidance

前定形： 预定形温度120°C，无须加染色助剂。
前处理： 可参考棉处理工艺，需要进行坯布、水洗、烧毛、水洗、定形、二次定形等工序。
后整理： 后定形温度建议160~180°C，需要加入酸、渗透剂及柔软剂。

Pre-setting: 120° C pre-setting temperature; no dyeing agents are needed.

Pre-treatment: Refer to the cotton treatment process, which requires blanking, washing, burning, washing, setting, and secondary setting.

Post-finishing: The recommended post-setting temperature is 160 ~ 180° C, with acid, penetrating agent and softeners added.

黑色循环再利用再生纤维素纤维下游应用实例
Examples of downstream applications of black recycled regenerated cellulose fiber

面料类型 Terminal field	原料配比 Raw material ratio	纤维规格 Fiber specifications	产品特性 Properties of the product
机织面料 Woven fabrics	70% 涤纶 / 棉 / 麻 / 30% 黑色循环再利用再生纤维素纤维 70% dacron/cotton/hemp/ 30% black recycled regenerated cellulose fiber	1.33dtex/38mm	较针织面料有强度高、耐磨损及易处理等多重优势、保形抗皱 Compared with knitted fabrics, it has multiple advantages such as strength, abrasion resistance, easy handling and wrinkle resistance
经编面料 Warp knitting fabric	50% 黑色循环再利用再生纤维素纤维 / 28% 涤纶 /22% 锦纶 70% 黑色循环再利用再生纤维素纤维 /30% 锦纶 50% black recycled regenerated cellulose fiber / 28% dacron / 22% chinlon 70% black recycled regenerated cellulose fiber/ 30% chinlon	1.67dtex/38mm	有舒适性、适应性、保暖性、透气性、弹性、变化多样性 Comfortable, adaptive, warm, breathable, elastic, versatile

纤维应用
Application of fibers

| 服装用纺织品
Clothing textiles | 婴儿服
Baby clothes | 牛仔
Jeans | 毛衣
Sweater | 高端成衣
High-end ready-to-wear |

Q：黑色循环再利用再生纤维素纤维在碳排放方面降低了多少？其省去印染环节对产业链减碳有哪些意义？

A：该产品取得了生命周期评估认证（LCA 认证），瑞士通用公证行（SGS）评估了从摇篮到大门阶段纤维对气候变化、富营养化、非生物耗竭、用水、人体毒性、生态毒性的影响。评估依据及方法符合 Worldly MSI 的标准，其中，Worldly MSI 数据显示，1kg 黏胶纤维全球平均碳排放为 8.36kg CO_2eq，而 1kg 黑色循环再利用再生纤维素纤维的碳排放为 3.10kg CO_2eq，较全球平均水平低 5.26kg CO_2eq。该产品省去印染环节，缩短纺织产业链，助力产业链减碳。

Q : How much does black recycled regenerated cellulose fiber lower carbon emissions? What is the significance of its elimination of the printing and dyeing process for carbon emission reduction in the industry chain?

A: The product is LCA certified, and SGS evaluated its cradle-to-gate impact on climate change, eutrophication, abiotic depletion, water consumption, human toxicity, and ecotoxicity. The basis and methodology of the assessment is in line with the Worldly MSI standards. The Worldly MSI data shows that the global average carbon emission of 1kg of viscose fiber is 8.36kg CO_2eq, while the carbon emission of 1kg of black recycled regenerated cellulose fiber is 3.10kg CO_2eq, which is 5.26kg CO_2eq lower than the global average. The product eliminates the printing and dyeing processes, shortening the textile industry chain, and helping the industry chain reduce carbon emissions.

rPET 基化学法再生氨纶
rPET-based Chemically Regenerated Elastane

推荐理由： 该纤维拓展了原料来源渠道，消费后再生原料的含量为 34%~36%，相对常规氨纶，可以减少 60% 的碳排放且低温可染，有效降低了能耗与环境负担。

Reasons for recommendation
The fiber expands the sources of raw materials; it contains 34%–36% post-consumer recycled raw materials; it can reduce carbon emissions by 60% when compared to traditional elastane; and it can be dyed at low temperatures, which significantly lowers energy consumption and environmental burden.

● 入选企业 COMPANY
连云港杜钟新奥神氨纶有限公司
LDZ New Aoshen Spandex Co., Ltd.

奥神 AOSHEN

制备技术
Preparative technique

以废旧聚酯瓶为原料，经化学法醇解制得聚酯二元醇，以此为主要原料通过预聚合、扩链反应生成聚酯型聚氨酯和聚氨酯脲高分子化合物，再经干法纺丝工艺制成纤维。

Using waste polyester bottles as raw materials, polyester glycol is obtained through chemical alcoholysis. This polyester glycol is then used as the main raw material to undergo pre-polymerization and chain extension reactions to produce polyester-based polyurethane and polyurethane-urea polymer compounds. Subsequently, the fiber is manufactured through a dry spinning.

纤维及制品特点
Features of fibers and finished products

主要规格 Main Specifications
长丝：20 旦 /1f，30 旦 /3f，40 旦 /3f，70 旦 /4f，150 旦 /14f，300 旦 /28f
Filament: 20D/1f, 30D/3f, 40D/3f, 70D/4f, 150D/14f, 300D/28f

相关标准 Relative Standards
《氨纶长丝》（FZ/T 54010—2014）
Elastane filament yarns (FZ/T 54010—014)

rPET 基化学法再生氨纶原貌图
The original appearance figure of rpet-based chemically regenerated elastane

纤维性能与制品特点

- 消费后再生，原料来源更加丰富，物理指标与原生氨纶基本一致。
- 分散染料低温（100~110℃）可染，高皂洗牢度和升华牢度。
- 产品可追溯。

Properties of fibers and features of finished products

- Post-consumer recycling provides a richer source of raw materials, and its physical indicators are basically the same as virgin elastane.
- Disperse dyes can be dyed at low temperature (100~110°C), with high soap washing fastness and sublimation fastness.
- Traceable products.

rPET 基化学法再生氨纶性能指标
Performance indexes of rpet-based chemically regenerated elastane

产品规格 Specifications	干断裂强度 (cN/dtex) Breaking tenacity (cN/dtex)	断裂伸长率 (%) Elongation at break(%)	300% 伸长时强度 (cN/dtex) Strength at 300% elongation (cN/dtex)	300% 时弹性回复率 (%) Elastic recovery rate at 300% elongation (%)	溶剂残存率 (%) Solvent residual rate (%)	消费后再生含量 (%) Content of post-consumer recycled material (%)	酸性染料上色率 (%) Acid dye dyeing rate (%)
40 旦	1.36	491	0.61	91.10	0.08	36	≥ 75

下游应用指导
The downstream application guidance

织造： 与常规氨纶一致。

染色： 分散染料低温 100~110℃染色。

Weaving: Same as conventional elastane.

Dyeing: Disperse dye is dyed at a low temperature of 100~110°C .

rPET 基化学法再生氨纶下游应用实例
Examples of downstream applications of rpet-based chemically regenerated elastane

终端领域 Terminal field	原料配比 Raw material ration	主要产品及特点 Mail products and properties
商务正装 Specillfication	86%75 旦再生涤纶 /10%40 旦氨纶 / 4%40 旦 rPET 基消费后再生氨纶 86% 75D recycle polyester/10% 40D spandex/ 4% 40D rPET-based post-consumer recycle spandex	商务男裤、外套等，环保、挺阔 Used for business men's trousers, coat, etc, with eco-friendly and crisp
运动休闲 Sports and leisure	96%120 旦涤纶 /4%40 旦 rPET 基消费后再生氨纶 96% 120D polyester/4%40D rPET-based post-consumer recycle spandex	用于 T 恤，吸湿排汗、耐磨、透气 Used for T-shirt, with moisture-wicking, breathable and wear-resistant
	92%75 旦涤纶 /8%30 旦 rPET 基消费后再生氨纶 92%75D polyester/8% 40D rPET-based post-consumer recycle spandex	用于运动服，吸湿排汗、耐磨、弹性好 Used for sportswear, with moisture-wicking, wear-resistant and elastic

纤维应用
Application of fibers

| 服装用纺织品 Clothing textiles | 运动服 Sportswear | 袜子 Socks | 泳衣 Swimsuit | 瑜伽服 Yoga clothes |

Q：rPET 基化学法再生氨纶的性能亮点和竞争优势体现在哪里？

A： 该纤维是部分原料来自消费后废旧 PET 的再生氨纶产品，解决了消费前再生产氨纶原料不稳定和产量受限等问题。同时，相较于常规氨纶，该产品具有分散染料低温易染（100~110°C）的优势，生产 1 吨 rPET 基化学法再生氨纶可以消耗废旧 PET 饮料瓶 36000 个，且生产过程有明显的减碳作用，相对于生产 1 吨普通氨纶可以减少 60% 的碳排放。

Q: What are the performance highlights and competitive advantages of rPET-based chemically regenerated elastane?

A: This fiber is a recycled spandex product with part of its raw materials sourced from post-consumer waste PET, addressing the issues such as the instability and limited production of raw materials for pre-consumer recycled spandex. Meanwhile, compared to conventional elastane, this product has the advantage of easy dyeing with disperse dyes at low temperature (100~110 °C). The production of 1 ton of rPET-based chemically regenerated elastane can consume 36000 waste PET bottles, and the production process has an significant carbon emission reduction effect, reducing carbon emissions by 60% compared to that of 1 ton of ordinary elastane.

低温热黏合纤维
LOW-TEMPERATURE HEAT-BONDABLE FIBER

低温热黏合纤维自带「天然亲和」与「智能自黏」属性，开启无胶黏新时代。凭借物理精妙设计的皮芯复合结构，无须化学胶水辅助，既能紧密相连又稳固持久，制作的卫材产品柔软蓬松、安全健康，每一次贴身接触都是与自然相拥，给予娇嫩肌肤极致呵护。

■ 推荐纤维及品牌

微细旦皮芯复合热黏合纤维
Micro-denier Sheath-Core Composite Heat-bondable Fiber

多组分复合改性聚乳酸纤维
Multi-component Composite Modified Polylactic Acid Fiber

MR FIBER PLON

Low-temperature heat-bondable fiber comes with the attributes of "natural affinity" and "intelligent self-bonding", opening a new era of glue-free. Its physically subtle composite sheath core structure allows it to be securely joined, stable, and long-lasting without the use of chemical glue. Sanitary products made from it are fluffy and soft, safe, and healthy, and every intimate touch is a hug with nature, providing the best care for sensitive skin.

纤·无界

127

微细旦皮芯复合热黏合纤维
Micro-denier Sheath-Core Composite Heat-bondable Fiber

推荐理由：成功打破国外产品的长期垄断，皮芯复合纤维实现细旦化。纤维黏合温度低、不含胶黏剂，尽显绿色环保属性。实现品质与环保层面双重跃升，为下游用户带来全新选择。

Reasons for recommendation
By achieving fine denier, the sheath-core composite fiber effectively breaks the long-standing monopoly of foreign products. With its low bonding temperature and free of adhesives, the fiber exhibits complete green and environmental protection qualities. It realizes the double leap in quality and environmental protection, and brings new options for downstream users.

● 入选企业 COMPANY
福建闽瑞新合纤股份有限公司
Fujian Mr Fiber Joint Co., Ltd.

制备技术
Preparative technique

由两种具有不同熔点的切片通过双螺杆纺丝机挤压挤出，采用皮芯复合纺丝技术制成以低熔点 PE 作为皮层，高熔点 PET 作为芯层的微细旦皮芯复合热黏合纤维。

Two kinds of chips with different melting temperature were extruded by twin-screw spinning machine to make the micro-denier sheath-core composite heat-bondable fiber with low melting temperature PE as sheath and high melting temperature PET as core using the sheath-core composite spinning technology.

纤维原貌图
Original appearance figure of the fiber

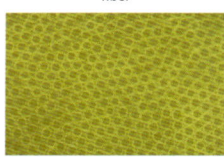

纤维截面图
Cross-section figure of the fiber

微细旦皮芯复合热黏合纤维原貌和截面图
The original appearance figure and cross-section figure of micro-denier sheath-core composite heat-bondable fiber

纤维及制品特点
Features of fibers and finished products

主要规格 Main Specifications
短纤：0.4dtex×51mm，0.6dtex×51mm，0.8dtex×51mm
Staple: 0.4dtex×51mm, 0.6dtex×51mm, 0.8dtex×51mm

相关标准 Relative Standards
《细旦聚乙烯/聚对苯二甲酸乙二醇酯（PE/PET）复合短纤维》
（T/CCFA 01051—2021）
Polyethylene/polyethylene terephthalate (PE/PET) bicomponent composite staple fiber (T/CCFA 01051—2021)

纤维性能与制品特点
- 无胶黏剂，低碳环保。
- 纤维制品手感柔软蓬松、亲肤性好。
- 回弹性、吸水性好。

Properties of fibers and features of finished products
- No adhesive, low-carbon and environmentally-friendly.
- Soft and fluffy fiber products with good skin-friendliness.
- Good elasticity and water absorption.

微细旦皮芯复合热黏合纤维性能指标
Performance indexes of micro-denier leather core composite heat-bondable fiber

产品规格 Specifications	含油率 (%) content (%)	比电阻 (Ω·cm) Specific resistance (Ω·cm)	干热收缩率 (%) Dry-thermal shrinkage (%)	断裂强度 (cN/dtex) Breaking strength (cN/dtex)	断裂伸长率 (%) Elongation at break (%)
0.8dtex×51mm	0.27	3.4×106	3.0	3.02	93.6

卷曲度 (%) Crimpness (%)	卷曲数 (个/25mm) Number of crimps (Pc/25mm)	超长纤维率 (%) Ultra-long fiber rate (%)	倍长纤维含量 (mg/100g) Extra-long fiber content (mg/100g)	疵点 (mg/100g) Defects (mg/100g)
15.2	11.2	99.1	0	0

下游应用指导
The downstream application guidance

混纺： 混纺比例可在 30%~70% 之间调整。对于需要更高强度的产品，可与高强度纤维进行合理搭配。

Blending: The blending ratio can be adjusted between 30%~70%. High-strength fibers can be properly integrated for products that require more strength.

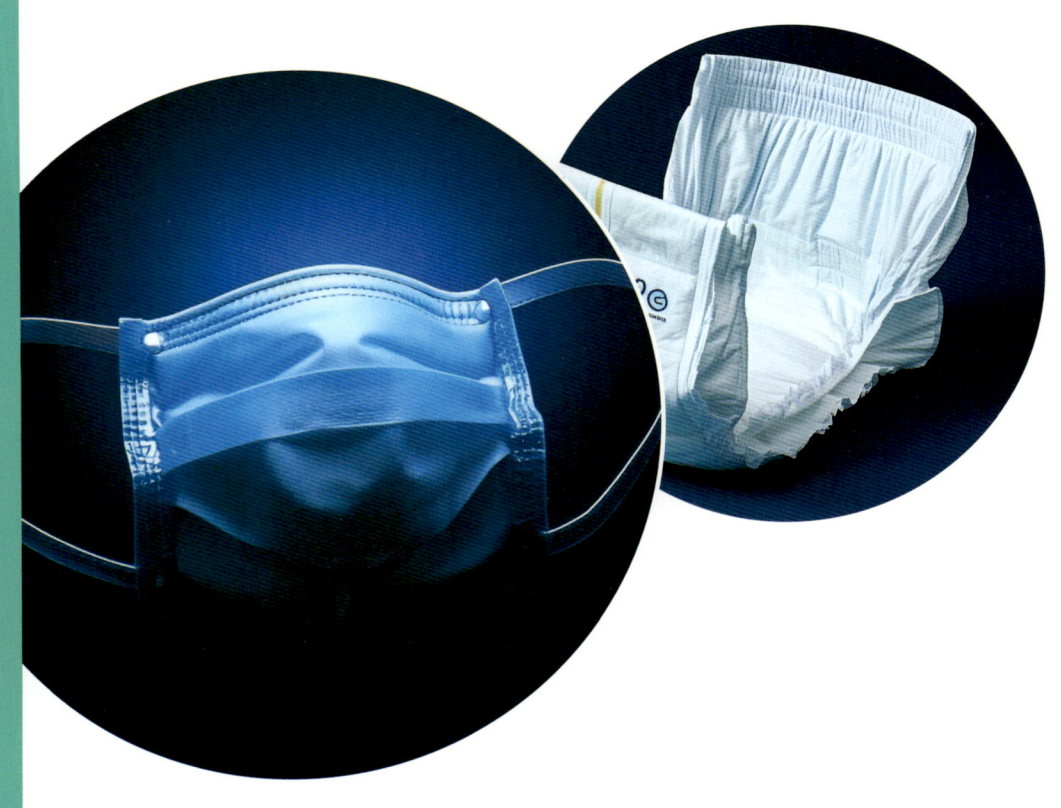

纤维应用
Application of fibers

产业用纺织品	纸尿裤	卫生巾	医疗防护用品	口罩
Industrial textiles	Paper diaper	Sanitary napkin	Medical protective equipment	Gauze mask

Q & A

Q：该产品是否在某些应用领域具有独特优势？
A： 该纤维的细旦化赋予纤维极致的柔软，用于纸尿裤能够给予婴儿娇嫩肌肤极致的呵护，减少摩擦带来的不适感。低熔点带来的良好的热黏合性能使纸尿裤结构更加稳定，不易分层或变形，确保在宝宝活动过程中始终保持良好的贴合度，有效防止侧漏。

Q: Does this product provide any distinct advantages in specific applications?
A: The fiber's fine denier provides it the utmost softness, making it suitable for use in diapers to provide the best possible care for infants' sensitive skin and lessen friction-induced discomfort. Because of the fiber's low melting point and strong heat-bonding qualities, diapers' structure is more stable and less likely to delaminate or deform, guaranteeing a snug fit throughout babies' activities and avoiding side leaks.

多组分复合改性聚乳酸纤维
Multi-component Composite Modified Polylactic Acid Fiber

推荐理由： 纤维皮层与芯层均为可降解材料，其制品天然抑菌、人体相容性优异，柔软亲肤，有效解决了卫材领域"用即抛"的废弃物污染问题，具有高价值绿色属性。

Reasons for recommendation
The fiber's core and sheath layers are made of biodegradable materials, and its products are naturally antibacterial, highly compatible with humans, soft and skin-friendly. It effectively addresses the issue of "use and throw" in the sanitary materials industry which leads to waste pollutions, while also having high green value qualities.

PLON 绿纶 PLON

● 入选企业 COMPANY
苏州金泉新材料股份有限公司
Suzhou Kingcharm New Materials Co., Ltd.

制备技术
Preparative technique

纤维皮层材料采用低熔点聚乳酸与微生物直接合成的可生物降解聚羟基脂肪酸酯(PHA)改性切片（熔点约118~135℃），芯层材料为高熔点聚乳酸切片（熔点约160~175℃），二者分别在线添加抗老化助剂、填料等工序挤出造粒，干燥后的切片通过双螺杆挤出机和异形喷丝板，经熔融复合纺丝工艺制备纤维。

The sheath layer material of the fiber is biodegradable chips (with a melting point of about 118~135 ℃) modified by low melting point polylactic acid and polyhydroxyalkanoate (PHA) directly synthesized from microorganism. The core layer material is high melting point polylactic acid chips (with a melting point of about 160~175 ℃). Both of them are extruded and pelletized by online addition of anti-aging additives and fillers. After drying, the chips are used to prepare the fiber by composite melt spinning process through twin-screw extruder and profiled spinneret.parallel composite spinning technology is used to produce isomeric composite elastic polyamide fibers.

纤维原貌图
Original appearance figure of the fiber

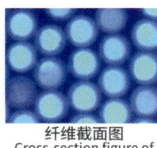

纤维截面图
Cross-section figure of the fiber

多组分复合改性聚乳酸纤维原貌和截面图
The original appearance figure and cross-section figure of multi-component composite modified polylactic acid fiber

纤维及制品特点
Features of fibers and finished products

主要规格 Main Specifications
短纤：1.8dtex×38mm，2.2dtex×38mm，1.5dtex×51mm，3.0dtex×51mm
Staple: 1.8dtex×38mm, 2.2dtex×38mm, 1.5dtex×51mm, 3.0dtex×51mm

相关标准 Relative Standards

《低熔点聚乳酸（LMPLA）/聚乳酸(PLA)复合短纤维》（FZ/T 52058—2021）
《聚乳酸短纤维》（FZ/T 52041—2015）
Low melting point polylactide (LMPLA)/polylactide (PLA) bicomponent staple fiber (FZ/T 52058—2021)
Polylactide staple fiber (FZ/T 52041—2015)

纤维性能与制品特点
- 生物基原料、绿色环保、可生物降解。
- pH 呈弱酸性，亲肤柔软，具有天然抑菌效果。
- 较好的导湿快干性。
- 强度保持率提升，耐用性良好。

Properties of fibers and features of finished products
- Bio-based raw materials, green and environmentally friendly, and biodegradable.
- Weakly acidic pH, skin-friendly and soft, with natural anti-bacteria effect.
- Good moisture-conducting and quick-drying properties.
- Improved strength retention, and good durability.

多组分复合改性聚乳酸纤维性能指标
Performance indexes of multi-component composite modified polylactic acid fiber

产品规格 Specifications	断裂强度 (cN/dtex) Breaking strength (cN/dtex)	断裂伸长率 (%) Elongation at break (%)	卷曲数 (个/25mm) Number of crimps (Pc/25mm)	90天断裂强度保持率 (%) 90-day breaking strength retention rate (%)	pH	可降解性 (%) Degradability (%)
1.8dtex×38mm	3.11	40.38%	14	99.40	6.1	100

面料 (100% 本纤维) 抑菌率 (%) Fabric (100% this fiber) antibacterial rate (%)			柔软度 (mN) 热风非织造布 (100% 本纤维) Softness (mN) Hot-air non-woven fabric (100% this fiber)		
金黄色葡萄球菌 Staphylococcus aureus	大肠杆菌 Escherichia coli	白色念珠菌 Candida albicans	克重 (g/㎡) Grammage (g/㎡)	纵向 Longitudinal	横向 Horizontal
96	95	92	89.25	69.50	3.375

下游应用指导
The downstream application guidance

织造：可用于生产热风非织造布。
热风工艺：建议初熔点设定在 129~133℃，生产线设置分区温度，生产前后阶段设定为低温度，生产中间阶段设定为高温度。

Weaving: It can be used to produce hot-air non-wovens.
Hot-air process: It is recommended that the initial melting point be set at 129~133° C, and that the production line be set up with zoned temperatures, with low temperatures set for the pre- and post-production stages, and high temperatures set for the middle production stage.

多组分复合改性聚乳酸纤维下游应用实例
Examples of the downstream applications of multi-component composite modified polylactic acid fiber

面料类型 Terminal field	原料配比 Raw material ratio	纤维规格 Fiber specifications	产品特性 Properties of the product
热风非织造布 Hot-air non-woven fabrics	100% 多组分复合改性聚乳酸纤维 100% multi-component composite modified polylactic acid fiber	1.8dtex×38mm 2.2dtex×38mm	应用在卫生巾、纸尿裤、日抛裤等产品的贴肤层，柔软亲肤，速渗透气 It is applied in the skin-contact layer of sanitary pads, diapers, and disposable pants, and is soft and skin friendly, with quick permeability and breathability

纤维应用
Application of fibers

产业用纺织品 | 卫生巾 | 日抛裤
Industrial textiles | Sanitary napkins | Disposable pants

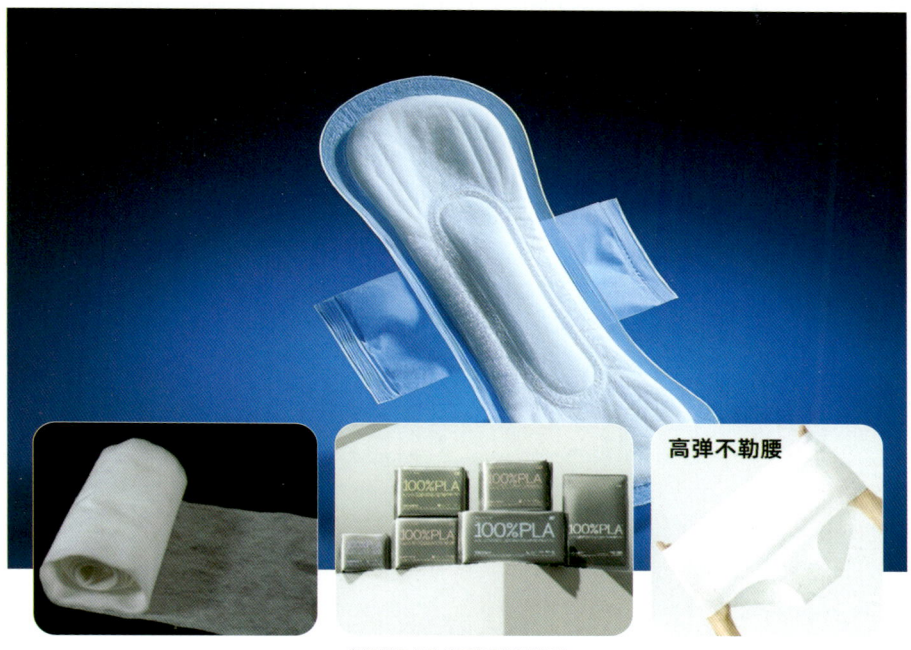

高弹不勒腰

多组分复合改性聚乳酸纤维制品
Products of multi-component composite modified polylactic acid fiber

Q：多组分复合改性聚乳酸纤维产品为消费者的生活带来了哪些全新体验呢？
A： 纯聚乳酸纤维制品手感偏硬及易老化问题得到有效解决，相较于纯聚乳酸纤维 90 天内的强度保持率，多组分复合改性聚乳酸纤维已从 87.1% 提升至 99.4%，终端产品更加耐用耐老化。良好的使用寿命与生物可降解特点，轻柔亲肤、抑菌除味、不易致敏、可迅速导出热气与湿气、舒适性显著提升等，进一步为消费者带来全新绿色舒爽体验。

Q: What new experiences have multi-component composite modified polylactic acid fiber products brought to consumers' lives?
A: The hard hand feel and easy aging of pure polylactic acid fiber products has been effectively solved. The strength retention rate of the multi-component composite modified polylactic acid fiber has risen from 87.1% to 99.4% in 90 days when compared to the strength retention rate of pure polylactic acid fiber. The final product is also more resilient to aging. Long service life, biodegradable qualities, gentleness and skin friendliness, antibacterial and deodorizing properties, non-allergenic properties, rapid heat and moisture dissipation, greatly enhanced comfort, etc., all contribute to giving customers a novel, green and cozy experience.

纤·无界

RECOMMENDED FIBERS

中国纤维流行趋势

入围纤维

RECOMMENDED FIBERS
CHINA FIBERS FASHION TRENDS 2025/2026

生物基化学纤维
BIO-BASED CHEMICAL FIBER

- DT 新溶剂法再生纤维素纤维
  DT new solvent method-regenerated cellulose fiber
- 沙棘改性再生纤维素纤维
  Sea buckthorn-modified regenerated cellulose fiber
- 可追溯低碳再生纤维素纤维
  Traceable low-carbon regenerated cellulose fiber
- 胶原蛋白改性竹莱赛尔纤维
  Collagen-modified bamboo Lyocell fiber
- 导湿快干原液着色聚乳酸纤维
  Moisture-conductive fast-drying dope-dyed PLA fiber

循环再利用化学纤维
RECYCLED CHEMICAL FIBER

- 海洋再生聚酯纤维
  Marine regenerated polyester fiber

原液着色化学纤维
DOPE-DYED CHEMICAL FIBER

- 亮彩轻柔聚酯纤维
  Bright-colored lightweight soft polyester fiber
- 原位聚合超黑聚酯纤维
  In-situ-polymerized ultra-black polyester fiber
- 原液着色仿麂皮海岛聚酯纤维
  Dope-dyed imitation suede sea-island polyester fiber

抗静电纤维
ANTI-STATIC FIBER

- 白色皮芯复合抗静电聚酯纤维
  White leather-core composite polyester fiber

抑菌纤维
ANTIBACTERIAL FIBER

稀土改性抑菌聚酯纤维
Rare earth-modified antibacterial polyester fiber

细旦多孔抑菌聚酯纤维
Fine-denier porous antibacterial polyester fiber

姜多酚改性抑菌再生纤维素纤维
Gingerol-modified antibacterial regenerated cellulose fiber

抑菌可降解再生纤维素纤维
Antibacterial degradable regenerated cellulose fiber

低熔点纤维
LOW-MELTING POINT FIBER

异形双组分低熔点聚酯纤维
Profiled double-component low-melting point polyester fiber

抗紫外纤维
ANTI-UV FIBER

无锑遮热聚酯纤维
Stibium-free heat-isolating polymerized fiber

抗紫外中空聚酰胺 6 纤维
Anti-UV hollow polyamide 6 fiber

舒感纤维
PLEASANT-FEEL FIBER

C 形扁平聚酯纤维
C-shaped flat polyester fiber

异形抗起球聚酯纤维
Profiled anti-pilling polyester fiber

亲水速干异形聚酯纤维
Hydrophilic fast-drying profiled polyester fiber

仿醋酸聚酯纤维
Imitation of cellulose acetate polyester fiber

桉树驱蚊防紫外聚酰胺 6 纤维
Eucalypt mosquito-dispelling anti-UV polyamide 6 fiber

抗起球干法聚丙烯腈纤维
Anti-pilling polyacrylonitrile fiber prepared by dry-jet wet spinning technique

调温抑菌再生纤维素纤维
Temperature-regulating antibacterial regenerated cellulose fiber

大豆牛奶蛋白复合改性聚乙烯醇纤维
Soybean and milk protein composite PVA fiber

石墨烯改性纤维
GRAPHENE MODIFIED FIBER

石墨烯原位聚合改性异形有色聚酯纤维
Graphene in situ polymerized modified profiled colored polyester fiber

石墨烯改性循环再利用聚酯纤维
Graphene modified recycled polyester fiber

石墨烯改性聚丙烯腈纤维
Graphene modified polyacrylonitrile fiber

阻燃纤维
FIRE-RESISTANT FIBER

原位聚合阻燃有色聚酯纤维
In situ polymerized fire-resistant colored polyester fiber

原液着色阻燃循环再利用聚酯纤维
Dope-dyed fire-resistant recycled polyester fiber

入围纤维

生物基化学纤维
BIO-BASED CHEMICAL FIBER
RECOMMENDED FIBERS

自然随身，绿色随行。 生物基化学纤维源于自然，自带绿色基因，从废旧棉纺织品、非粮作物、沙棘果实提取物再到胶原蛋白……自然精华萦绕于身，打造人体亲和、柔软舒适、生物可降解的绿色舒享，展现现代科技与自然资源的完美契合。

Natural and friendly, serving as a green product all the way. Originated from nature, bio-based chemical fiber has a green gene in itself, full of the essence of the nature from waste and ole textiles, non-food crops, and sea buckthorn extract to collagen, offering the green comfort of skin-friendliness, softness and comfortableness, and degradability, displaying the perfect compatibility between modern technology and natural resources.

DT 新溶剂法再生纤维素纤维

特点：	原料来源废旧棉纺织品，资源再利用、生产更环保，易染色、手感柔软、亲肤性好，具有生物降解性，穿着舒适度高
规格：	111dtex/38f，111dtex/44f，133dtex/38f，133dtex/44f
应用指导：	可直接用于生产针织或机织面料，建议使用分散低温染料，染色与热定形温度≤130℃
应用领域：	时装服饰、床上用品等各类生活用品

- 品牌：瑞赛尔
- 申报企业：新乡化纤股份有限公司

沙棘改性再生纤维素纤维

特点：	含沙棘果实提取物，富含维生素C；吸湿性良好、易染色；面料柔软亲肤，可有效清除外界自由基，具有抗氧化功能，可自然降解；含黄酮成分，具有抗氧化功效
规格：	1.33dtex×38mm
应用指导：	可适量考虑使用代碱剂；染色后处理等整个过程不可用氧化性物质
应用领域：	春夏家居服、内衣等

- 品牌：果维多
- 申报企业：宜宾惠美纤维新材料股份有限公司

DT new solvent method-regenerated cellulose fiber

Feature: Using waste cotton textiles as raw materials, achieving the recycling of resources, making production more environment-friendly, easy to dye, soft to the touch, skin-friendly, degradable, comfortable to wear
Specification: 111dtex/38f, 111dtex/44f, 133dtex/38f, 133dtex/44f
Application guidance: It can be used immediately to knit or weave fabric. It is suggested to use dispersive low-temperature dye with the dyeing and heat setting temperature $\leqslant$ 130°C
Application field: Daily use as fashionable dress and personal adornments, and bedding

- Brand: BlyuRecel
- Declaring enterprise: Xinxiang Chemical Fiber Co., Ltd.

Sea buckthorn-modified regenerated cellulose fiber

Features: Containing sea buckthorn extract, rich in vitamin C, good at absorbing moisture, easy to dye, enabling the fabric to be soft and skin-friendly, able to effectively eliminate external free radicals, inhibiting oxidation, naturally degradable, with its component flavone giving an anti-oxidation effect
Specification: 1.33dtex×38mm
Application guidance: An appropriate amount of alkaline substitute can be used. It is not allowed to use any substance that can cause oxidization throughout the entire process including dyeing and after-treatment
Application areas: Spring and summer home wear, underwear etc.

- Brand: G.VITO
- Declaring enterprise: Yibin Hmei New Fiber Co., Ltd.

生物基化学纤维
BIO-BASED CHEMICAL FIBER

RECOMMENDED FIBERS

可追溯低碳再生纤维素纤维

特点：	生产工艺低碳环保，采用双极膜技术实现碱液及硫酸盐回收利用。做成的面料柔软吸湿、透气亲肤、可自然降解，示踪技术实现全产业链可追溯
规格：	1.33dtex×38mm
应用指导：	可纯纺，也可与棉、涤纶等混纺，在梳棉过程中采用"重梳理轻打击"工艺，减少短纤维的断裂；在织造过程中，可提高牵伸或打纬的速度，且整个牵经张力处理上采用低张力工艺；染色工艺参考常规再生纤维素纤维；与棉混纺面料的丝光工艺中，碱浓度按≤120g/L进行控制
应用领域：	内衣、童装、卫衣、睡衣、床上用品等

- 品牌：宜可雅
- 申报企业：宜宾丝丽雅集团有限公司

胶原蛋白改性竹莱赛尔纤维

特点：	生物基属性，绿色环保，纤维光泽丝滑、天然抑菌、拥有良好的吸湿性与抗静电性，蛋白质含量达2.5%以上，可自然降解
规格：	1.56dtex×38mm，1.67dtex×38mm
应用指导：	可与天然纤维、化学纤维混纺，采用紧密纺，减少毛羽指数；采用莱赛尔纤维的印染处理工艺，使用活性染料，卷染浸染，低温烘干
应用领域：	内衣、高端商务运动服装、床品等

- 品牌：里奥
- 申报企业：上海里奥纤维企业发展有限公司

导湿快干原液着色聚乳酸纤维

特点：	生物基属性叠加原液着色，绿色环保。纤维颜色、截面可定制，天然抑菌防螨，本质阻燃、导湿快干、蓬松保暖、可降解
规格：	56dtex/48f，84dtex/72f，111dtex/72f，133dtex/72f，167dtex/144f，167dtex/288f，588dtex/432f DTY
应用指导：	一般选择分散染料染色，注意尽量选择同一染料厂家相同类型的染料进行匹配；染色温度为100~110℃，定形温度为135℃左右
应用领域：	休闲服、运动服、工装、衬衫、装饰物

- 品牌：玉绫丝
- 申报企业：绍兴迈宝科技有限公司 / 现代纺织技术创新中心（鉴湖实验室）

Traceable low-carbon regenerated cellulose fiber

Features: With the manufacturing technology being low-carbon and environment-friendly, using the bipolar membrane technique to achieve the recycling of alkaline liquor and sulfate, making its fabric feel soft and absorb moisture, breathable, skin-friendly, and naturally degradable, enabling traceability throughout the entire industry chain with the tracer technology

Specification: 1.33dtex×38mm

Application guidance: It can be spun pure or blended with cotton, polyester, etc. During the carding process, the "heavy combing and light impact" technique is used to reduce the breakage of short fibers; During the weaving process, the speed of stretching or beating can be increased, and a low tension process is used for the entire warp tension treatment; The dyeing process refers to conventional regenerated cellulose fibers; In the silk polishing process of cotton blended fabrics, the alkali concentration is controlled at ⩽ 120g/L

Application areas: Underwear, children's garments, jackets, pajamas, bedding etc.

- Brand: Ecosliya
- Declaring enterprise: Yibin Grace Group Co., Ltd.

Collagen-modified bamboo Lyocell fiber

Features: Bio-based, green and environment-friendly, shiny, naturally antibacterial, good at absorbing moisture and resisting static electricity, with a protein content up to 2.5% and above, naturally degradable

Specification: 1.56dtex×38mm, 1.67dtex×38mm

Application guidance: This fiber can be blended with natural and chemical fibers. Compact-spinning should be used to increase the hairiness index. Adopting the printing and dyeing process of Lyocell fiber, using reactive dyes, roll dyeing and immersion dyeing, and low-temperature drying

Application areas: Underwear, hi-end business suits, sportswear, bedding etc.

- Brand: LYO
- Declaring enterprise: Shanghai Lyocell Fibre Development Co., Ltd.

Moisture-conductive fast-drying dope-dyed PLA fiber

Features: Bio-based, dope-dyed, green and environment-friendly, with fiber's color and section customizable, able to inhibit bacteria and mites, naturally fire-retardant, moisture-conductive and fast drying, fluffy and warmth-retaining, degradable

Specification: 56dtex/48f, 84dtex/72f, 111dtex/72f, 133dtex/72f, 167dtex/144f, 167dtex/288f, 588dtex/432f DTY

Application guidance: Dispersive dye should be selected in general. It should be noted that preferably dyes of the same type and from the same vendor should be chosen to establish a match. The dyeing temperature should be 100~110°C, and the setting temperature at 135°C or so

Application areas: Casual clothes, sportswear, working suits, shirts, trimmings

- Brand: BMC
- Declaring enterprise: Marlboro Technologies (Shaoxing) Limited / Zhejiang modern textile technology innovation center (Jianhu Laboratory)

RECYCLED CHEMICAL FIBER

循环再利用化学纤维

高值利用，循环新生。 循环再利用化学纤维重塑再创新，品质求超越，海洋废弃瓶回收利用减轻对环境污染的压力，实现循环新生与高值利用的有机统一。

Valuable and reusable, having a new lease on life. Recycled chemical fiber is re-shaping innovations, delivering excellent quality. By recycling waste and discarded bottles from the ocean, environmental pollution is reduced, and the organic integration between recycled materials and new values is achieved.

海洋再生聚酯纤维

特点： 海洋瓶回收再利用，减少资源浪费与环境污染，纤维通过CU-OBP认证，品质媲美原生，其面料抗皱、保形性好

规格： 33dtex/72f、56dtex/72f、84dtex/72f、111dtex/144f、167dtex/144f、167dtex/288f、333D/96f DTY

应用指导： 纤维性能与常规涤纶基本一致，织造染整工艺可参照常规涤纶进行

应用领域： T恤、衬衫、床品、玩具、箱包、鞋帽等

- 品牌：鑫鸣远
- 申报企业：苏州佳海特种纤维有限公司

Marine regenerated polyester fiber

Features: Achieving the recycling of discarded bottles from the ocean, reducing resources waste and environmental pollution, successfully completing the CU-OBP certification, delivering a quality comparable to the original, enabling its fabric to resist wrinkles and maintain a good shape

Specification: 33dtex/72f, 56dtex/72f, 84dtex/72f, 111dtex/144f, 167dtex/144f, 167dtex/288f, 333D/96f DTY

Application guidance: This fiber's performance should be generally consistent with regular polyester. The weaving, dyeing, and finishing processes should be carried out by reference to regular polyester

Application areas: T-shirts, shirts, beddings, toys, bags and suitcases, shoes and hats etc.

- Brand: XINMINGYUAN
- Declaring enterprise: Suzhou Jiahai Special Fiber Co., Ltd.

原液着色化学纤维
DOPE-DYED CHEMICAL FIBER

绚丽灵动，炫彩生活。原液着色化学纤维将面料色彩表现得淋漓尽致，色彩斑斓、色度可控、绿色环保，让居家环境与生活场景焕发多彩活力，时刻展现灵动之美。

Gorgeous and vivid, livening up life. Dope-dyed chemical fiber gives a full play of fabric colors, adding bright luster, coming in controllable shades, green and environment-friendly, enabling home environment and living scenes to be more colorful and full of vitality, displaying a vivid beauty at any time.

入围纤维

亮彩轻柔聚酯纤维

- **特点**：纤维染色均匀性好，面料具有良好的透气性，耐磨抗皱、遮光性能优异，且易于清洁与保养
- **规格**：165dtex/72f DTY
- **应用指导**：避免长时间暴露在阳光下，建议环境温度保持在5~35℃之间；保持良好的通风环境，湿度应控制在50%~75%之间；使用过程中避免时间跨度大，不同批号的丝不可混用；制品避免与酸、碱等化学物质接触，避免与樟脑丸等具有挥发性的化学药剂存放在一起
- **应用领域**：西装、运动衣、运动裤、窗帘、装饰布、遮阳帽、手套、遮阳网

- 品牌：桐昆
- 申报企业：江苏桐昆恒阳化纤有限公司

原位聚合超黑聚酯纤维

- **特点**：原位聚合原液着色，产品黑度可控，色牢度高，超黑L值 ≈ 12，黑度远高于同品种，适用于细旦和多孔的黑色纤维产品
- **规格**：56dtex/72f，84dtex/36f，84dtex/144f，111dtex/144f，167dtex/48f DTY
- **应用指导**：应存放在阴凉、干燥、通风良好的仓库中，避免阳光直射和高温环境。运输过程中应注意防潮、防雨；加工前应对设备进行彻底清洁，避免杂质混入；应根据产品特性和下游客户需求进行合理搭配和使用
- **应用领域**：汽车内饰布、帐篷布、遮光服、黑色服装等

- 品牌：纤丝纺
- 申报企业：纤丝纺环保材料科技（苏州）有限公司

原液着色仿麂皮海岛聚酯纤维

- **特点**：绿色环保，仿麂皮效果良好；开纤前后色彩稳定、颜色丰富、色牢度高；面料透气性好
- **规格**：117dtex/36f DTY
- **应用指导**：注意开纤的温度及时间，推荐开纤温度100℃，时间15min，碱液浓度1.2%。同时要严格控制批与批之间的开纤时间与一致的碱液浓度
- **应用领域**：仿麂皮绒服装、鞋帽、沙发布、汽车内饰材料等

- 品牌：兴发
- 申报企业：绍兴诚邦高新纤维科技有限公司

DOPE-DYED CHEMICAL FIBER 原液着色化学纤维

Bright-colored lightweight soft polyester fiber

Feature: Good in color uniformity, enabling its fabric to breathe freely, endure wear, excellent shading performance, and easy to clean and maintain

Specification: 165dtex/72f DTY

Application guidance: Exposing this fiber to sun light for a long time should be avoided. It is suggested that the ambient temperature remain within the range of 5~35°C, good ventilation be maintained, and the humidity be kept within the range of 50%~75%. For use, mixing with the fibers that are produced a long time apart or in different batches should be avoided. Making the final products in contact with such chemical substances as acid and alkaline should be avoided. Storing it together with such volatile chemical medicament as camphor should be avoided

Application areas: Western dress, sport suits, sport pants, window curtains, decorating cloth, sun hats, gloves, shading nets

- Brand: TONGKUN
- Declaring enterprise: Jiangsu Tongkun Hengyang Chemical Fiber Co., Ltd.

In-situ-polymerized ultra-black polyester fiber

Feature: In-situ-polymerized and dope-dyed, controllable in blackness, high in color fastness, with the ultra-blackness value $L \approx 12$, far higher than those of the same type, suitable for fine denier and porous ultra-black fiber products

Specification: 56dtex/72f, 84dtex/36f, 84dtex/144f, 111dtex/144f, 167dtex/48f DTY

Application guidance: This fiber should be stored in a warehouse with shady, cool, dry, and well-ventilated conditions. Exposing this fiber directly to sunlight or to a high temperature should be avoided. During transportation, care should be taken to protect the fiber against moisture and rain. Before processing, equipment should be cleaned thoroughly so as to prevent and impurity from entering it. This fiber should be reasonably used and arranged in combinations according to product characteristics and downstream customers' requirements

Application areas: Automobile interior decorating cloth, tarps, sun-protective clothing, black garments etc.

- Brand: QSF
- Declaring enterprise: Suzhou Avant Environmental Sci-Tech Co., Ltd.

Dope-dyed imitation suede sea-island polyester fiber

Features: Green and environment-friendly, with a good effect of imitating suede, color-wise stable before and after splitting, rich in color, high in color fastness, enabling its fabric to be well breathable

Specification: 117dtex/36f DTY

Application guidance: Attention should be paid to splitting temperature and duration. A splitting temperature of 100°C, a duration of 15min, and an alkaline concentration of 1.2% are recommended. Meanwhile, the time between consecutive batches for splitting as well as the relevant consistent alkaline concentration should be strictly controlled

Application areas: Imitation suede clothes, sofa cloth, automobile interior decorating materials etc.

- Brand: Xingfa
- Declaring enterprise: Shaoxing Chengbang Hi-Tech Fiber And Technology Co., Ltd.

ANTI-STATIC FIBER
抗静电纤维

远离静电，舒适相伴。抗静电纤维是一种能够有效减少或消除静电积聚的特殊纤维材料。易于打理的舒心，让"你我"接触安心无忧，远离工作中的静电危害。

Free from static electricity, providing pleasant company. The anti-static fiber is a type of special fiber material able to effectively reduce or eliminate the buildup of static electricity. The comfort that it brings in its easy maintenance enables "you and me" to feel safe and relaxed when touching each other, and it keeps us away from the harm of static electricity at work.

白色皮芯复合抗静电聚酯纤维

特点：	解决了抗静电纤维浅色化的难题，白色纤维可染色、耐水洗、耐弯曲、不易断裂
规格：	22dtex/3f FDY
应用指导：	碱减量不能过高；在织造前需与其他纱线进行复合（空包/机包/倍捻）；在定形后整理加工时，温度应小于215℃；需注意磨毛、拉毛等工艺会把导电纤维扯断
应用领域：	防静电服、秋冬季服装、工业绳缆等

- 品牌：凡虎
- 申报企业：苏州凡虎导电纤维有限公司

入围纤维

White leather-core composite polyester fiber

Features: Solving the problem that anti-static fiber is light-colored, with white fiber able to be dyed, water-washed, and bent, difficult to break

Specification: 22dtex/3f FDY

Application guidance: The extent of alkali reduction should not be too high. Before the weaving process, the fibers need to be combined with other yarns (ACY/SCY/two for one twisted). In the finishing process after setting, the temperature should be less than 215℃. It needs to be noted that anti-static fiber may be pulled apart during such processes as sanding and napping.

Application areas: Anti-static clothes, autumn and winter clothes, industrial ropes and cables etc.

- Brand: Vistiger
- Declaring enterprise: Suzhou Vistiger fiber Co., Ltd.

ANTIBACTERIAL FIBER
抑菌纤维

抑菌防感,健康呵护。抑菌纤维实现抑菌效果新升级、更持久。纤维中稀土、姜多酚等抑菌材料,细旦多孔等工艺设计为消费者带来细微关怀,防螨、消臭助力生活安心、舒心。

Able to inhibit bacteria and protect against cold, delivering health care. Antibacterial fiber has an upgraded antibacterial effect, which lasts longer. The addition of such antibacterial materials as rare earth and gingerol to this fiber, as well as its fine-denier and porous design, provides customers with loving and tender care. It prevents mites and eliminates unpleasant odors, helpful in making life safer and happier.

稀土改性抑菌聚酯纤维

特点:	稀土添加,抑菌功能高效持久,具备远红外、负离子性能等特点
规格:	84dtex/48f DTY
应用指导:	可与其他纤维交织、包覆等组合使用,用于针织或机织面料;染色建议使用低温分散染料
应用领域:	袜子、家居服、工装、贴身内衣、床上寝具、沙发布、手术服等

- 品牌:稀贝丝
- 申报企业:中纺院(天津)科技发展有限公司

Rare earth-modified antibacterial polyester fiber

Features: With rare earth added, having a highly efficient and lasting antibacterial effect, characterized by far infrared and negative ion properties
Specification: 84dtex/48f DTY
Application guidance: This fiber can be interwoven and used in the covering process with other ones in combination for knitting or weaving fabrics. It is suggested that low-temperature dispersive dye be used in dyeing and finishing process.
Application areas: Socks, home wear, working suits, close-fitting underwear, bedding, sofa cloth, surgical gowns etc.

- Brand: REbase
- Declaring enterprise: China Textile Academy (Tianjin) Technology Development Co., Ltd.

细旦多孔抑菌聚酯纤维

特点： 具有良好的抑菌性，面料柔软透气，富有弹性与抗起球性，易护理

规格： 278dtex/288f，298dtex/288f，168~180dtex/288f POY、DTY

应用指导： 储存过程中应避免纤维暴露在阳光直射、高温高湿的环境中；对于不同机型的加弹机，加工车速应控制在680~750m/min的范围内；加弹丝加工变形温度应根据品种进行适当调整，变形温度不宜超过190°C

应用领域： 内衣、裙装、运动服、舞台服装等

- 品牌：桐昆
- 申报企业：江苏桐昆恒欣新材料有限公司

姜多酚改性抑菌再生纤维素纤维

特点： 发热保暖，植物基抑菌材料，抑菌功能持久，可自然降解

规格： 1.33dtex×38mm

应用指导： 在染色和整理过程中，pH严格控制在10以下；在添加氨纶生产针织面料时，尽量降低热定形温度，控制在195°C以内，缩短定形时间；避免使用阴离子型拒水类整理剂；针织产品配比不低于30%，机织产品配比不低于20%

应用领域： 针织内衣、T恤、衬衣、童装等

- 品牌：暖姜
- 申报企业：青岛邦特纤维有限公司

Fine-denier porous antibacterial polyester fiber

Features: Having a good antibacterial quality, with its fabric soft and breathable, highly elastic, able to resist pilling, easy to maintain

Specification: 278dtex/288f, 298dtex/288f, 168~180dtex/288f POY, DTY

Application guidance: During storage, exposing this fiber directly to sunlight, or to high-temperature or high-humidity conditions should be avoided. For different types of texturing machines, the processing speed should be kept within the range of 680~750m/min. The deforming temperature for textured yarn should be adjusted according to its type, and the deforming temperature should not be higher than 190°C

Application areas: Underwear, skirts, sportswear, costumes etc.

- Brand: TONGKUN
- Declaring enterprise: Jiangsu Tongkun Hengxin New Materials Co., Ltd.

Gingerol-modified antibacterial regenerated cellulose fiber

Features: Generating heat and retaining warmth, with bio-based antibacterial materials added, having a lasting antibacterial effect, naturally degradable

Specification: 1.33dtex×38mm

Application guidance: During the dyeing and finishing process, the pH should be kept strictly below 10. When polyurethane fiber is added to manufacturing knitted fabrics, the heat setting temperature should be as low as possible, which should be kept lower than 195°C. The duration of the setting should be shortened. Using a negative-ion water-repellent finishing agent should be avoided. The proportion of knitted products should be no less than 30%, while woven products no less than 20%

Application areas: Knitted underwear, T-shirts, shirts, children's garments

- Brand: WarmGinger
- Declaring enterprise: Qingdao BetterTex Fiber Co., Ltd.

抑菌纤维 / ANTIBACTERIAL FIBER

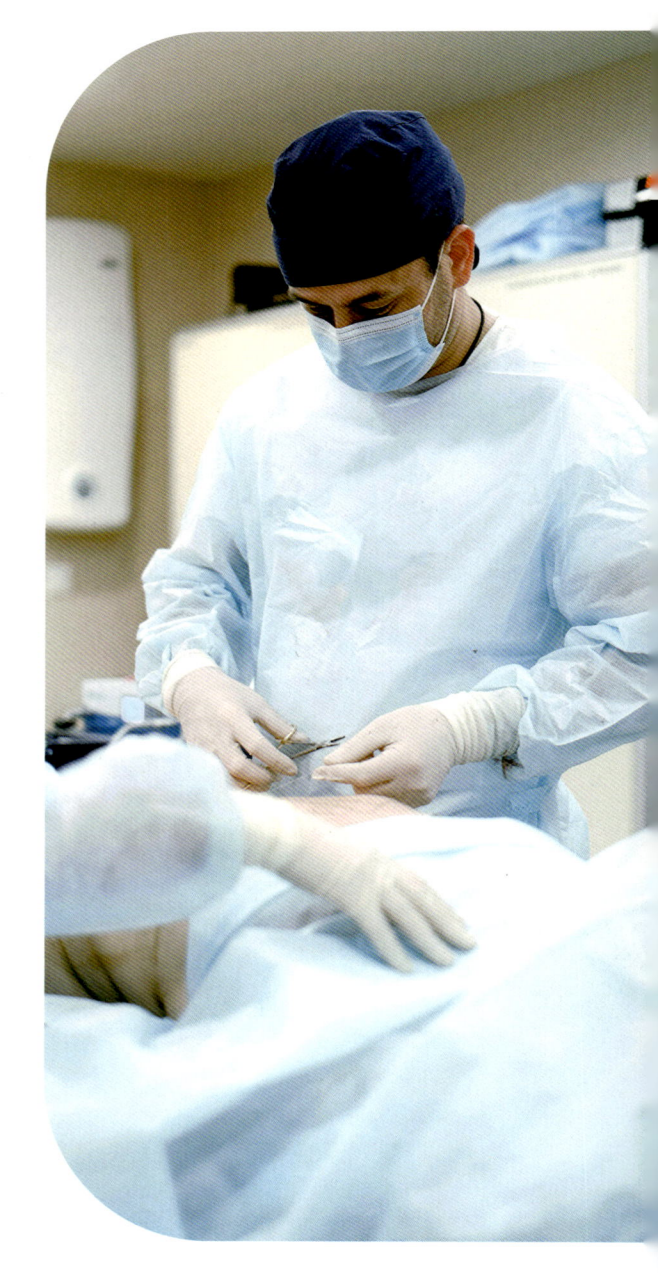

抑菌可降解再生纤维素纤维

- **特点**：手感柔软、光泽好、吸湿透气、抑菌、可自然降解；染色性好，色彩纯正、艳丽
- **规格**：1.33dtex×38mm
- **应用指导**：使用活性染料染色时，应注意染色温度为30℃，固色温度为40℃
- **应用领域**：内衣、牛仔、家居服、家纺等

- 品牌：兰丝尔
- 申报企业：太极石股份有限公司

Antibacterial degradable regenerated cellulose fiber

Features: Having a soft feel and a good shine, able to absorb moisture and breathable, antibacterial, naturally degradable, easy to dye, pure and bright in color
Specification: 1.33dtex×38mm
Application guidance: When active dye is used for dyeing, it should be noted that the dyeing temperature is 30℃, and the fixation temperature is 40℃
Application areas: Underwear, jeans, home wear, home textiles etc.

- Brand: lansir
- Declaring enterprise: Tai Chi Stone Co., Ltd.

LOW-MELTING POINT FIBER
低熔点纤维

热熔免胶、绿色环保。 低熔点纤维持续替代化学胶黏剂，具有热熔黏合温度低、黏合迅速、剥离强度高的特点，安全健康，环境更友好。

Thermally fused without adhesive, going green and protecting the environment. Low-melting point fiber has been continuously replacing chemical adhesive, low in thermal fusion temperature, fast in bonding, high in cracking strength, safe, healthy, and more environment-friendly.

异形双组分低熔点聚酯纤维

特点： 具备良好的吸湿导湿性能，热黏合技术可替代传统的胶水，绿色环保，具有成本优势
规格： 255dtex/72f, 365dtex/72f, 444dtex/144f DTY
应用指导：定形温度需控制在 180~230°C之间
应用领域：电子烟储油棉、香烟过滤嘴、马克笔笔头等

- 品牌：DP110
- 申报企业：凯泰特种科技有限公司

入围纤维

Profiled double-component low-melting point polyester fiber

Features: Good at absorbing and conducting moisture, giving so efficiently a thermal bonding performance as to replace conventional adhesive, green and environment-friendly, having a cost advantage
Specification: 255dtex/72f, 365dtex/72f, 444dtex/144f DTY
Applied technique: The setting temperature needs to be kept within the range of 180~230°C
Application areas: Electronic cigarette oil-storing cotton, cigarette filters, maker pen tips etc.

- Brand: DP110
- Declaring enterprise: CTA High-tech Fibre Co., Ltd.

ANTI-UV FIBER 抗紫外纤维

优异防护，无惧骄阳。随着户外热潮与健康意识的双重崛起，抗紫外纤维成为户外活动的"刚性需求"，叠加遮热、轻盈、柔软、透气等优异性能，完美适配夏日多彩缤纷的美好场景。

Excellent in protectiveness, braving the blazing sun. As both the wave of outdoor activity and the awareness of health have risen, the "rigid demand" for anti-UV fiber is becoming more urgent. Besides protecting against heat, and being lightweight, soft, and breathable, the anti-UV fiber fits perfectly in the colorful and beautiful scene of a summer day.

无锑遮热聚酯纤维

- 特点： 采用无锑催化技术，不含重金属，其面料可有效地阻挡紫外线，遮热效果明显
- 规格： 1.67dtex×38mm，84dtex/72f，167dtex/144f DTY
- 应用指导： 纤维在织物中的比例建议在30%以上，用量越多，遮热效果越明显；后处理工艺可按照普通的涤纶织物进行
- 应用领域： 户外运动服、防晒服、夏季休闲服、工装等

• 品牌：洁宜康
• 申报企业：上海洁宜康化工科技有限公司

抗紫外中空聚酰胺6纤维

- 特点： 纤维具有亚光风格以及抗紫外性能，中空结构赋予面料轻盈柔软质感
- 规格： 77.8dtex/36f×2 DTY
- 应用指导： 织造时应注意大圆机的换针，注意避免勾丝
- 应用领域： 瑜伽服、无缝内衣、针织T恤

• 品牌：雅达
• 申报企业：烟台华润锦纶有限公司

Stibium-free heat-isolating polymerized fiber

Features: Using antimony-free catalytic technology, containing no heavy metal, enabling the fabric to effectively block out UV light, having a remarkable heat-isolating effect

Specification: 1.67dtex×38mm, 84dtex/72f, 167dtex/144f DTY

Application guidance: It is suggested that the proportion of this fiber in fabric should be more than 30%. The higher the proportion is, the more remarkable the heat-isolating effect will be. The after-treatment can be carried out by reference to ordinary polyester textiles

Application areas: Outdoor sportswear, sun-blocking suits, summer casual clothes, working suits etc.

- Brand: JIECON
- Declaring enterprise: Shanghai Jiecon Chemicals Hi-tech Co., Ltd.

Anti-UV hollow polyamide 6 fiber

Features: In a matt style, able to resist UV light, with its hollow structure giving the fabric a quality of being lightweight and soft

Specification: 77.8dtex/36f ×2 DTY

Application guidance: In the weaving process, attention should be paid to any change in stitching by the machine. Care should be taken to avoid snagging

Application areas: Yoga suits, seamless underwear, knitted T-shirts

- Brand: YADA
- Declaring enterprise: China Resources Yantai Nylon Co., Ltd.

舒感纤维
PLEASANT-FEEL FIBER

舒适悦享，温馨感受。 舒感纤维是舒适性与功能性结合的高端体验，通过特殊工艺设计，赋予纤维柔软、亲肤、透气、调温及吸湿排汗等特性，有效提高面料的亲和触感与健康舒适的穿着体验，为生活增添温馨感受。

Comfortable and delightful, giving a warm feeling. The pleasant-feel fiber represents a high-end experience of comfortableness and functionality. The special technological design enables this fiber to be soft, skin-friendly, breathable, able to regulate temperature, absorb moisture, and get rid of sweat, effectively improving the fabric's pleasant and sweet feel, as well as the experience of feeling healthy and comfortable when wearing it, adding a mild and fragrant quality to life.

C形扁平聚酯纤维

- **特点：** 截面为C形，密度小，质轻，面料保暖性强，能够快速吸汗、导湿，保持人体皮肤的干爽感
- **规格：** 262dtex/144f POY
- **应用指导：** 纤维需存放在干燥、清洁、通风且不会阳光直晒的场所；加弹速度不超700 m/min，温度在180~190°C
- **应用领域：** 贴身内衣、户外服饰、衬衫、毛毯等

- 品牌：桐昆
- 申报企业：桐昆集团浙江恒腾差别化纤维有限公司

异形抗起球聚酯纤维

- **特点：** 纤维手感柔软、蓬松度高、光泽柔和，面料具有一定的防透效果
- **规格：** 1.33dtex×38mm，1.67dtex×38mm，3.9dtex×51mm，11dtex×88mm，11dtex×102mm
- **应用指导：** 下游应用参考常规涤纶短纤
- **应用领域：** 毛衫、针织内衣、家居服、休闲服、衬衫、牛仔服等

- 品牌：柔软聚酯纤维
- 申报企业：江苏垶恒复合材料有限公司

C-shaped flat polyester fiber

Features: Having a C-shaped section, low in density, lightweight, with the fabric highly capable of retaining the warmth, able to fast absorb sweat and get rid of moisture, keeping human skin dry
Specification: 262dtex/144f POY
Application guidance: This fiber needs to be stored under dry, clean, and ventilated conditions and should not be exposed directly to sunlight. The texturing speed should not exceed 700 m/min, and the temperature of the upper heating part should be within the range of 180~190°C
Application areas: Close-fitting underwear, outdoor clothes, shirts, woolen blankets etc.

- Brand: TONGKUN
- Declaring enterprise: Tongkun Group Zhejiang Hengteng Differential Fiber Co. Ltd.

Profiled anti-pilling polyester fiber

Features: Soft to the touch, highly fluffy, mildly shiny, enabling its fabric to be opaque in some way
Specification: 1.33dtex×38mm, 1.67dtex×38mm, 3.9dtex×51mm, 11dtex×88mm, 11dtex×102mm
Application guidance: Downstream applications should be by reference to regular polyester staple
Application areas: Sweaters, knitted underwear, home wear, leisure wear, shirts, jeans etc.

- Brand: Soft polyester fiber
- Declaring enterprise: Jiangsu Xingheng Composite Material Co., Ltd.

舒适感纤维
PLEASANT-FEEL FIBER
RECOMMENDED FIBERS

桉树驱蚊防紫外聚酰胺 6 纤维

特点：	蚊虫驱避率 B 级，天然植物安全环保，织物具有接触凉感、防紫外、吸湿透气等功能
规格：	77dtex/68f，154dtex/136f DTY，FDY
应用指导：	参照普通聚酰胺 6 纤维的染整工艺
应用领域：	婴童类服装、防晒驱蚊衣等

- 品牌：桉树驱蚊纤维
- 申报企业：青岛尼希米生物科技有限公司

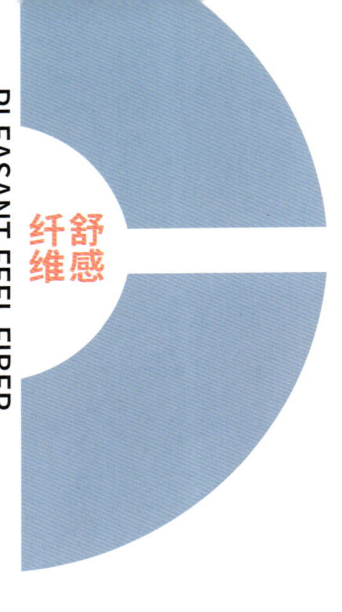

亲水速干异形聚酯纤维

特点：	纤维回潮率高，亲水性与抗静电性良好，其织物柔软抗皱、吸湿速干性能优异、蒸发速率高达 0.53（标准值为 ≥0.20）
规格：	56dtex/144f，167dtex/288f DTY
应用指导：	面料中纤维应用比例建议在总含量 30% 以上；混纺前预处理应根据实际使用情况进行松弛热定形；染色温度应控制在 100~130℃，pH 应控制在 4~5；后整理过程中定形温度建议不超过 180℃
应用领域：	运动服、休闲服、时尚女装、衬衣等

- 品牌：麻丽
- 申报企业：青岛新维纺织开发有限公司

仿醋酸聚酯纤维

特点：	光泽度好，可定制扁平形、三叶形截面，异形度高；八角形截面带来良好的吸湿性与仿醋酸纤维效果
规格：	30~150dtex/36~72f
应用指导：	织物组织、纬密会对织物光泽产生影响，建议机织物选用缎纹组织，适当提高纬密
应用领域：	女士连衣裙、礼服、衬衫等

- 品牌：桐昆
- 申报企业：江苏嘉通能源有限公司

Hydrophilic fast-drying profiled polyester fiber

Features: High in moisture-regaining rate, highly hydrophilic and anti-static, enabling its fabric to be soft, prevent pilling, absorb moisture, and fast dry, with evaporating rate up to 0.53 (nominal value is ≥ 0.20)
Specification: 56dtex/144f, 167dtex/288f DTY
Application guidance: It is suggested that the proportion of applied fiber should be more than 30% of the total content in the fabric. The relaxed heat setting process in the pretreatment before blending should be carried out according to actual application conditions. The dyeing temperature should be kept within the range of 100~130°C, and the pH value 4~5. It is suggested that the setting temperature should be less than 180°C during the after-treatment
Application areas: Sportswear, leisure wear, fashionable women's dresses, shirts etc.

- Brand: MALI
- Declaring enterprise: Qing Dao XINWEI Textile Development Co. Ltd.

Imitation of cellulose acetate polyester fiber

Features: Having a good shine, tailor-made to have a flat or trilobed leaf-shaped section, highly profiled, able to have an octagonal section so as to absorb moisture and produce an acetate fiber-imitating effect
Specification: 30~150dtex/36~72f
Application guidance: Because the structure and the weft density in a textile will affect its shine, it is suggested that the structure of satin weave should be selected for use in woven textiles, and weft density should be properly increased
Application areas: Women's dresses, ceremonial dress, shirts etc

- Brand: TONGKUN
- Declaring enterprise: Jiangsu Jiatong Energy Co., Ltd.

Eucalypt mosquito-dispelling anti-UV polyamide 6 fiber

Features: Having its mosquito-dispelling rate reaching Class B, natural plant-based, safe and environment-friendly, enabling its fabric to have a cool feel, able to block out sun light, protect against UV light, absorb moisture, and breathe freely
Specification: 77dtex/68f, 154dtex/136f DTY, FDY
Application guidance: The dyeing and finishing process for ordinary polyamide 6 fiber should be referred to
Application areas: Infant and children's clothes, sun-blocking mosquito-dispelling clothes etc.

- Brand: MosquitoSpell®
- Declaring enterprise: Qingdao Niximi Biotechnology Co., Ltd.

PLEASANT-FEEL FIBER 舒感纤维

抗起球干法聚丙烯腈纤维

特点：	犬骨形截面具有独特的芯吸功能，吸湿排汗性能优异；织物蓬松保暖、手感柔软，抗起球性较常规产品高 0.5 级以上
规格：	1.33dtex×38mm，1.67dtex×38mm，1.67dtex×52mm，2.22dtex×52mm，2.44dtex×5mm
应用指导：	干、湿法聚丙烯腈纤维混纺时，根据所染颜色深浅程度，染色保温时间至少 30~60min，染深色时需要延长时间至 90min
应用领域：	保暖内衣、仿羊绒制品等

- 品牌：中国石化
- 申报企业：中国石化集团齐鲁石化

调温抑菌再生纤维素纤维

特点：	生物基属性，绿色环保，具有可纺性好、焓值高（15J/g）、安全低敏、控温性能优越等特点
规格：	1.33dtex×38mm，1.67dtex×38mm，3.33dtex×51mm
应用指导：	纤维存放应避免高温、潮湿或阳光直射的环境；后道的生产环节中，应避免接触强酸、强碱，浸泡或染色温度不宜超过 100℃，烘干温度不超过 140℃
应用领域：	保暖内衣、针织衫、婴童恒温睡袋、袜子、冲锋衣、凉席、枕头、睡袋

- 品牌：Dukk® 生物基控温技术
- 申报企业：杭州尚选科技有限公司

大豆牛奶蛋白复合改性聚乙烯醇纤维

特点：	添加植物与动物蛋白，蛋白质含量在 30% 左右，与人体皮肤具有较好的亲和性，穿着舒适；具有抑菌、远红外保暖、负氧离子保健功效
规格：	1.65dtex×38mm
应用指导：	可与棉、黏胶纤维等混纺，也可作为家纺填充物；染整过程中，染色温度建议≤100℃
应用领域：	内衣、家居服、衬衣、床品填充物、面膜等

- 品牌：天绒
- 申报企业：上海全宇生物科技遂平有限公司

Anti-pilling polyacrylonitrile fiber prepared by dry-jet wet spinning technique

Features: With a dog bone-shaped section uniquely able to produce capillary action, good at absorbing moisture and getting rid of sweat, enabling its fabric to be fluffy, warm, and soft, and have its anti-pilling level being at least 0.5 points higher than regular ones
Specification: 1.33dtex×38mm, 1.67dtex×38mm, 1.67dtex×52mm, 2.22dtex×52mm, 2.44dtex×5mm
Application guidance: When the polyacrylonitrile fiber is made using dry and wet methods, the temperature-keeping duration for dyeing should be at least 30~60 minutes, depending on the shade of color. In the case of a dark shade, the duration needs to be extended until it has reached 90 minutes
Application areas: Thermal underwear, imitation cashmere products etc.

- Brand: SINOPEC
- Declaring enterprise: Sinopec Qilu Petrochemical Company

Temperature-regulating antibacterial regenerated cellulose fiber

Features: Bio-based, green and environment-friendly, easy to spin, high in enthalpy (15J/g), safe and less sensitive, good at controlling temperature
Specification: 1.33dtex×38mm, 1.67dtex×38mm, 3.33dtex×51mm
Application guidance: This fiber should be stored in a place where there is no high-temperature, no moisture, and the fiber is not exposed directly to sunlight. In the subsequent processes, this fiber should be prevented from being in contact with strong acids or strong alkaline. The bathing or dyeing temperature should be less than 100°C, and the drying temperature less than 140°C
Application areas: Thermal underwear, knitted shirts, infant and children's constant-temperature sleeping bags, jackets, summer sleeping mats, pillows, sleeping bags

- Brand: Dukk®BIO—BASEDTEMPERATURE CONTROL TECHNOLOGY
- Declaring enterprise: Hangzhou Shangxuan Technology Co., Ltd.

Soybean and milk protein composite PVA fiber

Features: With the addition of plant and animal protein, having its protein content at 30% or so, skin-friendly, comfortable to wear, antibacterial, producing far infrared-enabled warmth-retaining and negative ion-enabled health care effects
Specification: 1.65dtex×38mm
Application guidance: This fiber can be blended with cotton and viscose fiber, and also can be used as fillings for home textiles. It is suggested that the dyeing temperature should be ≤100°C during the dyeing and finishing process
Application areas: Underwear, home textiles, shirts, bedding fillings, facial masks

- Brand: TIANRONG
- Declaring enterprise: Shanghai Quanyu Biotechnology Ping Co., Ltd.

石墨烯改性纤维
GRAPHENE MODIFIED FIBER
RECOMMENDED FIBERS

科技铸就，聚势赋能。石墨烯改性纤维具有抑菌、抗紫外、远红外、保暖、抗静电等功能，广泛应用于智能纺织、健康护理、运动服饰等领域，为品质生活提供有力的材料支撑。

Scientifically built, gaining strength and bringing energy. Graphene modified fiber is antibacterial, able to resist UV light, having a far infrared-enabled warmth-retaining effect, anti-static, widely used in such fields as intelligent spinning, health care, and sportswear, giving significant material support for a quality life.

石墨烯原位聚合改性异形有色聚酯纤维

特点：	抑菌保暖、抗紫外、远红外和抗静电性好，色牢度高；中空及十字异形截面可定制
规格：	55dtex/48f，82.5dtex/48f，82.5dtex/72f，110dtex/96f，165dtex/72f，165dtex/144f
应用指导：	参考常规聚酯纤维
应用领域：	登山服、滑雪服、骑行服、床上用品、过滤材料、帐篷、睡袋等

- 品牌：烯纳斯
- 申报企业：常州恒利宝纳米新材料科技有限公司

石墨烯改性聚丙烯腈纤维

特点：	与羊绒混纺可提升面料的保暖性，具有抑菌、抗紫外、消臭等复合功能
规格：	1.33dtex×38 mm
应用指导：	参考常规腈纶
应用领域：	毛线、内衣、羊毛外套、西服等

- 品牌：泰鼎
- 申报企业：绍兴泰鼎石墨烯科技有限公司

石墨烯改性循环再利用聚酯纤维

特点：	纤维呈现螺旋立体卷曲状态，具有弹性优异、抑菌防霉、远红外、蓄热保暖等特点，此外，采用循环再利用材料做纤维基体，产品绿色环保
规格：	2.5dtex×38mm
应用指导：	在加工和使用过程中，避免与强酸或强碱性物质接触，避免长时间暴露于高温条件；储存在阴凉、通风、干燥的地方，避免受潮
应用领域：	服装、玩具、靠枕等填充物

- 品牌：海科云绒
- 申报企业：江苏海科纤维有限公司

Graphene in situ polymerized modified profiled colored polyester fiber

Features: Antibacterial and thermally functional, UV-resistant, far infrared-enabled, anti-static, good in color fastness, able to be customized and have a hollow or cross-shaped profiled section
Specification: 55dtex/48f, 82.5dtex/48f, 82.5dtex/72f, 110dtex/96f, 165dtex/72f, 165dtex/144f
Application guidance: Refer to regular polyester fiber
Application areas: Climbing wear, ski wear, cycling wear, bedding, filtering materials, tents, sleeping bags etc.

- Brand: PHENAX
- Declaring enterprise: Highbery New Nano Materials technology Co., Ltd.

Graphene modified recycled polyester fiber

Features: In the state curling around spirally and in a three-dimensional manner, excellently elastic, antibacterial and mold-proof, far infrared-enabled, able to store heat and retain warmth, and additionally, with the fiber body made of recycled materials being green and environment-friendly.
Specification: 2.5dtex×38mm
Application guidance: When being processed or used, this fiber should be prevented from being in contact with strong acid or strong alkaline, and from long exposure to high-temperature conditions. This fiber should be stored in a shady, cool, ventilated, and dry place so as not to become damp
Application areas: Garment fillings, toy fillings, back cushion fillings etc.

- Brand: OCEANTEX
- Declaring enterprise: Jiangsu Oceantex Fiber Co., Ltd.

Graphene modified polyacrylonitrile fiber

Features: Blended with cashmere can enhance the warmth of the fabric and has composite functions such as antibacterial, UV resistant, and deodorizing
Specification: 1.33dtex×38 mm
Application guidance: Refer to regular acrylic
Application areas: Knitting wool, underwear, woolen coats, Western suits etc.

- Brand: TAIDING
- Declaring enterprise: Shaoxing Taiding Graphene Technology Co., Ltd.

FIRE-RESISTANT FIBER
阻燃纤维

卓越安全，阻燃提升。 阻燃纤维为消费者提供持续守护。在具备永久阻燃特性的同时，还叠加原液着色技术，赋予纤维靓丽色彩，更加注重环保、可持续性和实用性，打造全方位的安全保障。

Excellent and safe, enhancing fire resistance. Flame retardant fibers provide continuous protection for consumers. In addition to possessing permanent flame retardant properties, it also combines original liquid coloring technology to give fibers beautiful colors, paying more attention to environmental protection, sustainability, and practicality, and creating a comprehensive safety guarantee.

原位聚合阻燃有色聚酯纤维

特点：	原液着色与阻燃共聚技术相融合，做成的纤维极限氧指数高，阻燃效果好，色泽鲜艳持久，强度高，无须印染，节水节能
规格：	89dtex/36~48f，135dtex/36~72f，150dtex/36f，278dtex/72~96f FDY；55dtex/36~48f，82.5dtex/36~72f，167dtex/72~144f DTY
应用指导：	可与其他纤维交织混用，后处理时应注意协同效应，此效应会影响阻燃效果
应用领域：	消防服、工装服、地毯、墙布、遮阳帘、窗帘等

- 品牌：新丝维
- 申报企业：诸暨市新丝维纤维有限公司

原液着色阻燃循环再利用聚酯纤维

特点：	绿色环保，再生的高端化利用；纤维具有阻燃、蓬松柔软、色彩鲜艳等特性；无须印染，节水节能
规格：	1.33dtex×38mm，1.56dtex×38mm
应用指导：	纤维存放应避免高温，高湿或阳光直射的环境；远离酸、碱、氧化剂等具有腐蚀性或氧化性的化学品；与其他纤维混纺染色时应控制在130℃左右、30~90min，烘干定形温度220℃
应用领域：	服装衬布、皮革基布、汽车地毯、后备厢地毯、汽车衣帽架、脚垫、工装吸音装饰板、家居家装

- 品牌：奔马
- 申报企业：杭州奔马化纤纺丝有限公司

In-situ polymerized fire-resistant colored polyester fiber

Features: embodying the combination of dope-dyeing and fire-resistant co-polymerizing technologies, high in maximum oxygen index; Good flame retardant effect, bright and long-lasting color, high strength, no need for printing and dyeing, water-saving and energy-saving
Specification: 89dtex/36~48f, 135dtex/36~72f, 150dtex/36f, 278dtex/72~96f FDY; 55dtex/36~48f, 82.5dtex/36~72f, 167dtex/72~144f DTY
Application guidance: This fiber can be interwoven and used with other ones. At the time of after-treatment, attention should be paid to the synergic effect, which will have an impact on fire resistance
Application areas: Fire suits, carpets, wall cloth, sun-blocking curtains, window curtains etc.

- Brand: Sansiwell
- Declaring enterprise: Zhuji Xinsiwei Fiber Co., Ltd.

Dope-dyed fire-resistant recycled polyester fiber

Features: Green and environment-friendly, regenerated for high-end use, fire-resistant, fluffy, soft, bright-colored, without the need for dyeing and printing processes, saving water and energy
Specification: 1.33dtex×38mm, 1.56dtex×38mm
Application guidance: Fiber storage should be avoided in environments with high temperature, high humidity, or direct sunlight; Stay away from corrosive or oxidizing chemicals such as acids, bases, and oxidants; When dyeing with other fibers, it should be controlled at around 130 °C for 30~90 minutes, and the drying and setting temperature should be 220 °C
Application areas: lining cloth, leather substrate, automobile rugs, automobile trunk carpets, automobile hat racks, food pads, industrial sound-absorbing decorating panels, home textiles

- Brand: BENMARPET
- Declaring enterprise: Hangzhou Benma Chemfibre and Spinning Co., Ltd.

当无限的创造力柔软地延伸于现实与幻想之间,我们在大自然中撷取生物基材料的潜力,在创意的探索中超越传统界限,让纱线的世界因智慧共融而拓展。此刻,AI 的理性精准与新享乐主义的浪漫审美彼此依存,于高性能面料的微妙触感中,生成一曲多元文化交响乐。面对未知,我们以敏锐的感知力、蓬勃的好奇心,跨越学科与领域的阻隔,在彼此激荡的创意脉搏中孕育新生。于此,我们以谦卑与宏观视野,让纱线在协作中延展维度,以柔性智慧为未来谱写无边的艺术长卷。

As the unlimited creative power is finely developed from reality to fantasy, we unlock the potential of natural resources as bio-based materials, go beyond traditional limits when looking for originality, and expand the world of yarn with Intelligent Sharing. Right now, AI's rational accuracy and new hedonism's romantic aesthetics depend on each other for existence, setting the tone for multiculturalism in the subtle feel of high-performance fabric. Facing the unknown, we break through the barrier between disciplines and domains with keen perception and intense curiosity, giving birth to new things of great originality in each other. Then, in all modesty and in a grand vision, we add dimensions to yarn through integration, flexibility wise intelligently writing a long chapter about future unconventional artistry.

白鲨・中国纱线流行趋势 2025/2026

WHITE SHARK ·
CHINA YARNS FASHION TRENDS
2025/2026

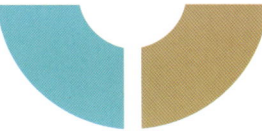

智享 协创

Intelligent Sharing
Collaborative Innovation

白鲨·中国纱线流行趋势

主题解读

2025/2026白鲨·中国纱线流行趋势以"智享·协创"为核心,掀起了一股行业创新的浪潮。这股浪潮中,创造力如细流般温柔地延展于现实与幻想的边缘,引领我们深入自然的肌理,挖掘生物基材料的无限潜能。我们以创意为笔,跨越传统束缚,将纱线世界拓宽至智慧与自然的完美交融。

智能制造技术的广泛应用,为纺纱领域注入了新的活力。从原料筛选到成品生产,每一步都融入了智能的精髓,显著提升了生产效率与产品质量。同时,AI技术的逐步介入,使纱线产品的开发与呈现经历了一场前所未有的智能升级。其理性与精准,与新享乐主义的浪漫审美相辅相成,共同作用于高性能面料之上,赋予织物细腻的触感,并在多元文化的交织中,演绎出和谐而丰富的交响乐章。在纱线产品的呈现阶段,AI通过虚拟现实(VR)和增强现实(AR)技术,创建出逼真的展示效果,让消费者在虚拟环境中体验产品的触感和外观。这种沉浸式的展示方式,不仅激发了消费者的购买意愿,还为纱线产品的推广和销售开辟了新的渠道和机遇。

面对未来的不确定性,我们以敏锐的洞察力和无限的好奇心,跨越学科与领域的界限,激发创意的火花。上下游企业的紧密联动,推动了产品的创新与开发,从纤维到面料,从设计到生产,每一个环节都紧密相连,共同绘制出未来图景的生动轮廓。

展望未来,纱线行业如同一位优雅的舞者,在"智享·协创"的旋律中翩翩起舞。她以环保、再生和绿色纺织品为舞鞋,轻盈跳跃在高端化、智能化、绿色化的舞台上;她身披高科技功能的华服,在提升产品质量和个性化设计的璀璨灯光下闪耀;她以市场需求为舞台,用品牌建设和市场拓展的舞步,演绎出在国际市场上翩翩起舞的乐章。

在此,我们以谦卑之心,秉持宏观视野,让纱线在协作与共享中拓展其维度。我们以柔性智慧为未来纺织业编织出一幅无边的艺术长卷,这不仅是对美的追求,更是对行业智慧与创新的深刻致敬。未来,纱线行业将在"智享·协创"的引领下,持续创新,不断前行,共同书写纺织业的新篇章。

Theme interpretation

A wave of industrial innovation has been rising, thanks to 2025/2026 White Shark · Prevailing Trends in Yarn of China, at the core of which is "Intelligent Sharing · Collaborative Innovation". On this wave, creative power, like a small stream peacefully running its course, is being developed along the boundary between reality and fantasy, leading us to go deep into natural texture and explore the unlimited potential of bio-based materials. With originality, we break traditional barriers, expanding the world of yarn toward the perfect integration of intelligence and nature.

The wide application of intelligent manufacturing techniques injects new energy into the field of spinning. From raw material selection to final products, the essence of intelligence is combined with every step, remarkably increasing productive efficiency and product quality. Meanwhile, the gradual penetration of AI technology makes yarn products undergo an unprecedented intelligent upgrade on their development and presentation. Its rationality and precision, and the romantic aesthetics of new hedonism complement each other, jointly acting on high-performance fabric, giving the textile a delicate feel, telling a harmonic and colorful story in the process of cultural combination. At the stage of yarn products' presentation, AI brings about a lifelike effect of presentation through Virtual Reality (VR) and Augmented Reality (AR) technologies, enable customers to experience the feel and appearance of products under virtual conditions. Not only does this immersing way of presentation arouses customers' desire to buy, it also provides new channels and opportunities for promoting and marketing yarn products.

Facing the uncertainty of the future, with perceptive insight and insatiable curiosity, we break the boundary between disciplines and domains, igniting sparks of originality. The strong interaction between upstream and downstream enterprises has pushed forward the innovation and development of products, with all the links closely connected with each other, from fiber to fabric, and from design to production, jointly creating a lovely picture of the future.

With the future in view, the yarn industry rises majestically like a graceful dancer to the song about "Intelligent Sharing · Collaborative Innovation". With environmental protection, regeneration and green textile products as its dance shoes, it dances lively on the stage for high-end, intelligent, and green products; with hi-tech functionality as its lavish costume, it shines under the spotlight that falls on the promotion of product quality and personalized design; with market demand as the stage, performing the dance steps towards brand building and market exploration, it gives a brilliant performance on the international stage.

Here, we modestly hold a macroscopic view, adding more dimensions to yarn in the process of collaboration and sharing. We flexibility-wise intelligently build up an artistic picture of the future yarn industry, not only representing the pursuit of beauty, but also paying a fine tribute to industrial intelligence and innovation. In the future, driven by "Intelligent Sharing · Collaborative Innovation", the yarn industry will keep innovation, continuously progress, and jointly open a new chapter.

永续
UNBROKEN CONTINUITY
A poem about the nature, fulfilling the dream about the future

自然之诗，织就未来绮梦

关键词：环保、再生、绿色

Key words: Environmentally friendly, regeneration, greening

自然的轻吟与人类的智思交织间，纱线领域正绽放出一场前所未有的绿色梦幻。废旧纺织品的循环利用，犹如一场资源的重生仪式，不仅彰显了对自然的敬畏与珍视，更以创新技术为笔，勾勒出旧物新生的温柔画卷。植物染色技术的细腻运用，让纱线色彩回归自然的怀抱，与大自然共舞，演绎出和谐共生的美妙乐章。环保再生原料，如再生聚酯、再生纤维素纤维，正缓缓铺展成主流趋势的绿意长廊，它们以轻盈之姿，减轻地球的负担，赋予纱线更加丰富而深邃的质感与性能。可生物降解材料的温柔介入，更为地球的未来添上一抹希望的绿意，让绿色纱线成为时尚与自然和谐共融的诗意见证。柔和色调与天然质感渐成美学趋势，让纱线不止于纺织，更是绿色未来的织梦者。

As the nature interacts with human wisdom, an unprecedented dream about the greening of yarn industry is being chased. Recycling waste and old textiles, like a ceremony for the rebirth of resources, not only displays reverence and respect for nature, but also paints a charming scene of old things being reborn with innovative technologies. The delicate use of plant-dyeing technology enables yarn colors to return back to the nature, and to be blended with the nature, creating a beautiful picture of harmonic coexistence. Environmentally friendly raw materials, e.g. regenerated polyester, regenerated cellulose fiber, are gradually paving the way to go mainstream, which reduces the burden on earth by being light, and giving yarn richer and deeper texture and functionality. The smooth introduction of biodegradable raw materials even offers more reasonable hope that the earth will become greener in the future, enabling green yarn to witness the harmonic integration between fashion and nature. Gentle color and natural texture have gradually set aesthetic trends, making yarn go beyond spinning to build a green future.

环锭纺植物染色纺纱
RING-SPUN PLANT-DYED YARN

BROS

● **关键词：植物染色纺、环保健康**

原料及规格： 环锭纺 100% 棉纤维 30 英支

推荐理由： 植物染作为古老染色工艺，采用植物的根、茎、叶、果实等进行发酵或者化学提纯等现代工艺，汲取植物色素精华并实现纺织纤维着色。百隆选用以板栗壳、桑葚、栀子、桑叶等一系列农林废产物提取的植物染料，结合有机棉进行散纤维染色，运用色纺工艺，成功开发了多色天然有机植物染纱线，具有天然性、再生性、环保利用性、自然降解性。同时实现了植物本身的药用价值，为人体健康提供保障，广泛用于内衣、床品、休闲运动及时尚服装

适用范围： 服装（内衣、休闲运动及时尚服装等）、家纺（床品）

代表企业： 百隆东方股份有限公司

Key words: plant-dyed spinning, environmentally friendly and healthy

Raw materials and specifications:
Ring-spinning 100% cotton fiber 30^S

Reasons for recommendation:
As a conventional dyeing process, plant-dyeing means using the roots, stems, leaves, and fruits of plants for modern technologies such as fermentation and chemical purification, extracting plant pigment and achieving fiber dyeing. For BROS, pigments extracted from a series of waste and old products of agriculture and forestry, such as chestnut shell, mulberry, jasmine, and folium mori, are selected to combine with organic cotton for dyeing loose fiber, while the technology for spinning with pigment is applied, and multi-color yarn dyed with natural organic plants is successfully developed, which has the quality of being nature, regenerated, usable for environmental protection, and naturally degradable, fulfilling the medicinal value of plants, providing human health protection, widely applicable to underwear, bedding, sportswear and fashionable dress

Scope of application:
Clothing (underwear, sportswear and fashionable dress etc.)
Home textile (bedding)

Representing enterprises:
BROS Eastern Co., Ltd.

永续 Unbroken Continuity

环锭纺无水上色棉纱
RING-SPUN WATERLESS-DYED COTTON YARN

魏桥纺织 WEIQIAO TEXTILE

● 关键词：无染上色、无水色纺、喷染色牢度

原料及规格：
①环锭纺 微纳镶嵌纺无染上色 棉 100% 21~60 英支
②赛络紧密纺 无染上色棉网喷染 莫代尔 100% 21~80 英支

推荐理由：通过微纳米镶嵌纺静电纺丝液原液着色与棉网喷染方式，在纺纱工序的梳棉阶段实现有色微纳米纤维与普通棉纤维的复合成纱或对梳棉网进行喷染上色，相较于传统染色加工技术，该技术使染色加工流程更加高效，减少了大量废水排放，加工过程更加绿色环保，具有广阔的市场前景与应用价值

适用范围：针织、机织服装、家纺等
代表企业：魏桥纺织股份有限公司
品牌：魏桥牌棉纱、嘉嘉家纺、向尚运动

产品获得认证 / 专利：
①《一种无水色纺纱线染色设备及染色方法》
②《一种无水染色生物基可降解防螨纺丝液及其制备与应用》
③《一种色纺纱线及其制备方法和应用》

Key words: pigment-free dyeing, waterless dyed-spinning, web spray-dyed color fastness

Raw materials and specifications:
① Ring-spinning micro-nanometer inlay pigment-free dyeing cotton 100% 21~60^S
② Compact siro-spinning pigment-free spray-dyeing modal 100% 21~80^S

Reasons for recommendation: Using the methods of dyeing with micro-nanometer inlay static spinning solution and of web spray-dyeing, the combination of colorful nanometer fiber and ordinary cotton fiber into yarn or the spray-dyeing of carded web is achieved at the cotton carding stage in a spinning process, and this technology enables the dyeing process to be more efficient as compared to traditional dyeing technology, resulting in a significant reduction in the amount of discharged water, more green and environmentally friendly manufacturing process, offering better market prospects and application values

Scope of application: Knitted and woven clothing, home textile, etc.
Representing enterprises: Weiqiao Textile Co., Ltd.
Brand: Weiqiao cotton yarn, Jiajia home textile, Xiangshang sportswear

Product certification/patent obtained:
① "The waterless yarn-dyeing equipment and the dyeing method"
② "The waterless-dyed biodegradable mite-resisting spinning solution and the preparation and application"
③ "The pigment-spun yarn and the preparation method and application"

检测结果 Test results

目前已实现浅粉、浅蓝、浅紫、浅绿色面料开发，产品色牢度均可达到 4 级及以上，同规格常规面料色牢度测试对比见下表

At present, light pink, light blue, light purple, and light green fabric have been developed, with these products' color fastness up to grade 4 and above, for comparison in color fastness with common fabric of same specifications, seeing the table below

项目 Items	摩擦牢度（级） Rubbing fastness (grade)		皂洗牢度（级） Soaping fastness (grade)		水渍牢度（级） Water stain fastness (grade)		汗渍牢度（酸性）（级） Perspiration fastness (acidity) (grade)		汗渍牢度（碱性）（级） Perspiration fastness (alkalinity) (grade)	
	干摩 Dry friction	湿摩 Wet grinding	变色 Color change	沾色 Color transfer	变色 Color change	沾色 Color transfer	变色 Color change	沾色 Color transfer	变色 Color change	沾色 Color transfer
无水色纺面料 Waterless pigment-spun fabric	4~5	4~5	4	4~5	4~5	4~5	4	4~5	4	4~5
常规染色面料 Regularly dyed fabric	4	3~4	4	3~4	4	4~5	4	4~5	4	4~5

赛络紧密纺再生莱赛尔超高支纱
COMPACT SIRO-SPUN REGENERATED LYOCELL ULTRA-HIGH-COUNT YARN

● **关键词**：再生莱赛尔、环保、超高支

原料及规格：赛络紧密纺 100% 再生莱赛尔 100 英支

推荐理由：以再生莱赛尔纤维为原料开发再生莱赛尔超高支纱线产品，工艺技术水平处于国内领先，可满足国内外高端纺织品市场需求。该产品的开发不仅可以大幅度缓解我国原料资源不足的问题，同时也为资源循环再利用起到很好的引导作用，推动我国再生资源的资源整合、技术研发、生产销售等企业化发展进程

适用范围：服装、家纺

代表企业：江苏大生集团有限公司

品牌：大吉

产品获得认证/专利：通过江苏省新产品新技术鉴定，苏工信鉴字〔2023〕485号；再生莱赛尔超高支纱线鉴定证书

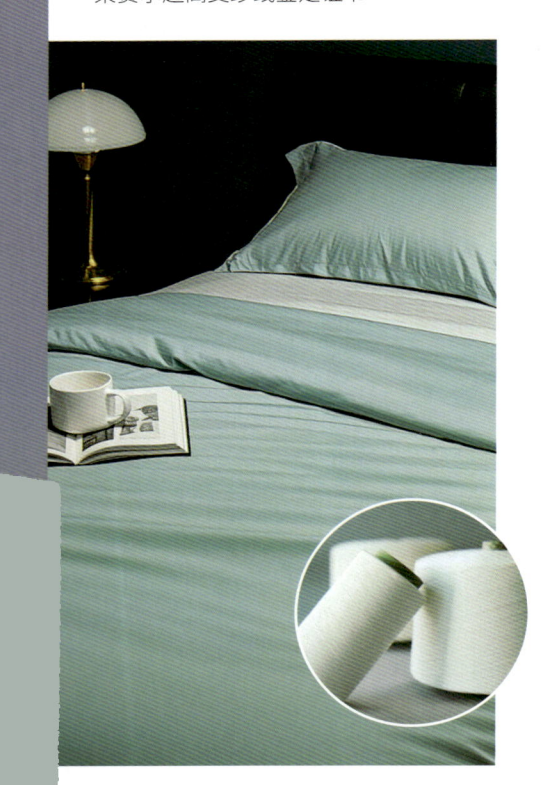

Key words: regenerated Lyocell, environmentally friendly, ultra-high-count

Raw materials and specifications:
Compact siro-spinning 100% regenerated Lyocell 100^S

Reasons for recommendation: The regenerated Lyocell ultra-high-count yarn products are developed with regenerated Lyocell fiber as raw material, taking lead domestically at technical levels, able to satisfy the market demand for high-end textiles at home and abroad. The development of these products not only largely mitigates the problem of raw material shortage in our country, but also plays a good leading role in resources recycling, facilitating the process of enterprise-oriented development in our country such as regenerated resources integration, technical research and development, and production and marketing

Scope of application: Clothing, home textiles

Representing enterprises: Jiangsu Dasheng Group Co., Ltd.

Brand: Daji

Product certification/patent obtained: Having passed the new product and new technology certification in Jiangsu province, by Su Gong Xin Jian〔2023〕No.485; Regenerated Lyocell Ultra-high-count yarn certificate

赛络纺菠萝麻纤维混纺纱
SIRO-SPUN PINEAPPLE-HEMP-FIBER BLENDED YARN

● **关键词**：天然环保、吸湿排汗、抑菌

原料及规格：赛络纺 棉纤维 70%~90%/ 菠萝麻纤维 30%~10% 6~21 英支

推荐理由：菠萝麻纤维具有易种植、价格低、生长周期短、运输便利等优势，与亚麻相比，在具有吸湿透气、抗过敏的功能上，其手感、缩水稳定性、染色牢度等优于亚麻。利用一定比例的菠萝麻纤维与天然棉纤维混纺开发的纱线及面料，环保抑菌。在服装领域功能显著，具有较大的市场潜力

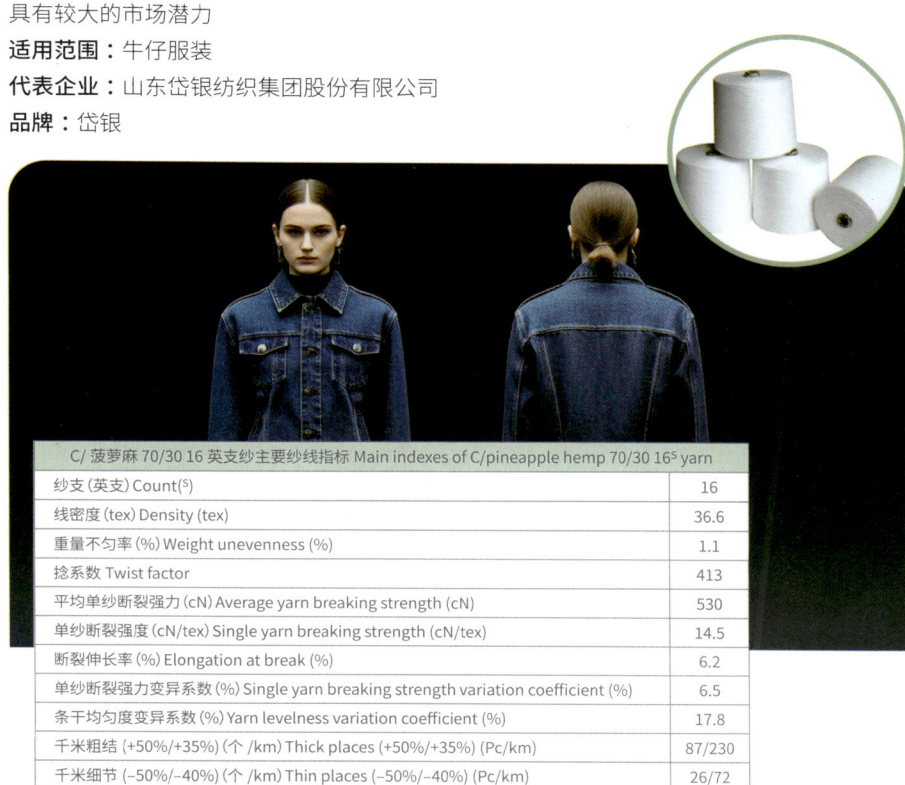

适用范围：牛仔服装

代表企业：山东岱银纺织集团股份有限公司

品牌：岱银

C/ 菠萝麻 70/30 16 英支纱主要纱线指标 Main indexes of C/pineapple hemp 70/30 16^S yarn	
纱支（英支）Count(^{S})	16
线密度 (tex) Density (tex)	36.6
重量不匀率 (%) Weight unevenness (%)	1.1
捻系数 Twist factor	413
平均单纱断裂强力 (cN) Average yarn breaking strength (cN)	530
单纱断裂强度 (cN/tex) Single yarn breaking strength (cN/tex)	14.5
断裂伸长率 (%) Elongation at break (%)	6.2
单纱断裂强力变异系数 (%) Single yarn breaking strength variation coefficient (%)	6.5
条干均匀度变异系数 (%) Yarn levelness variation coefficient (%)	17.8
千米粗结 (+50%/+35%) (个 /km) Thick places (+50%/+35%) (Pc/km)	87/230
千米细节 (-50%/-40%) (个 /km) Thin places (-50%/-40%) (Pc/km)	26/72
千米棉结 (+200%/+140%) (个 /km) Cotton knot (+200%/+140%) (Pc/km)	50/200

Key words: naturally environmentally friendly, moisture-absorbing and breathable, antibacterial

Raw materials and specifications:
Siro-spinning cotton fiber 70%~90% / Pineapple hemp fiber 30%~10% 6~21^S

Reasons for recommendation: Pineapple hemp fiber has the merit of being easy to plant, low in price, short in growth time, suitable for transportation, better than flax in terms of feel, stability at shrinkage, color fastness, and moisture-absorbing, breathable and anti-allergic functions. At a certain proportion, the yarn and fabric made by blending pineapple hemp fiber with natural cotton fiber are environmentally friendly and inhibit bacteria. They stand out in the field of garment, having a relatively good market prospect

Scope of application: Jeans

Representing enterprises: Shandong Daiyin Textile Group Limited Company

Brand: Daiyin

赛络紧密纺聚乳酸纯纺纱
COMPACT SIRO-SPUN POLYLACTIC ACID MONO-FIBER YARN

● **关键词**：生物基可降解、柔软、透气、聚乳酸纯纺

原料及规格：赛络紧密纺 100% 聚乳酸 21~120 英支

推荐理由：聚乳酸是由玉米、木薯等农作物糖化后，经微生物发酵产生的乳酸聚合而成。聚乳酸制成的纱线具有良好的光泽、柔软的手感和一定的强度，同时具有生物相容性和生物可降解性，用于制作服装、家居用品、卫生用品等。在可持续发展和生态保护方面具有广泛的应用前景

适用范围：服装、家纺、产业用（卫生用品）

代表企业：绍兴迈宝科技有限公司

品牌：BMC、玉绫丝

Key words: biodegradable, soft, breathable, polylactic acid mono-fiber yarn

Raw materials and specifications:
Compact siro-spinning 100% polylactic acid 21~120^S

Reasons for recommendation: Polylactic acid is made through polymerizing lactic acid that is produced from fermentation of saccharified crops such as corn and cassava with microorganisms. Yarn made of polylactic acid has a good shine, a soft feel to the touch, and certain strength, and moreover, it is compatible with the organism, biodegradable, for use in making clothes, articles at home, and sanitary products. With respect to sustainable development and ecological protection, it has good prospects of wide applications

Scope of application: Clothing, home textile, industrial textiles (sanitary products)

Representing enterprises: Shaoxing Maibao Scientific Co., Ltd.

Brand: BMC, Yulingsi

● **主要质量指标与性能** Main quality indexes and performances

聚乳酸 PLA 纤维 100% 纯纺纱
PLA fiber 100% mono-fiber yarn

规格 Specifications	条干均匀度变异系数 CV(%) ⩽ Yarn levelness variation coefficient CV (%) ⩽	平均单纱断裂强力 (cN) ⩾ Average yarn breaking strength (cN) ⩾	千米棉结 (+200%) (个/km) ⩽ Neps per 1000 meters (+200%) (Pc/km) ⩽	千米细节 (-50%) (个/km) ⩽ Thin places per 1000 meters (-50%) (Pc/km) ⩽	千米粗节 (+50%) (个/km) ⩽ Thick places per 1000 meters (+50%) (Pc/km) ⩽
32^S	13.0	230	50	15	20
40^S	14.0	210	60	20	30
50^S	15.0	190	70	30	40

低扭纺生物基抑菌全棉纱
LOW-TWIST BIO-BASED ANTIBACTERIAL PURELY COTTON YARN

BIOSERICA ERA 禾素时代

● 关键词：生物基抑菌低扭矩纱、抑菌＋超柔

原料及规格：低扭纺 精梳棉／长绒棉／OPHB 抑菌棉 55/35/10 32~40 英支

推荐理由：OPHB 是一种具有特定聚合度的、非离子型生物基环保有机抑菌剂，属于迭代型抑菌技术，可以在堆肥条件下完全生物降解为二氧化碳与水，源于自然又归于自然，所制成的产品使用安全。通过绿色生态的 SCF 先进施加技术，使 OPHB 牢固地附着在纤维浅表，在保持纱线物理和染色性能的基础上，兼具耐洗涤、抑菌、抗病毒效果。OPHB 生物基抑菌超柔全棉纱是在原有环锭纺细纱机上增加假捻器，有效提升须条内纤维抱合力和纺纱速度，减少断头。与常规环锭纺相比，纱线扭矩减少一半，产量提高 20%，同时有效降低针织物纬斜，使纱线结构蓬松、易吸色，布面柔软舒适、色泽均匀。

适用范围：服装

代表企业：南京禾素时代抗菌材料科技集团有限公司，现代纺织技术创新中心（鉴湖实验室）

品牌：禾素时代

产品获得认证／专利 Product certification/patent obtained:

知识产权类别 Intellectual Property Type	知识产权名称 Intellectual Property Title	国家 Country	申请／授权号 Certificate No.
实用新型专利 Practical patent of new type	一种采用 OPHB 抗菌剂纤维的抗菌除臭袜 Antibacterial deodorant socks made of OPHB antibacterial fiber	中国 China	ZL202222415460.3
实用新型专利 Practical patent of new type	一种采用 SCF 工艺含羟基酸酯低聚物生物基材料的抗菌袜子 Antibacterial socks made of bio-based materials containing alcohol ester oligomer with SCF technology	中国 China	ZL202222374884.X
实用新型专利 Practical patent of new type	一种 OPHB 禾素生物基抗菌去异味 T 恤 OPHB Bioserica bio-based antibacterial deodorant T-shirts	中国 China	ZL2023218265270
发明专利 Invention patent	一种基于改性低熔点 PET 的 PHBV 复合纤维 PHBV composite fiber based on modified low-melting point PET	中国 China	ZL202311552789.7

纱线流行趋势

Unbroken Continuity

Key words: bio-based antibacterial low-twist yarn, antibacterial + super-soft

Raw materials and specifications:
Low-twist combed cotton/long-staple cotton/OPHB antibacterial cotton 55/35/10 32~40^S

Reasons for recommendation: OPHB is a bio-based environmentally friendly organic antibacterial agent of non-ion type with a high level of polymerization, attributed to an updated antibacterial technology, able to be completely biodegraded into carbon dioxide under composting conditions, coming from nature and going back to nature, and products made of it are safe to use. With the advanced SCF applying technology for green ecology, OPHB firmly adheres to the surface layer of fiber, and besides keeping yarn's physical and dyeing performance, it has wash-enduring, antibacterial, antiviral effects. OPHB bio-based antibacterial super-soft purely cotton yarn is made by adding false twisting device to the original ring-spinning frame, which effectively improves the bonding between fibers in a silver and spinning speed, and reduces cracked ends. Compared with commonly ring-spun yarn, this yarn's torque is reduced by half, and its production increased by 20%, while the instances where weft is skewed in fabric have been effectively reduced, so that yarn is structurally fluffy, easy to absorb pigment, and fabric is comfortable to the touch, and uniform in color

Scope of application: Clothing

Representing enterprises: Nanjing Bioserica Era Antibacterial Materials Scientific Group Co., Ltd., Modern Textile Technological Innovation Center (Jianhu Laboratory)

Brand: Bioserica Era

生物基抑菌纤维混纺纱系列
BIO-BASED ANTIBACTERIAL FIBER BLENDED YARN SERIES

邯郸纺织有限公司
HAN DAN TEXILE CO., LTD.

● **关键词**：生物基、抑菌、绿色环保

原料及规格：

① 涤纶/生物基抑菌棉 65/35 23~100 英支

② 涤纶/棉/生物基抑菌棉 65/25/10 23~100 英支

③ 棉/生物基抑菌棉 90/10 32~100 英支

④ 棉/涤纶/生物基抑菌涤纶 80/10/10 45~100 英支

⑤ 涤纶/黏胶/棉/生物基抑菌黏胶 50/20/20/10 32~80 英支

推荐理由：利用天然生物基抑菌原液，通过物理技术结合，赋予原料抑菌功效，抑菌短纤配以适当比例纯纺或混纺抑菌纱线，面料抑菌性能提高，相较于传统抑菌方式，该产品既避免了某些潜在危害和环保问题，实现了"天然绿色抑菌"。其抑菌效果经过认证，针对医院常见病菌如金黄色葡萄球菌、白色念珠菌、大肠杆菌等具有显著抗性。此外，还能有效抑制或杀灭人体中分布的致臭菌，从源头上消除臭味，实现持久抑菌抑臭。其长效的抑菌功效和天然生物基抑菌的安全相容性，符合绿色环保和健康安全的发展理念

适用范围：服装、家纺、产业用

代表企业：邯郸纺织有限公司

品牌：海盛威和博特

Key words: bio-based, antibacterial, green and environmentally friendly

Raw materials and specifications:

① polyester/bio-based antibacterial cotton 65/35 23~100^S

② polyester/cotton/bio-based antibacterial cotton 65/25/10 23~100^S

③ cotton/bio-based antibacterial cotton 90/10 32~100^S

④ cotton/polyester/bio-based antibacterial polyester 80/10/10 45~100^S

⑤ polyester/viscose/bio-based antibacterial viscose/cotton 50/20/10/20 32~80^S

Reasons for recommendation: Raw materials are provided with antibacterial effects by combining natural bio-based antibacterial dope with physical technology, fabric made by blending antibacterial staple with mono-fiber-spun yarn or antibacterial blended yarn in an appropriate proportion has an enhanced antibacterial performance, and as compared with traditional antibacterial methods, this product not only avoids some potential harm and problems with environmental protection, but also has achieved "naturally green and antibacterial effects". Its antibacterial effect has been certified, able to remarkably resisting the pathogenic bacteria commonly seen at hospitals such as Staphylococcus aureus, Candida albicans, and E. coli. In addition, it can also effectively inhibit or kill the odor-producing bacteria in a human body, eliminating odor from its source, achieving a long-lasting antibacterial effect of inhibiting odor. The safe compatibility between its long-acting antibacterial effect and natural bio-based antibacterial effects conforms to the idea of being green, environmentally friendly, healthy, and safe for development

Scope of application: Clothing, home textile, industrial textiles

Representing enterprises: Handan Textile Co., Ltd.

Brand: Haishengwei and Bote

Unbroken Continuity

赛络紧密纺原液着色海藻纤维多组分混纺纱

COMPACT SIRO-SPUN DOPE-DYED ALGINATE-FIBER MULTI-COMPONENT BLENDED YARN

● **关键词**：环保轻量、抑菌阻燃、吸湿排汗

原料及规格：赛络紧密纺 细旦零碳莫代尔/精梳棉/海藻纤维 50/30/20 80 英支

推荐理由：海藻纤维源自海洋，天然具备抑菌、防霉等特性，其舒适感可与蚕丝、羊绒媲美，能够赋予织物更佳的保暖性能。当在纺织面料中添加量达到或超过 10% 时，可大幅提高服装的穿着舒适性，因此是制作秋衣裤的理想材料。此外，海藻纤维还具有阻燃、抑菌和生物降解等特性，广泛应用于训练服、消防服、抑菌内衣、除臭袜、儿童服装等。原液着色海藻纤维混纺纱优选海藻纤维与细旦莫代尔、莱赛尔、羊绒等纤维混纺，开发了多组分 80~100 英支高支纱线面料，这些面料不仅具有抑菌防霉、阻燃特性，还兼具轻量、柔软和舒适等特点，满足了面料的高品质要求

适用范围：服装（内衣、除臭袜、秋衣裤、训练服、消防服等）

代表企业：山东联润新材料科技有限公司

品牌：联润

Key words: environmentally friendly and lightweight, antibacterial and fire-retardant, moisture-absorbing and breathable

Raw materials and specifications:
Compact siro-spinning fine-denier zero-carbon modal/combed cotton/alginate fiber 50/30/20 80[S]

Reasons for recommendation: Alginate fiber is from the ocean, naturally characterized by being antibacterial and mould-proof, giving a comfortable feel that is comparable to silk and cashmere, able to provide textiles with better warmth-retaining performance. When its addition to textile fabric reaches or exceeds 10%, it can significantly improve their quality of being comfortable to wear, proving, thus making them the ideal material for long underwear. Moreover, alginate fiber also has fire-retardant, antibacterial, and biodegradable effects, widely applied in training suits, fire suits, antibacterial underwear, deodorant socks, and children's garments. Dope-dyed alginate-fiber blended yarn is made by blending preferentially selected alginate fiber with such fibers as fine-denier modal, Lyocell, and cashmere, the fabrics featuring multi-component 80-100[S] high-count yarn have been developed, and these fabrics not only have antibacterial, mould-proof, and fire-retardant effects, but also are lightweight, soft, and comfortable, satisfying the requirements for high-quality fabrics

Scope of application: Clothing (underwear, deodorant socks, long underwear, training suits, fire suits etc.)

Representing enterprises: Shandong Longrun New Materials Scientific Co., Ltd.

Brand: Longrun

产品获得认证 / 专利：
①项目列入 2023 年度山东省工信厅企业技术创新项目计划
②产品开发过程中形成专利

Product certification/patent obtained:
① This product is listed in the plan of the Department of Industry and Information Technology in Shandong province for the corporate technical innovation projects in 2023
② Patents are obtained during the product development

类别 Type	知识产权名称 Intellectual Property Title	国家 Country	申请 / 授权号 Application/Certificate No.
发明专利 Invention patent	一种低强力短纤维纺纱的加工工艺 A process of spinning low-strength staple yarn	中国 China	ZL2022113254570
发明专利 Invention patent	一种减碳环保可染花灰赛络紧密纱及其生产工艺 Carbon-reducing environmentally-friendly dyeable siro-spun compact yarn and its manufacturing process	中国 China	ZL2022114826083
实用新型专利 Practical patent of new type	一种梳棉管道泄压风口 A cotton-carding pipe decompression tuyere	中国 China	ZL202222961780.9

智护

INTELLIGENT PROTECTION
The light to science and technology, livening life up

关键词：高性能、黑科技
Key words: high performance, black technology

科技之光，点亮生活诗篇

在科技的璀璨星河中，纱线与科技的邂逅，正编织出一幅幅智能时代的绚丽图景。吸湿速干、高效抑菌、智能调温等功能性纱线的诞生，如同智慧的使者，不仅满足了人们对健康生活品质的无尽向往，更在科技的引领下，开启了纱线产品创新的新纪元。这些功能性纱线，如同科技的笔触，以先进的材料技术和智能设计为墨，勾勒出贴心、实用的生活画卷，让纱线产品更加人性化、个性化，成为生活中不可或缺的温馨伴侣。这一趋势，正引领着纱线行业向更加智能化、功能化的方向迈进，为人们的生活增添一抹科技的诗意与温馨。

In the brilliant star river of the scientific world, science and technology have reached into yarn, creating a wonderful picture of an intelligent era. As the yarn emerges like a wisdom envoy that can absorb moisture and dry off rapidly, that are highly efficient and antibacterial, and that can intelligently regulate temperatures, not only does people's insatiable the desire for a healthy life is fulfilled, a new chapter about the innovation in yarn products are also opened, with science and technology taking the leading role. These functional yarn, like a scientific pen with advanced material technology and intelligent design as its ink, draws a picture of life where they are helpful and practical, enabling yarn products to be more human-centered and personalized, becoming an indispensable mate in life. This trend is leading the yarn industry to be more intelligent and functional, bringing scientifically enabled poetic flavor and warmth into people's lives.

紧密纺腈纶多组分混纺导湿抑菌单染纱

COMPACT-SPUN ACRYLIC FIBER MULTI-COMPONENT-BLENDED MOISTURE-CONDUCTING ANTIBACTERIAL SINGLE-DYED YARN

● **关键词**：抑菌、保暖、导湿、单染

原料及规格：紧密纺 腈纶 / 火山岩黏胶 / 涤纶 40/35/25 40 英支

推荐理由：该纱线应用了细旦腈纶、火山岩黏胶、抑菌涤纶，并结合精混技术、紧密纺技术、细纱集体落纱技术纺制，具有手感柔软、强度高、毛羽少、抗起毛起球性好、条干均匀度好等特点。织成的纺织品，布面光洁，轻蓬暖柔，悬垂性、耐磨性好，具有蓄热升温、改善微循环、抑菌等功能，产品附加值高

适用范围：服装、家纺

代表企业：南通双弘纺织有限公司

品牌：双弘

Key words: antibacterial, warmth-retaining, moisture-conducting, single-dyed

Raw materials and specifications:
Compact-spun acrylic fiber/ volcanic rock viscose/ polyester 40/35/25 40^S

Reasons for recommendation: This yarn is made of fine-denier acrylic fiber, volcanic rock viscose, antibacterial polyester fiber by using precision-blending, compact-spinning, and spun yarn-collective doffing technologies in combination, and it is characterized by feeling soft to the touch, high strength, and less hairiness, being good at preventing fluffing and pilling, and having a good yarn levelness. The textiles that are made of it have a bright and clean surface, lightweight, fluffy, warm, soft, and good in drapeability and wear resistance, feature heat-storing, temperature-rising, microcirculation-improving, and antibacterial functions, and hold high value-added commodities

Scope of application: Clothing, home textile

Representing enterprises: Nantong Double Great Textile Co., Ltd.

Brand: Double Great

Intelligent Protection

产品获得认证 / 专利：

① 乌斯特产品认证
② 《一种混合梳理机及抗菌混纺纱生产方法》，ZL202110831082.4
③ 《一种涤棉混纺单染纱的生产方法》，ZL202210850963.5

Product certification/patent obtained:

① Uster certification
② "Mix-carding machine and the method of manufacturing antibacterial blended yarn Patent", ZL202110831082.4
③ "The method of manufacturing polyester-and-cotton-blended single-dyed yarn Patent", ZL202210850963.5

● 主要质量指标与性能　Main quality indexes and performances

产品名称 Product name	紧密纺 腈纶 / 火山岩黏胶 / 抑菌涤纶 40/35/25 40 英支 Compact-spun acrylic fiber/volcanic rock viscose/antibacterial polyester 40/35/25 40^S		
项目 Items	标准指标 Standard index		产品指标 Product index
抑菌率（水洗 150 次） Antibacterial rate (water-washed 150 times)	金黄色葡萄球菌抑菌率 ≥ 85% *Staphylococcus aureus* antibacterial rate ≥ 85%		99%
	大肠杆菌抑菌率 ≥ 70% *E. coli* antibacterial rate ≥ 70%		99%
	白色念珠菌抑菌率 ≥ 70% *Candida albicans* antibacterial rate ≥ 70%		99%

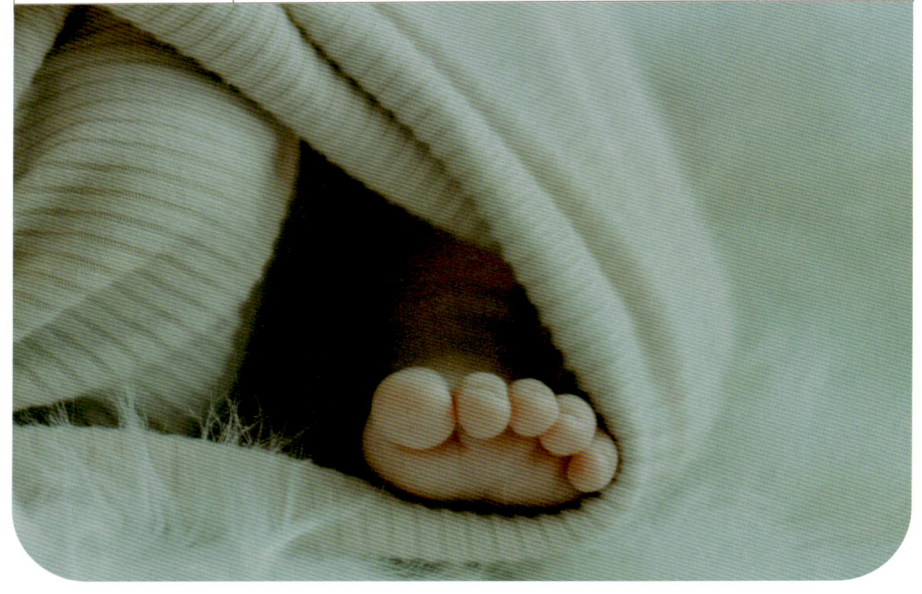

赛络紧密纺抑菌棉混纺纱
COMPACT SIRO-SPUN ANTIBACTERIAL COTTON-BLENDED YARN

海纤® 生物 Healcell

● **关键词**：生物抑菌、瞬间消臭

原料及规格：赛络紧密纺 海丝林抑菌棉／莫代尔 50/50 20~60 英支

推荐理由：海丝林多功能纤维，采用纳米技术将海洋藻类中萃取海洋生物提取物等活性成分注入纤维素纤维内部，在纤维分子链上形成大量羧基基团，该基团可分解反应去除碱性和酸性异味，利用该纤维制成的纺织品具有优异的抑菌、消臭功能，产品经 150 次水洗，抑菌率＞99%，可有效抑制氨气、醋酸、壬烯醛、异戊酸等臭味且可瞬间分解臭味。产品基材灵活，品质稳定，抑菌形式为生物抑菌，健康环保

适用范围：服装、家纺

代表企业：山东海纤生物材料科技有限公司

品牌：海丝林

Healthly 海丝林

Key words: organisms inhibiting bacteria, instant deodorization
Raw materials and specifications:
Compact siro-spinning, Healthly antibacterial cotton/modal 50/50 20~60^S
Reasons for recommendation: Healthly multi-functional fiber is made by using nanometer technology to inject active ingredients such as marine organisms extracted from marine algae into cellulose fiber, so that a large amount of COOH carboxyl groups are formed in the molecular chains of the fiber, able to cause a decomposition reaction to eliminate acidity, alkalinity, and unpleasant odor, and the textiles that are made of this fiber have excellent antibacterial and deodorant functions, with an antibacterial rate > 99% after being water-washed 150 times, able to inhibit foul odors such as ammonia, acetic acid, nonenal, and isovaleric acid, and to eliminate unpleasant odors immediately. This product is variable in base materials but invariable in quality, and its antibacterial effect is based on organisms that inhibiting bacteria, which is healthy and environment-friendly
Scope of application: Clothing, home textile
Representing enterprises:
Shandong Healcell Organisms Materials Scientific Co., Ltd.
Brand: Healthly

Intelligent Protection
智护

● 主要质量指标与性能 Main quality indexes and performances

产品名称 Product name	项目 Items	标准指标 Standard index	产品指标 Product index
50 英支海丝林多功能布 Multi-functional cloth for 50^S Healthly socks			
抑菌率（水洗 150 次） Antibacterial rate (water-washed 150 times)		金黄色葡萄球菌抑菌率 ≥ 85% Staphylococcus aureusanti antibacterial rate ≥ 85%	99%
		大肠杆菌抑菌率 ≥ 70% E. coli antibacterial rate ≥ 70%	94%
		白色念珠菌抑菌率 ≥ 70% Candida albicans antibacterial rate ≥ 70%	96%
消臭性能 Deodorizing performance		氨气异味成分浓度减少率 ≥ 70% Odor-wise reduction in the concentration of ammonia ≥ 70%	96.2%
		异戊酸异味成分浓度减少率 ≥ 85% Odor-wise reduction in the concentration of isovaleric acid ≥ 85%	93.9%
		2- 壬烯醛异味成分浓度减少率 ≥ 75% Odor-wise reduction in the concentration of 2-Nonenal ≥ 75%	87.0%
		醋酸异味成分浓度减少率 ≥ 70% Odor-wise reduction in the concentration of acetic acid ≥ 70%	91.4%
耐唾液牢度 Saliva fastness		变色 ≥ 4 级 color change ≥ grade 4	4~5 级 grade 4~5
		沾色 ≥ 4 级 color transfer ≥ grade 4	4~5 级 grade 4~5
耐光色牢度 Color fastness to light		≥ 4 级 ≥ grade 4	> 4 级 > grade4

赛络紧密纺再生聚酯莱赛尔混纺纱
COMPACT SIRO-SPUN REGENERATED PET AND LYOCELL BLENDED YARN

● **关键词**：环保、抑菌（微纳米）、吸湿排汗
原料及规格：赛络紧密纺 再生涤纶／交联型天丝™ 莱赛尔 65/35 26 英支 /2
推荐理由：采用微纳米纤维跨尺度复合纺纱技术，将静电纺丝与传统纺纱方法相结合，通过抑菌载体微纳米纤维混纺赋予纱线功能性，是颠覆传统功能后整理的技术。该产品的生产有效解决了抑菌纺织品功能耐久性差、试剂添加量大、废水难回收等难题，制成的面料具有较好的吸湿排汗功能，市场前景广阔
适用范围：鞋材、服装
代表企业：山东联润新材料科技有限公司
品牌：联润

Key words: environmentally-friendly, antibacterical (micro-nanometer), moisture-absorbing and breathable
Raw materials and specifications:
Compact siro-spinning regenerated polyester/Cross-linked Tencel™ Lyocell 65/35 26^S/2
Reasons for recommendation: The static spinning method is combined with traditional spinning methods by using the micro-nanometer fiber cross-dimensional composite yarn technology, and the yarn is made functional after spinning the bacteria-inhibiting micro-nanometer fiber into it, which is a finishing technology that revolutionizes traditional functionalities. The fundamental tricky problems of antibacterial textiles' functionally short endurance, large addition of reagent, and difficult recycling of wastewater are effectively solved, and the fabric made in this way has better moisture-absorbing and breathable functions, with a bright market prospect.
Scope of application: Materials for shoes, clothing
Representing enterprises: Shandong Longrun New Materials Scientific Co., Ltd.
Brand: Longrun

智护 Intelligent Protection

产品获得认证 / 专利：
①获得认证：项目列入山东省工信厅企业技术创新项目计划
②产品开发过程中形成专利

Product certification/patent obtained:
① product certification: this product is listed in the plan of the Department of Industry and Information Technology in Shandong province for corporate technical innovation
② patents are obtained during the product development

类别 Type	知识产权名称 Intellectual Property Title	国家 Country	申请 / 授权号 Application/ Certificate No.
发明专利 Invention patent	一种抑菌聚氨酯纳米纤维 / 短纤维混纺鞋材用纱及其制备方法 The antibacterial polyurethane nanometer fiber /staple blended yarn for use in shoes and its preparing method	中国 China	ZL2022115587770
发明专利 Patent for innovation	一种多轨道环形静电纺丝装置及其使用方法 The multi-track ring-shaped static spinning device and its usage	中国 China	ZL2024100169973
发明专利 Patent for innovation	一种按需打印的激光熔体静电纺丝方法及装置 The on-demand printing laser melt static spinning method and device	中国 China	ZL2024103973340
实用新型专利 Practical and new	一种阻止抓管帽掉落纱车装置 The device preventing a grabbing pipe cap from falling into charka	中国 China	ZL2023230141785
实用新型专利 Practical patent of new type	一种梳棉管道泄压风口 The cotton carding pipe decompression tuyere	中国 China	ZL202222961780.9

● 主要质量指标与性能 Main quality indexes and performances

该项目采用再生涤纶、莱赛尔纤维混纺，通过电离镶嵌纺技术赋予面料更好的抑菌、吸湿排汗等功能，实现织物性能与风格的多样化和高档化

In this project, regenerated polyester and Lyocell fiber are blended, and the fabric made with the ionization inlay spinning technology has better antibacterial, moisture-absorbing and breathable functions, enabling textiles to be diversified in performance and style and of the best quality

序号 No.	项目 Items	项目产品 Product in the project	常规产品 Common product
1	单纱断裂强度（cN/tex） Single yarn breaking strength (cN/tex)	25.8	22
2	条干均匀度变异系数（%） Yarn levelness variation coefficient (%)	7.2	9
3	千米棉结（+200%）（个/km） Neps per 1000 meters(+200%) (Pc/km)	1	5
4	金黄色葡萄球菌抑菌率（%） Staphylococcus aureus antibacterial rate (%)	≥ 99	≥ 70
5	大肠杆菌抑菌率（%） E. coli antibacterial rate (%)	≥ 99	≥ 70
6	白色念珠菌抑菌率（%） Candida albicans antibacterial rate (%)	≥ 88	≥ 60

汉麻棉混纺抑菌锦纶弹力复合纱

HEMP-BLENDED ANTIBACTERIAL NYLON ELASTIC COMPOSITE YARN

● **关键词**：抑菌、高品质汉麻、复合纱

原料及规格：21.6tex 棉／汉麻（60/40）混纺纱 +75 旦 抑菌锦纶弹力丝复合纱

推荐理由：汉麻素有"天然纤维之王"美誉，与纯棉织物相比，汉麻纤维制成的服装可使体感温度降低 5°C 左右，且具备抑菌性、化学吸附性、抗紫外线和吸音消波等性能，可用作各种军用服装、高档服饰的原料。该纱线利用复合纱线技术使纱线具有优良的弹性和耐磨性，既丰富了纱线的功能，同时提高了纱线抑菌效果，产品天然环保、吸湿速干透气、抑菌性好，易于打理

适用范围：针织品、服装

代表企业：浙江麻银佳纺织科技有限公司，现代纺织技术创新中心（鉴湖实验室）

品牌：麻银佳

Key words: antibacterial, high-quality hemp, composite yarn

Raw materials and specifications:
21.6 tex cotton/hemp (60/40) blended yarn+75D antibacterial nylon elastic composite yarn

Reasons for recommendation: Hemp always enjoys the good reputation as 'king of natural fiber', and as compared with purely cotton textiles, a clothes made of hemp can make sensible temperature go down by 5 °C or so, and have bacteria-inhibiting, chemical-absorbing, ultraviolet ray-resisting, sound-absorbing, and wave-eliminating functions, able to be used as the raw materials for various military uniforms, and high-grade clothes. This yarn is made very elastic and wear-resistant with the composite yarn technology, having not only its functionalities enhanced, but also its antibacterial effects improved, and this product is naturally environment-friendly, able to absorb moisture and dry off rapidly, breathable, antibacterial and easy to keep

Scope of application: Textiles, Clothing

Representing enterprises: Zhejiang Mayinjia Textile Scientific Co., Ltd. Modern Textile Technology Innovation Center (Jianhu Labortary)

Brand: Mayinjia

Intelligent Protection

产品获得认证 / 专利：

① 《一种汉麻纤维混纺复合纱的制备方法》，ZL2024107159690

② 《一种汉麻纤维精梳装置》，ZL2024211837451

Product certification/patent obtained:

① "The method of preparing the hemp fiber-blended composite yarn", ZL2024107159690

② "The hemp fiber carding device", ZL2024211837451

● 主要质量指标与性能　Main quality indexes and performances

序号 No.	检验项目 Tested item		检验结果 Test result
1	强伸性能 Tensile property	断裂强力（cN） Breaking strength (cN)	350
		断裂伸长率（%） Elongation at break (%)	8.6
		单纱断裂强度（cN/tex） Single yarn breaking strength (cN/tex)	11.2
2	耐皂洗色牢度（级） Soap-enduring color fastness (grade)	变色 Color change	4~5
		沾色 Color transfer	4
3	耐酸汗渍色牢度（级） Acid-enduring perspiration color fastness (grade)	变色 Color change	4~5
		沾色 Color transfer	4~5
4	耐碱汗渍色牢度（级） Alkaline-enduring perspiration color fastness (grade)	变色 Color change	4~5
		沾色 Color transfer	4~5
5	耐干摩擦色牢度（级） Dry friction-enduring color fastness (grade)	沾色 Color transfer	4
6	耐湿摩擦色牢度（级） Wet grinding-enduring color fastness (grade)	沾色 Color transfer	3
7	大肠杆菌抑菌率（%） E. coli antibacterial rate (%)	未水洗 Not water-washed	>99
		洗涤50次 Washed 50 times	>99
8	金黄色葡萄球菌抑菌率（%） Staphylococcus aureus antibacterial rate (%)	未水洗 Not water-washed	>99
		洗涤50次 Washed 50 times	>99
9	白色念珠菌抑菌率（%） Candida albicans antibacterial rate (%)	未水洗 Not water-washed	>99
		洗涤50次 Washed 50 times	93

紧密纺棉凉感乙纶混纺纱
COMPACT-SPUN COTTON COOL POLYETHYLE-BLENDED YARN

● **关键词**：天然凉感、吸湿、减碳、防霉抑菌

原料及规格：紧密纺 精梳棉／乙纶 70/30 30~60 英支

推荐理由：聚乙烯纤维，又称乙纶，是一种综合性能优良的纤维新材料，具有较高的导热速率，常被用作凉感材料。使用该纤维与精梳棉混纺的纱线织成的面料手感丝滑，具有仿真丝的效果，接触皮肤后可产生2℃左右的瞬间凉感，降低出汗率及闷热感，同时具有棉的天然亲肤性和优良的吸湿透气性，产品通过了专业的冷温感检测认证，广泛应用于服用面料、家纺制品等领域

适用范围：服装、家纺

代表企业：邯郸纺织有限公司、凯泰特种纤维科技有限公司

品牌：海盛威

检测报告 Test report

检测结果 Test result

接触凉感系数 XT-max $[J/(cm^2 \cdot s)]$ Cool feel factor XT-max $[J/(cm^2 \cdot s)]$		
标准(称)值 Standard (nominal) value	实测值 Actually measured value	单项判定 Judgments on single item
≥ 0.15	0.16	具有接触瞬间凉感性能 Having the quality of instantly feeling cool to the touch

Key words: natural cool feeling, moisture-absorbing, carbon-reducing, mould-proof, antibacterial

Raw materials and specifications:
Compact-spinning combed cotton/polyethyle 70/30 30~60^S

Reasons for recommendation:
Polyethyiene fiber is a good general performance new material with a high heat-conducting rate, often used for the material that give a cool feel. The fabric made of the yarn that is developed by blending this fiber with combed cotton is slick to the touch, having the effect of artificial silk, giving a feeling that the temperature is 2℃ or so as soon as it is in contact with skin, able to reduce perspiration and relive sweltering feelings, as naturally skin-friendly as cotton is, excellent in moisture absorption, breathable, and this product has been professionally tested and certified for cool and warm feel, widely applied in such fields as apparel fabrics and home textiles

Scope of application: Clothing, Home textile

Representing enterprises:
Handan Textile Co., Ltd., Kaitai Special Fiber Scientific Co., Ltd.

Brand: Haishengwei

智护
Intelligent Protection

赛络紧密纺莱赛尔玉精纤维混纺纱
COMPACT SIRO-SPUN LYOCELL AND YUJING FIBER-BLENDED YARN

GOLDSUN

● **关键词**：十字截面、透气丝滑、凉感、远红外

原料及规格：赛络紧密纺 莱赛尔 / 玉精纤维 70/30 60 英支

推荐理由：玉精纤维是在聚酯纤维的纺丝制备过程中加入了微纳米级天然玉石母粒，横截面为十字形，具有凉感、远红外和负离子功能，十字型的截面使纤维具有良好的吸湿透气性能。莱赛尔纤维是一种绿色纤维，绿色环保、亲肤舒适、光泽细腻。将玉精纤维与莱赛尔纤维混纺的纱线兼具两种纤维的优良性能，其与人体皮肤接触时丝滑微凉，亲肤舒适，多用于生产夏季套件面料

适用范围：家纺面料

代表企业：江苏金太阳纺织科技股份有限公司

产品获得认证 / 专利：玉精纤维绿叶认证证书

Key words: cross-section, breathable and slick, cool feel, far infrared

Raw materials and specifications:
Compact siro-spinning, Lyocell/Yujing fiber 70/30 60^S

Reasons for recommendation: Yujing fiber is made by adding natural jade-in-master-batch in the process of preparing PET for spinning, featuring a cross-section in the shape, giving a cool feel, far infrared and negative-ion functions, and its cross-shaped cross-section enables the fiber to have good moisture-absorbing and breathable quality. Lyocell fiber is a green product, environment- and skin-friendly, comfortable, having a fine and smooth shine. The yarn made by blending Yujing fiber with Lyocell fiber has both the good properties of the two, feeling slick and slightly cool when in contact with skin, being skin-friendly and comfortable, and mostly used in fabrics for summer suits

Scope of application: Home textile fabric

Representing enterprises: Jiangsu Goldsun Textile Scientific Limited Company

Product certification/patent obtained: Intertek certificate for Yujing fiber

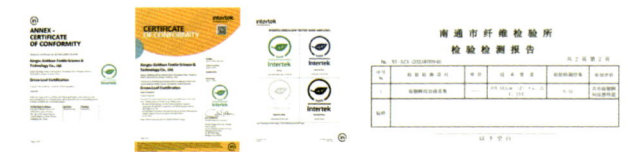

检测报告
Test report

● **主要质量指标与性能** Main quality indexes and performances

序号 No.	规格 Specifications	本产品 This product	常规品 Common products
1	接触凉感系数 [J/(cm²·s)] Cool feel factor [J/(cm²·s)]	0.32q-max	≥ 0.15
2	平均单纱断裂强力（cN） Average yarn breaking strength (cN)	210	—
3	面料相对手感值 Fabric relative feel value	0.45	4.87
4	面料透气率（mm/s） Fabric air permeability (mm/s)	431.83	283.94
5	面料褶皱恢复率 (%) Fabric wrinkle recovery rate (%)	76.24	63.18
6	远红外发射率 Far infrared emissivity	0.93	—
7	负离子发生量 (cm³) Amount of generated negative-ion (cm³)	1251	—

赛络紧密纺腈纶稀土黏胶莫代尔混纺纱

COMPACT SIRO-SPUN ACRYLIC FIBER AND RARE EARTH VISCOSE MODAL BLENDED YARN

● **关键词**：蓄热保暖、吸光升温、安全亲肤

原料及规格：赛络紧密纺 腈纶 / 稀土黏胶 / 莫代尔 60/30/10 50 英支

推荐理由：采用无锡四棉自主设计研发的"精密紧密纺"生产工艺，该功能原纱所制服饰改变了传统保暖面料仅有的保暖性能，在进一步提升蓄热保温的同时具有吸光发热和远红外发热的功效，并且具备良好的抑菌功能。改变了传统保暖面料仅有的蓄热特性，吸光发热性能突出，可吸收冷光源发热，光蓄热性能最大升温值为 7.6°C（国标 6°C），远红外发射率为 0.93（国标 0.88），远红外辐射温升值为 1.9°C（国标 1.4°C），水洗 50~199 次仍可保持 7A 级抑菌，对皮肤零刺激，安全亲肤，有助于打造健康安全的冬日穿着体验。独特的肌理与线条，强大的发热性能为时尚人士提供新选择

适用范围：服装（户外运动、商务休闲、贴身内衣等）

代表企业：无锡四棉纺织有限公司

品牌：球鹤

Key words: Heat storage and warmth, light absorption, safe and skin-friendly

Raw materials and specifications:
Compact siro-spinning acrylic fiber/rare earth viscose/modal 60/30/10 50^S

Reasons for recommendation: The "precision compact spinning" technology designed and developed independently by Wuxi Fourth Cotton Spinning Co., Ltd. is used to spin yarn, and the clothes made of this yarn have caused a change in traditional warmth-retaining fabrics that only have a warmth-retaining function, and they further enhance the heat-storing and warmth-retaining quality while light-absorbing, heat-generating, and far infrared heat-generating functions, as well as producing good antibacterial effects. These clothes have caused traditional warmth-retaining fabrics to change from only having a heat-storing quality, their light-absorbing and heat-generating functions stand out, able to absorb the heat from a cold light source, their heat-storing function has seen the maximum temperature rise reaching 7.6 °C (6 °C as per national standards), far infrared emissivity 0.93 (0.88 as per national standards), far infrared radiation temperature rise 1.9 °C (1.4 °C as per national standards), and they can still remain Class 7A antibacterial after being water-washed 50~199 times, without skin irritation, safe and skin-friendly, helpful in providing an experience of wearing clothes in a healthy and safe way in winter days. Unique textures and lines, and powerful heat-generating performance offer new options for fashionable people.

Scope of application: Clothing (outdoor sportswear, business suits and leisurewear, close-fitting underwear etc.)

Representing enterprises: Wuxi Fourth Cotton Spinning Co., Ltd.

Brand: Qiu He

赛络紧密纺 Polarwarm 多组分混纺弹力牛仔用纱

COMPACT SIRO-SPUN POLARWARM MULTI-COMPONENT-BLENDED ELASTIC YARN FOR USE IN JEANS

● 关键词：Polarwarm 纤维、轻质、保暖

原料及规格：赛络纺 腈纶/黏胶/Polarwarm 纤维 50/30/20 6~21 英支弹力纱

推荐理由：采用了功能性纤维与粘胶纤维、腈纶等混纺，并与包芯纺相结合，开发出单包、双包超保暖系列纱线，与普通腈纶及粘胶纱线面料相比，其在保温率及克罗值等指标上显著提高，是传统保暖牛仔面料用纱的升级产品，具有较高的使用推广价值

适用范围：牛仔服装面料

代表企业：山东岱银纺织集团股份有限公司

品牌：岱银

主要质量指标与性能　Main quality indexes and performances

赛络紧密纺 Polarwarm 多组分混纺弹力牛仔用纱
Compact siro-spun Polarwarm multi-component-blended elastic yarn for use in jeans

序号 No.		测试项目（计量单位） Tested item (Measurement unit)	测试结果 Test result
1	生理舒适性 Physiological comfortableness	热阻值 ($m^2 \cdot K/W$) Thermal resistance value ($M^2 \cdot K/W$)	0.0568
		克罗值 clo value	0.366
		保温率 (%) Warmth-retaining rate (%)	46.4
2	远红外性能 Far infrared performance	远红外发射率 Far infrared emissivity	0.93
		远红外辐射温升值 (℃) Far infrared radiation temperature rise value (℃)	2.2

Key words: Polarwarm fiber, lightweight, warmth-retaining

Raw materials and specifications:
Siro-spinning Polarwarm fiber/acrylic fiber/viscose 6~21^S elastic yarn

Reasons for recommendation: Single- and double-pack warmth-retaining yarn series is developed by blending functional, viscose, and acrylic fibers before combing them with corn-spun yarn, and as compared with ordinary fabrics made of acrylic and viscose fibers, their performance on such indexes as warmth-retaining rate and clo value is remarkably enhanced, and they are the products upgraded from the yarn for use in traditional warmth-retaining jeans fabrics, having a relatively high value in terms of application and popularization

Scope of application: Jeans fabrics
Representing enterprises: Shandong Daiyin Textile Group Co., Ltd.
Brand: Daiyin

环锭纺棉调温纤维混纺纱
RING-SPUN COTTON TEMPERATURE-REGULATING FIBER-BLENDED YARN

● 关键词：双向调温、原纤抑菌、吸湿排汗

原料及规格：环锭纺 棉／调温纤维 60/40 12~41 英支

推荐理由：控温纱线是一种革命性的功能性产品，采用微胶囊软膜包裹技术，将生物基控温材料植入纤维。这种纱线拥有独特的控温功能，能够吸收、储存和释放热量。在不同温度环境下，通过固液转换的方式，其能够调节温度，从而在皮肤表层形成稳定的温度环境，为人体带来无与伦比的舒适感。这种纱线主要应用于服装、运动装备等领域，可维持人体 28~32℃的舒适体表温度

适用范围：服装、家纺、产业用（运动设备等）

代表企业：河北晟科纺织品有限公司

品牌：晟科

检测报告 Test report

Key words: bi-directional thermoregulation, original fiber anti-bacteria, moisture wicking

Raw materials and specifications:
Ring-spinning cotton/temperature-regulating fiver 60/40 12—41^S

Reasons for recommendation: It is a revolutionary functional product, which is made by using microcapsule soft film technology to plant bio-based temperature-regulating materials into fibers. This yarn has a unique temperature-regulating function, able to absorb, store and discharge heat. Under different temperature conditions, with the method of solid-liquid conversion, it can regulate temperature, so as to create stable temperature conditions on the surface layer of skin, giving the human body a wonderful comfortable feeling. This yarn is mainly used in such fields as apparel and sportswear, able to maintain a comfortable body surface temperature of 28—32°C

Scope of application: Clothing, home textile, industrial textiles (sports equipment etc.)
Representing enterprises: Hebei SK Textile Co., Ltd.
Brand: SK

智护 INTELLIGENT PROTECTION

紧密纺丙纶纯纺纱
COMPACT-SPUN POLYPROPYLENE MONO-FIBER YARN

魏桥纺织 WEIQIAO TEXTILE

● 关键词：丙纶纯纺、单向导湿、吸湿速干

原料及规格： 紧密纺 100% 丙纶 21~60 英支

推荐理由： 丙纶又称聚丙烯纤维，具有质量轻、强度高、疏水快干、芯吸能力强、回潮率 0% 等特点，是生产吸湿快干、单向导湿类产品的理想材质。紧密纺丙纶纯纺纱通过纺纱技术创新成功解决了因丙纶短纤蓬松、回潮率低、静电严重而无法成纱的行业技术难题，其纱线条干指标好、强力高、毛羽少，实现了丙纶纯纺纱线的规模化生产，为吸湿速干、单向导湿等专业运动的功能性面料应用提供了有力支撑，具有广阔的应用前景及市场空间

适用范围： 服装（专业运动面料）

代表企业： 魏桥纺织股份有限公司

品牌： 魏桥牌棉纱、嘉嘉家纺、向尚运动

产品获得认证／专利：《一种丙纶短纤纯纺纱线及生产方法》，ZL202010192448.3

Key words: Polypropylene mono-fiber, unidirectional moisture gui, moisture-absorbing and rapid drying

Raw materials and specifications:
Compact-spinning 100% Polypropylene 21~60^S

Reasons for recommendation: Polypropylene is characterized by lightweight, high strength, hydrophobicity, fast drying, and strong core-absorption ability, making it an ideal material for the production of moisture-absorbing, fast-drying, and unidirectional moisture-conducting products. With compact-spun Polypropylene mono-fiber yarn and the innovation in spinning technology, the industrial technical problem of being unable to spin yarn because Polypropylene staple is fluffy, has low moisture-regaining rate, and high static electricity is successfully solved, and the yarn has good levelness, high strength, low hairiness, making possible to manufacturing Polypropylene mono-fiber yarn on a large scale, significantly helpful in applying functional fabrics for use in professional sportswear that has moisture-absorbing, fast-drying, one-way moisture-conducting functionalities, having a good application prospect and marketing potential

Scope of application: Clothing (professional sportswear fabrics)

Representing enterprises: Weiqiao Textile Co., Ltd.

Brands: Weiqiao, Jiajia, Xiangshang

Product certification/patent obtained: "the Polypropylene staple mono-fiber yarn and manufacturing method", ZL202010192448.3

● 主要质量指标与性能　Main quality indexes and performances

采用丙纶纯纺纱线作为里料导湿层，细旦涤纶作为外料速干层所开发单向导湿的吸湿速干面料与常规市面吸湿速干面料性能对比：

The one-way moisture-conducting, moisture-absorbing and fast-drying fabric are developed by using Polypropylene mono-fiber yarn as the moisture-conducting lining, and fine-denier polyester as the fast-drying outer layer, for the comparison in the moisture-absorbing and fast-drying performance with common fabrics:

品种 Type	滴水扩散时间 (s) Drip diffusion time (s)	吸水率 (%) Water-absorbing rate (%)	芯吸高度 (mm) Core suction height (mm)	干燥速率 (克 / 小时) Drying rate (g/hour)	评判 Judgments
CP 丙纶 60sk/ 涡流纺 T48 涤盖丙纶短纤单向导湿网眼 CP Polypropylene 60sk/Jet vortex spun T48 Polyester-covered Polypropylene staple one-way moisture-conducting mesh	1.1	210	118	0.4	Ⅲ级
常规涤纶短纤单向导湿网眼 Common polyester fiber one-way moisture-conducting mesh	3.5	105	82	0.25	Ⅰ级

纱线流行趋势

Intelligent Protection

赛络紧密纺棉麦卢卡乳木果复方再生纤维素纤维混纺纱

COMPACT SIRO-SPUN COTTON AND MANUKA SHEA BUTTER COMPOUND REGENERATED CELLULOSE FIBER BLENDED YARN

● **关键词**：含有麦卢卡精油＋乳木果油、抑菌＋亲肤

原料及规格：赛络紧密纺 精梳棉／麦卢卡乳木果复方可再生纤维素纤维 50/50 40~60英支

推荐理由：麦卢卡乳木果复方纱线融合了棉的亲肤舒适性以及麦卢卡和乳木果的特定功能。纱线内的麦卢卡精油是纯天然蒸馏产物，其香气能舒缓压力、促进放松、净化空气。麦卢卡精油含有ß三酮，能抗病毒、抗霉菌，具有强效杀菌能力，可用于辅助舒缓感冒症状，缓解喉咙痛，保养皮肤，舒缓皮肤敏感、斑点、烫伤、疔疖、溃疡等皮肤问题，尤其适用于久伤不愈的伤口。乳木果种仁脂肪含量高达45%~55%，具有高油溶性，安全无毒，良好的皮肤渗透和防晒功能，在化妆品、医药等领域也有应用

适用范围：服装（贴身内衣、手套、袜子等）、家纺、产业用

代表企业：响水六棉纺织科技有限公司

品牌：乳木果 麦卢卡

产品获得认证/专利：
《一种含乳木果油的再生纤维素纤维及其制备方法》，ZL 201910827633.2

Key words: containing Manuka essential oil and shea butter, antibacterial and skin-friendly

Raw materials and specifications:
Compact siro-spinning combed cotton/Manukashea butter compound regenerable cellulose fiber 50/50 40~60^S

Reasons for recommendation: The skin-friendliness and comfortableness of cotton and the particular functions of Manuka and shea butter are combined into Manuka shea butter compound yarn. The Manuka essential oil in the yarn is a purely natural product of distillation, and its sweet smell can relieve stress, facilitate relaxation, and purify the air. Manuka essential oil contains ß triketone, able to resist viruses, inhibit mould, and highly effectively eliminate bacteria, helpful in relieving cold symptoms, throat sores, protecting skin, and addressing skin problems of allergies, spots, burns, furuncle, and ulcers, especially in healing wounds that are difficult to heal. Shea butter has a fat content is as high as 45%~55%, and a high oil solubility, safe and non-toxic, able to permeate into skin and sun protection, and also applicable to such fields as cosmetics and medicine

Scope of application: Clothing (close-fitting underwear, gloves, socks etc.), home textile, industrial textiles

Representing enterprises: Xiangshui Sixth Cotton Spinning Scientific Co., Ltd.

Brand: Shea Butter Manuka

Product certification/patent obtained: "The regenerated cellulose fiber containing shea butter and its preparation method", ZL 201910827633.2

赛络紧密纺蚕蛹蛋白多组分混纺纱
COMPACT SIRO-SPUN SILKWORM CHRYSALIS AND MULTI-COMPONENT BLENDED YARN

● 关键词：健康、环保、舒适、蚕蛹蛋白

原料及规格：
赛络紧密纺 蚕蛹蛋白 / 腈纶 / 丝光防缩毛条 / 聚乳酸 / 羊绒 30/25/20/15/10 63 英支

推荐理由： 蚕蛹蛋白纤维是一种新型生物质纤维，通过综合利用高分子技术、化纤纺丝技术、生物工程技术，将蚕蛹蛋白与天然纤维素共混后，制成的新型生物质纤维。将蚕蛹蛋白纤维与聚乳酸纤维、羊绒纤维、丝光防缩毛条、腈纶等混合纺纱，具有亲肤、抗紫外、吸湿透气等优点，织成的面料克服了真丝织物娇嫩、色牢度差、易缩易皱、易泛黄、遇强碱易脆损等缺陷，兼具真丝和生物质纤维色泽亮丽、光泽柔和、吸湿透气、悬垂性好、抗折皱性好等优点

适用范围： 服装（内衣、衬衫）、家纺、产业用（医疗行业）

代表企业： 德州彩诗禾纺织有限公司

Key words: healthy, environment-friendly, comfortable, silkworm chrysalis

Raw materials and specifications:
Compact siro-spinning silkworm chrysalis/acrylic fiber/Mercerized Shrink-Proof Wool Tops/Polylactic Acid/cashmere 30/25/20/15/10 63^S

Reasons for recommendation: As a new type of biomass fiber, silkworm chrysalis fiber is made by comprehensively using macromolecular technologies, chemical fiber spinning, and biological engineering technologies to blend silkworm chrysalis with natural cellulose. The yarn made by blending silkworm chrysalis fiber with Polylactic Acid, cashmere, Mercerized Shrink-Proof Wool Tops, and acrylic fiber has the merit of being skin-friendly, resisting UV light, absorbing moisture, and absorbent and breathable, and the fabric made of it has overcome the shortcomings of real silk fabric, which is frail, poor in color fastness, easy to wrinkle, yellowed, and easily brittle when exposed to strong alkali. Moreover, it has the merits of both real silk and biomass fibers, which have a bright color, a smooth shine, and are able to absorb moisture and absorbent and breathable, well drapable, and prevent wrinkling

Scope of application: Clothing (underwear, shirts), home textile, industrial textiles (medical industry)

Representing enterprises: Dezhou Caishihe Textile Co., Ltd.

Intelligent Protection

复合聚绒纺木棉多组分养生纱
PLUSH COMPOSITE SPUN KAPOK MULTI-COMPONENT HEALTHCARE YARN

● **关键词**：天然、抑菌、驱螨、润肤、透气、桑蚕丝、木棉

原料及规格：聚绒复合纺 莱赛尔 / 精梳棉 / 木棉 / 蚕丝 42/24/18/16 38~40 英支

推荐理由：木棉纤维被誉为"植物软黄金"，以其细、轻、高中空度及优越保暖性著称，兼具防霉、防蛀、抑菌、驱螨等多重优点。该纱线采用创新的"聚绒纺"纺纱技术，巧妙融合桑蚕丝，复合成纱，保留了木棉的天然功能，兼具了桑蚕丝的润肤养肤等特性，具有除臭、抑菌、驱螨、润肤等效果。可用作机织、针织用纱，常用于衬衫、内衣、家纺、休闲服等

适用范围：服装（衬衫、内衣、休闲服）、家纺

代表企业：江苏东华纺织有限公司

Key words: natural, antibacterial, mite repellent, emollient, breathable, silk, kapok

Raw materials and specifications:
Plush composite spinning Lyocell/combed cotton/kapok/silk 42/24/18/16 38~40^S

Reasons for recommendation: Kapok fiber is praised as "plant soft gold", well known for its thin, light, and high hollowness, and good warmth-retaining quality, while it also has the merit of inhibiting mould, moth, bacteria, and mites. This yarn is made by using the innovative "Plush spinning" technology to delicately blend with silk, and while maintaining the natural functionalities of kapok, it also has the quality and effects of silk, which can tone up skin, eliminate unpleasant odor, and inhibit bacteria and mite, able to be used in woven and knitted fabrics, commonly for use in shirts, underwear, home textile, and casual wear

Scope of application: Clothing (shirts, underwear, casual wear), home textile

Representing enterprises: Jiangsu Huadong Textile Co., Ltd.

● **主要质量指标与性能　Main quality indexes and performances**

（参考标准：Q/SWSE 8—2016 木棉多组分混纺本色纱线）
(reference standards: Q/SWSE 8—2016 Kapok multi-component blended natural color yarn)

序号 No.	质量指标 Quality index	指标 Index	实测 Actual measurement
1	纤维含量（%） Fiber content (%)	±1.5	天丝 / 精梳棉 / 木棉 / 桑蚕丝 Tencel/combed cotton/kapok/silk 42.2/24.5/18.2/15.1
2	单纱断裂强力变异系数（%） Single yarn breaking strength variation coefficient (%)	≤ 7	6.3
3	百米重量变异系数（%） 100-meter weight variation coefficient (%)	≤ 1.5	0.5
4	单纱断裂强度（cN/tex） Single yarn breaking strength (cN/tex)	15.0	16.8
5	百米重量偏差（%） 100-meter weight deviation (%)	±1.5	0.6
6	抑菌率（金黄色葡萄球菌）（%） Antibacterial rate (*Staphylococcus aureus*) (%)	70	75
7	抑菌率（大肠杆菌）（%） Antibacterial rate (*E. coli*) (%)	70	82
8	抑菌率（白色念珠菌）（%） Antibacterial rate (*Candida albicans*) (%)	60	63
9	驱螨率（%） Mite-repellant rate (%)	60	63.5

石墨烯混纺纱线系列
GRAPHENE BLENDED YARN SERIES

金常山 GOLD CHANGSUN

● **关键词：石墨烯、调温**

原料及规格：
①家纺产品纱线：如80英支、100/2英支、60英支、50英支、40英支，以黏胶基石墨烯纤维和棉、天丝、天竹纤维、黏胶纤维、莫代尔等混纺
②医护产品纱线：如21英支、23英支、45/2英支、26英支，以涤纶基石墨烯纤维和棉混纺
③男装衬衣纱线系列：如40英支、80/2英支、100/2英支等，以黏胶基石墨烯纤维和涤纶、棉、天丝、天竹纤维、黏胶纤维、莫代尔等混纺，基本是三组分产品
④防静电工装纱线：如32英支、21英支、45/2英支、16英支，以涤纶基石墨烯纤维和棉、天竹混纺
⑤户外休闲产品纱线：如21/2英支、21英支、16英支，以涤纶基石墨烯纤维和棉混纺
⑥针织产品纱线：40英支、32英支、50英支，有S捻和Z捻，以黏胶基石墨烯纤维和棉、天丝、天竹纤维等混纺

推荐理由： 石墨烯系列纱线，包含石墨烯黏胶、石墨烯涤纶、石墨烯腈纶等含石墨烯纤维，开发了不同石墨烯纤维与棉、涤纶、各种差别化纤维天竹、天丝、莱赛尔、莫代尔、麻等不同含量配比共80多种纱线，以赛络紧密纺为主，纱线全部达到Uster25%以上水平，纱线条干均匀，结杂少，布面光洁匀整，满足了高档针织、机织产品的要求

适用范围： 服装（内衣、功能性服装、保健袜）、家纺、产业用（户外帐篷布等）
代表企业： 石家庄常山恒新纺织有限公司恒盛分公司

Intelligent Protection

● 主要质量指标与性能 **Main quality indexes and performances**

Graphene bedding fabric test result

No.	Quality index	Specifications	Actual measurement
1	表面电阻率 （Ω） Surface electric resistance rate (Ω)	$\geq 1\times 10^{10}$, $\leq 1\times 10^{13}$	1.8×10^{11}
2	远红外发射率 Far infrared emissivity	≥ 0.88	0.92
3	远红外辐照温升（℃） Far infrared radiation temperature rise (℃)	≥ 1.4	2.0
4	趋避率（%） Avoidance rate (%)	≥ 60	75.6
5	百米重量偏差（%） 100100-meter weight deviation (%)	±1.5	0.6
6	抑菌率（金黄色葡萄球菌）（%） Antibacterial rate (Staphylococcus aureus)(%)	70	> 99
7	抑菌率（大肠杆菌）（%） Antibacterial rate (E. coli)(%)	70	> 99
8	抑菌率（白色念珠菌）（%） Antibacterial rate (Candida albicans)(%)	60	91

Key words: Graphene, thermoregulation

Raw materials and specifications:

① Yarn for home textile products: e.g. 80.100/2.60.50.40 count, made by blending viscose-based Grapheme fiber with cotton, Tencel, bamboo fiber, viscose fiber, modal etc.

② Yarn for medical products: e.g. 21 count, 23.45/2.26 count, made by blending polyester-based Grapheme fiber with cotton

③ Yarn for men's shirts: e.g. 40 count, 80/2.100/2 etc, made by blending viscose-based Graphene fiber with polyester, cotton, Tencel, bamboo fiber, viscose fiber, modal etc, generally featuring three components

④ yarn for anti-static work clothes: e.g. 32 count, 21.45/2.16 count, made by blending polyester-based Graphene fiber with bamboo fiber

⑤ Yarn for outdoor casual wear: e.g. 21/2 count, 21.16 count, made by blending polyester-based Graphene fiber with cotton

⑥ Yarn for knitted wear: 40.32.50 count, with S and Z twists, made by blending viscose-based Grapheme fiber with cotton, Tencel, bamboo fiber

Reasons for recommendation: Graphene series of yarn includes Grapheneviscose, Grapheme polyester, Graphene acrylic fibers that contain Graphene fiber, and more than 80 types of yarn have been developed by blending different Graphene fibers with cotton, polyester, various differential fibers, bamboo fiber, Tencel, Lyocell, modal, and hemp in different proportions, with compact Siro-spinning as the main technology, all the yarn reaching the Uster level of 25% or above, high in levelness, low in unevenness, apparently shiny and uniform, satisfying the requirements for high-end woven and knitted products

Scope of application: Clothing (underwear, functional clothes, healthcare socks), home textile, industrial textiles (outdoor tarp etc.)

Representing enterprises: Shijiazhuang Changsun Hengxin Textile Co., Ltd. Hengsheng Branch

石墨烯腈纶多组分混纺纱
GRAPHENE ACRYLIC FIBER MULTI-COMPONENT BLENDED YARN

● **关键词**：石墨烯、抑菌、保暖、远红外、抗紫外、抗静电、抗辐射、长时间有效

原料及规格：石墨烯腈纶／再生黏胶／羊毛 40/40/20 48 英支

推荐理由：石墨烯是世界上发现的最薄、强度最大、导电导热性能最强、延展性最好的新型纳米材料之一，被称为"黑金""新材料之王"。添加石墨烯后的腈纶纱线具有体温远红外、超高热传导、持久抑菌、除异味、抗辐射等优异康护特性，应用领域广泛

适用范围：服装

代表企业：绍兴泰鼎石墨烯科技有限公司

Key words: Grapheme, antibacterial, warmth-retaining, far infrared, anti-UV light, anti-static, anti-radiation, long effectiveness

Raw materials and specifications:
Grapheme acrylic fiber/regenerated viscose/wool 40/40/20 48^S

Reasons for recommendation: As a new type of nano-material, Graphene is one of the thinnest, the strongest, the most electric-conductive, and the most extensible that has ever been discovered in the world. It is named "black gold" and "king of new material". The yarn made of acrylic fiber with Graphene has a special quality of resisting UV lig ht, highly effectively conducting heat, continuing inhibiting bacteria, eliminating unpleasant odor, and protecting against radiation, and is widely applied

Scope of application: Clothing

Representing enterprises: Shaoxing Taiding Grapheme Scientific Co., Ltd.

Intelligent Protection

● 主要质量指标与性能 Main quality indexes and performances

防紫外线性能 GB/T 18830—2009 Anti-UV light performance GB/T 18830—2009		
UPF 平均值 UPF average value	—	199
UPF 紫外线防护系数 UPF UV light protection factor	>40	>50
UVA 平均透射比 (%) UVA average transmittance (%)	<5	0.61
UVB 平均透射比 (%) UVB average transmittance (%)	—	0.47
异味成分浓度减少率（体味）(%) GB/T 33610.2—2017 GB/T 33610.3—2019 Reduction in concentration of unpleasantly odorous ingredient (body odor) (%) GB/T 33610.2—2017 GB/T 33610.3—2019		
氨气 (%) Ammonia (%)	≥ 70	86.0
醋酸 (%) Acetic acid (%)	≥ 70	86.7
异戊酸 (%) Isovaleric acid (%)	≥ 85	98.4
2- 壬烯醛 (%) 2-Nonenal (%)	≥ 75	94.7

	标准（称）值 Requirement	实测值 Results	单项判定 Judgement
远红外发射率 GB/T 30127—2013 Far infrared emissivity GB/T 30127—2013	≥ 0.88	0.93	符合
远红外辐射温升 (℃) GB/T 30127—2013 Far infrared radiation temperature rise (℃) GB/T 30127—2013	≥ 1.4	2.4	符合
肺炎克雷白氏菌 (ATCC4352) 抑菌率 (%) GB/T 20944.2—2007 Klebsiella pneumonia (ATCC4352) antibacterial rate (%) GB/T 20944.2—2007	≥ 99	>99	具有良好抑菌效果 Having a good antibacterial effect
大肠杆菌 (8099) 抑菌率 (%) GB/T 20944.3—2008 E. coli (8099) antibacterial rate (%) GB/T 20944.3—2008	≥ 70	93	具有抑菌效果 Having a good antibacterial effect
金黄色葡萄球菌 (ATCC 6538) 抑菌率 (%) GB/T 20944.3—2008 Staphylococcus aureus (ATCC 6538) antibacterial rate (%) GB/T 20944.3—2008	≥ 70	>99	具有抑菌效果 Having a good antibacterial effect
白色念珠菌 (ATCC 10231) 抑菌率 (%) GB/T 20944.3—2008 Candida albicans (ATCC 10231) antibacterial rate (%) GB/T 20944.3—2008	≥ 60	98	具有抑菌效果 Having a good antibacterial effect
热阻 (m²·K/W) Thermal resistance (m²·K/W)	—	0.00960	
克罗值 clo value	—	0.0619	
折算保温率 (%) Converted warmth-retaining rate (%)	—	13.0	
热导率 [W/(m·K)] Heat-conducting rate [W/(m·K)]	—	0.0697	

EXCELLENT QUALITY
A unique ingenuity in play, embodying the great charm of a classic

关键词：品质、匠心
Key words: quality, ingenuity

臻品

匠心独运，诠释经典之美韵

在品质生活的温柔呼唤下，高品质纱线正成为市场的璀璨明珠，如同艺术品般精致，每一根都蕴含着匠人的心血与智慧。柔软低捻纱线以其细腻的触感优雅的外观正引领着纱线品质提升的新风尚如同细腻的笔触，勾勒出生活的精致轮廓。锦纶短纤纯纺及混纺纱线，以其耐磨、抗皱、易打理的特性成为高品质服饰的首选以其坚韧编织出服饰的优雅与实用。喷气涡流纺高支纱包芯纱等新型纱线的研发和应用不仅丰富了产品线，更提升了产品的艺术价值，如同创新的音符，为纱线行业奏响了一曲品质与创新的交响曲。羊毛、天然麻、绢丝等混纺纱线，更是将自然元素与时尚潮流完美融合，为消费者提供了更多元化的选择，如同自然的馈赠，让纱线产品更加丰富多彩，充满生机与活力。

Friendlily driven by quality life, high-grade yarn is becoming the brilliant star of the market, as exquisite as a work of art, with every detail reflecting a craftsman's painstaking effort and wisdom. With its delicate feel and graceful appearance, the soft low-twist yarn is setting a new trend in enhancing the quality of yarn products, as if a picture of a beautiful life is being painted with delicate strokes. Characterized by enduring wear, resisting wrinkle, and being easy to maintain, the yarn made of nylon staple using mono-fiber-spinning and blending methods has become the first choice for high-quality clothes, and it works like a strong silk thread, enabling clothes to have a beautiful appearance and a practical value. As new types of yarn e.g. the jet vortex spun high-count yarn and the covering yarn are developed and applied, not only are the lines in products enriched, but the artistic value of products is also improved, and this seems as if a chapter about quality and innovation in yarn industry is being written. It goes further to show the perfect merge between natural elements and fashion trends that yarn is made by blending wool, natural hemp, and silk, which provide customers with more diversified choices, and this seems like a natural endowment that enables yarn to be more colorful, and full of vigor and energy.

纱线流行趋势

意柔纺长绒棉锦纶羊毛高强包覆纱

YIROU-SPUN LONG-STAPLE COTTON NYLON WOOL HIGH-STRENGTH COVERING YARN

● **关键词**：高强、抗起球、意柔纺纱技术

原料及规格：长绒棉/锦纶长丝/羊毛 38/37/25 20~50 英支

推荐理由：意柔纺是在嵌入式系统定位新型纺纱技术（如意纺）上实现升级，运用两根长丝和短纤维组合的长短复合加工技术、提高纱线强力，同时可根据产品需求调整长丝短纤材料及喂入方式。FDY 的特殊收缩性能赋予织物一定的膨胀度和弹性，使产品表面光洁、抗起球性好，产品耐磨、有骨感。目前多用在军工领域，未来可在民用、户外等领域广泛应用

适用范围：服装

代表企业：汶上如意技术纺织有限公司

品牌：天容

Key words: high-strength, anti-piling, Yirou spinning technology

Raw materials and specifications:
Ring-spinning long-staple cotton/nylon filament/wool 38/37/25 20~50^S

Reasons for recommendation: Yirou-spinning is an upgraded version of what is called the new type of spinning technology (Ruyi spinning) in embedded systems, and it is a compound processing technology to use two filaments and staple for combination, improving yarn's strength, able to adjust filament and staple materials as well as the feeding method according to product requirements. FDY's special shrinking quality enables textiles to have a certain expansion and elasticity, so that the product has a shiny and clean surface, effectively prevents pilingpilling, endures wear, and produces a body-shaping effect. At present, it is mostly used in the military field, and is expected to see wider applications in civil and outdoor fields

Scope of application: Clothing
Representing enterprises: Wenshangruyi Technical Spinning Co., Ltd.
Brand: Tianrong

● 主要质量指标与性能　Main quality indexes and performances

（参考标准：FZ/T 12014—2014 针织用棉色纺纱）
(reference standards: FZ/T 12014-2014 knitting-specific cotton dye-spinning)

项目 Item	线密度 变异系数 Yarn density variation coefficient	单纱断裂强力 变异系数（%）≤ Single yarn breaking strength variation coefficient (%) ≤	单纱断裂 强度 (cN/tex) ≥ Single yarn breaking strength (cN/tex) ≥	耐皂洗色牢度（级） 变色、沾色 Soap-enduring color fastness (grade) Color change　Color transfer	耐汗渍色牢（级） 变色、沾色 Perspiration-enduring color fastness (grade) Color change　Color transfer	耐干摩擦色牢度（级） Dry friction-enduring color fastness (grade)	耐湿摩擦色牢度（级） Wet grinding-enduring color fastness (grade)
标准要求 Standard	1.8	9.5	13.5	≥ 4，≥ 3~4	≥ 4，≥ 3~4	≥ 4	≥ 3~4
常规产品 Common products	1.5	7.8	14.9	4，4	4，4	4	4
本产品 This product	1.5	5.0	15.7	4~5，4~5	4~5，4~5	4~5	4~5

喷气涡流纺再生纤维素纤维锦纶 PBT 包芯纱

AIR- JET VORTEX CORE-SPUN YARN OF REGENERATED CELLULOSE FIBER/ NYLON BLENDED COVER PBT

● 关键词：芯纱坚韧、手感细腻、涡流纺包芯

原料及规格：喷气涡流纺 再生黏胶／锦纶＋聚对苯二甲酸丁二酯（PBT）50 旦 70/30 28 英支

推荐理由：包芯纱以其独特的复合结构，巧妙融合多种纤维优势，展现出高效益与广阔的增长前景。不仅提升了织物的强度与耐磨性，还保留了优异的吸湿排汗与透气性能，适用于服装、家居及医疗等多个领域。其独特的性能与广泛的应用前景，使包芯纱成为高效益且潜力巨大的纺织产品

适用范围：服装、家纺、产业用

代表企业：吴江京奕特种纤维有限公司

Key words: heart yarn firm and tensile, delicate feel, Jet vortex spinning core-covering

Raw materials and specifications:
Jet vortex spinning regenerated viscose/nylon +Polybutylene-terephthalate(PBT)50D 70/30 28^S

Scope of application: With its unique compound structure, and the advantage of delicately combining several types of fiber, it has significant benefits and a bright growth prospect. It not only improves the textile's strength and wear-enduring quality, but also maintains excellent moisture-absorbing and breathing functions, applicable to many fields such as apparel, home articles and medical industry. Its unique performance and broad application prospects enable covering yarn to become the textile product that brings enormous benefits and has huge potential

Scope of application: Clothing, home textile, industrial textiles

Representing enterprises: Wu jiang Jingyi Special Fiber Co., Ltd.

● 主要质量指标与性能　Main quality indexes and performances

测试项目 Tested item	再生黏胶／锦纶＋聚对苯二甲酸丁二酯（PBT）50 旦 70/30 27.5 英支 Regenerated viscose/nylon + Polybutylene-terephthalate (PBT) 50 denier 70/30 27.5^S
条干均匀度变异系数（%） Yarn levelness variation coefficient (%)	12.5
千米细节（-50%）（个/km） Thin places per 1000 meters (-50%) (Pc/km)	0
千米粗结（+50%）（个/km） Thick places per 1000 meters (+50%) (Pc/km)	20
千米棉结（+200%）（个/km） Neps per 1000 meters (+200%) (Pc /km)	10
毛羽指数 H 值 Hairiness index H value	3.75
平均单纱断裂强力（cN） Average yarn breaking strength (cN)	277
单纱断裂强力变异系数（%） Single yarn breaking strength variation coefficient (%)	4.8
平均单纱最低断裂强力（cN） Average single-yarn minimum breaking strength (cN)	235
断裂伸长率（%） Elongation at break (%)	14.2
单纱断裂强度（cN/tex） Single yarn breaking strength (cN/tex)	12.8
耐磨指数 Wear-enduring index	20

臻品
Excellent Quality

喷气涡流纺莱赛尔聚酯包芯纱
AIR-JET VORTEX CORE-SPUN OF LYOCELL COVER PET

pure + fiber
普路通

● **关键词**：高效、多样、舒适、质量稳定

原料及规格：喷气涡流纺 莱赛尔/涤纶 30 英支，L30 英支/50 旦包芯纱

推荐理由：涡流纺包芯纱是一种采用涡流纺纱技术生产的包芯纱线，由两种或多种不同纤维组合而成，其中芯部纤维被外部纤维包裹，形成一种特殊的纱线结构。该产品结合了涡流纺纱的高效性与包芯纱的多样性，广泛用于纺织行业中。由于其独特的结构和性能特点，该涡流纺包芯纱在高档纺织品、功能性纺织品等领域具有广阔的应用前景

适用范围：服装（工业防护服）、家纺、产业用

代表企业：苏州普路通纺织科技有限公司

品牌：普路通

产品获得认证/专利：
《一种涡流纺复合包缠强力纱》，ZL201921685183.X

Key words:
high efficiency, diversity, comfortable, invariable quality

Raw materials and specifications:
Jet vortex spinning Lyocell/polyester 30^S, L30^S/50D covering yarn

Reasons for recommendation: This covering yarn is made by using Jet vortex spinning technology to blend two or more types of fiber, where, the fiber at the core is covered with the fiber at the outer part to form a special structure in the yarn. It combines Jet vortex spun yarn's quality of being highly efficient with covering yarn's quality of being diversified, and it is widely used in the textile industry. Thanks to its unique structure and performance, this Jet vortex spun covering yarn has a bright application prospect in such fields as textile products, and functional textile products

Scope of application: Clothing (industrial protective clothes), home textile, industrial textiles

Representing enterprises: Suzhou Pure Fiber Textile Scientific Co., Ltd.

Brand: Pure Fiber

Product certification/patent obtained:
The Jet vortex spun compound wrapped strong yarn (patent No.: ZL201921685183.X)

● **主要质量指标与性能** Main quality indexes and performances

产品名称 Product name	条干均匀度变异系数（%） Yarn levelness variation coefficient (%)	平均单纱断裂强力（cN） Average yarn breaking strength (cN)	单纱断裂强力变异系数（%） Single yarn breaking strength variation coefficient (%)	百米重量变异系数（%） 100-meter weight variation coefficient (%)	支数偏差（%） Count deviation(%)	耐磨指数 Wear-enduring index
包芯纱（30^S） Covering yarn (30^S)	11.8	406.4	7.1	0.2	−1.5	10.0
黏胶纱（30^S） Viscose yarn (30^S)	12.94	282.3	7.04	0.56	0.6	10.0
麻灰纱3%灰（30^S） Duey yarn 3% (30^S)	12.39	315.4	5.89	0.69	−2.9	10.0
涤黏混纺纱（30^S） Polyester-viscose-blended yarn (30^S)	12.98	440.1	7.51	0.54	−1.5	8.9

紧密纺普梳超柔纯棉纱
COMPACT-SPUN REGULARLY CARDED SUPER-SOFT PURELY COTTON YARN

● **关键词：超柔**

原料及规格： 紧密纺 100% 棉 32 英支

推荐理由： 采用特殊的纺纱设备和工艺，通过调整纺纱扭矩，生产出捻度比常规纱线低 20%~30% 的产品。在保持纱线强力等关键指标不变的前提下，纱线依然保持了蓬松的质地和柔软的手感。紧密纺普梳超柔纯棉纱毛羽少、强力高、强力不匀率低、捻度不匀率小、纱线光滑、条干均匀、纱体蓬松、手感柔软。用其织成的面料具有亲肤、吸湿、透气和保暖的特性，非常适合用于运动休闲服装、内衣、睡衣以及婴幼儿产品。此外，结合其舒适手感和弹性纤维的高弹力塑形，可制备超柔弹力牛仔面料，具有良好的市场前景

适用范围： 服装（牛仔、运动休闲服装、内衣、睡衣、婴幼儿用品等）

代表企业： 利泰醒狮（太仓）控股有限公司

Key words: Super-soft

Raw materials and specifications:
Compact-spinning 100% cotton 32^S

Reasons for recommendation: This product is produced using special spinning equipment and technology by regulating yarn torque so that its twist is 20%~30% lower than ordinary yarn. Besides keeping key indicators such as yarn strength unchanged, this yarn still maintains a fluffy texture and a soft feel. This compact-spun regularly carded super-soft purely cotton yarn is low in hairiness, high in strength, low in strength unevenness, and in twist unevenness, high in slickness, and levelness, with the yarn body fluffy, and soft to the touch. The fabric made of it is skin-friendly, absorbs moisture, breathes freely, and retains warmth, especially suitable for use in sportswear, casual clothes, underwear, pajamas, and infant products. Moreover, if its comfortable feel is combined with the high-elasticity shaping quality of elastic fiber, super-soft elastic jeans fabric can be made, which has a good market prospect

Scope of application: Clothing (jeans, sportswear, casual clothes, underwear, pajamas, infant products etc.)

Representing enterprises: Litai Xingshi (Taicang) Holding Co., Ltd.

● **主要质量指标与性能   Main quality indexes and performances**

（参考标准：T/CCTA 30102—2021 棉本色平衡纱）
(reference standards: T/CCTA 30102—2021 cotton natural color reeled yarn)
普梳紧密纺 32 英支超柔纱主要物理指标
Main physical indexes of regularly carded compact-spun 32^S super-soft yarn

	卷装 Packed in rolls	管纱 Packed with thin tubes	筒纱 Packed with thick tubes
	品种 Type	紧密纺 100% 棉 32 英支 Compact-spun 100% cotton 32^S	
捻度 Twist	上机捻度 T/10cm On-loom twist T/10cm	66.0	64.0
	实测下机捻度 T/10cm Actually measured off-loom twist T/10cm	68.1	65.7
	捻度均匀度变异系数 CV(%) Twist evenness variation coefficient CV (%)	2.8	3.8
	捻系数 Twist factor	292	282

Excellent Quality

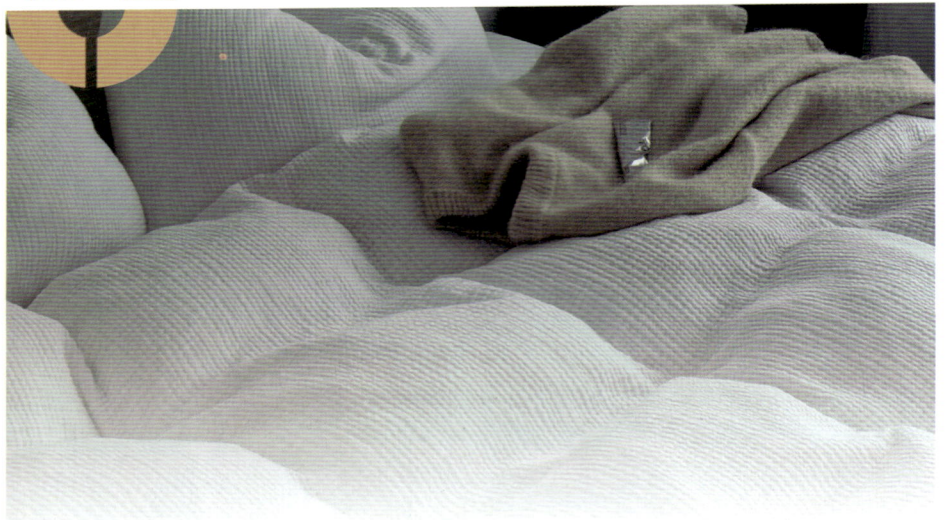

赛络紧密纺精梳匹马棉超柔纱
COMPACT SIRO-SPUN COMBED SUPIMA COTTON SUPER-SOFT YARN

● **关键词**：精梳赛络紧密纺、Supima 棉、低捻

原料及规格：精梳赛络紧密纺 Supima 棉 100% 50 英支超柔纱

推荐理由：充分利用美国 Supima 棉纤维长度长、强力高以及特殊的纤维光泽性，配合集聚赛络纺纱机理，使纺制成的纱线在捻度比正常纱线低 25% 时仍保持较好的强力、条干、毛羽指标。该纱线捻度小、纱体蓬松、手感好，后道工序处理方便。由其制成的面料光滑靓丽，既有棉的亲肤、吸湿排汗透气，又有化纤的光泽。产品附加值是普通产品的 1.5 倍

适用范围：服装、家纺

代表企业：河北宁纺集团广和纺织有限公司

品牌：广新

产品获得专利：《一种纺织生产用梳棉机》，ZL202211675684.6

Key words: combed compact siro-spinning, Supima cotton, low twist

Raw materials and specifications:
Combed compact siro-spinning Supima cotton 100% 50^S super-soft yarn

Reasons for recommendation: By making better use of American Supima cotton fiber that is long, strong, and shiny, and with the help of Siro-spun yarn polymerizing mechanism, the yarn made in this way can still maintain good performance in terms of such indexes as strength, levelness and hairiness when its twist is 25% lower than ordinary yarn. This yarn has a low twist, a fluffy body, and a good feel, making it easier to go through follow-up processes. The fabric made of it is slick and beautiful, not only skin-friendly, able to absorb moisture, and breathable, but also shiny. This product is 1.5 times the added value of an ordinary product

Scope of application: Clothing, home textile

Representing enterprises: Hebei Ningfang Group Guanghe Textile Co., Ltd.

Brand: Guangxin

Product patent obtained: "The cotton carding machine for textile production", ZL202211675684.6

紧密纺精梳匹马棉高支股线
COMPACT-SPUN COMBED SUPIMA COTTON HIGH-COUNT PLIED YARN

● 关键词：纯棉、特高支

原料及规格：精梳紧密纺 Supima 棉 100% 200 英支股线

推荐理由：选用高品质的美国 Supima 棉，通过 CAS 配棉系统进行精确配棉，对各生产工序的工艺参数进行优化，精心挑选纺织专用配件，并由技艺精湛的手工操作车工进行操作，确保了纺纱过程轻定量、慢速度、低断头。该精梳紧密纺 200 英支股线，条干均匀、强力高、毛羽少，单纱截面仅包含约 20 根纤维，生产过程难度大，是制作高支数高档面料的首选

适用范围：服装

代表企业：山东华强纺织有限公司

品牌：禧麻

Key words: purely cotton, extremely high-count

Raw materials and specifications:
Combed compact-spinning Supima cotton 100% 200^S plied yarn

Reasons for recommendation: High-quality American Supima cotton is selected for use, cotton is accurately fed through the CAS cotton-feeding system, the technological parameters for every process have been optimized, and accessories especially for use in textiles are carefully chosen and manually operated by a skillful lathe worker to ensure small amounts to feed, slow speed, and less broken ends. This combed compact-spun 200^S plied yarn is high in levelness and strength, and low in hairiness, with the cross-section of a single yarn only containing about 20 fibers, difficult to manufacture, being the first choice for manufacturing high-count top-grade fabrics

Scope of application: Clothing

Representing enterprises:
Shandong Huaqiang Textile Co., Ltd.

Brand: Xima

Excellent Quality

紧密纺棉绢丝混纺特高支纱
COMPACT-SPUN COTTON SILK BLENDED EXTREMELY HIGH-COUNT YARN

TALAK 太湖

● 关键词：亲肤舒适、柔软细腻、透气、特高支纱

原料及规格：紧密纺 棉/绢丝 90/10 200 英支

推荐理由：该纱线巧妙融合了棉纤维的柔顺与绢丝的华贵，其天然成分赋予产品卓越的吸湿和透气性能。棉花的柔软与绢丝的光滑细腻相得益彰，为织物带来了无与伦比的触感，非常适合贴身穿着。此外，200英支的特高纱支数保证了织物的高密度和精致度，从而赋予产品更佳的光泽和良好的悬垂性。该特高支纱线在保持轻盈的同时，也提升了耐久性和抗皱性，使衣物更易于打理，持久保持新衣状态。所制成的面料不仅柔软细腻，色彩鲜艳，还具备良好的抗皱和耐用特性，适用于高端面料市场，为服装领域带来了新的增长潜力，并能为品牌带来显著的市场竞争优势和高附加值

适用范围：服装

代表企业：无锡一棉纺织集团有限公司

品牌：TALAK

Key words: skin-friendly, soft and delicate, breathable, extremely high-count yarn

Raw materials and specifications:
Compact-spinning cotton/silk 90/10 200^S

Reasons for recommendation: It subtly combines the softness of cotton fiber with the luxury of silk, with its natural components giving an excellent moisture-absorbing and freely breathing performance. The softness of cotton complements the slickness and exquisiteness of silk, enabling the textile to have a wonderful feel, especially suitable for close-fitting underwear. Additionally, its extremely high 200^S ensures a high density and a high level of exquisiteness in textile, so that the product has a good shine, and a high drapability. While remaining lightweight, this extremely high-count yarn also has improved the enduring and wrinkle-resisting performance, so that the clothes are easier to maintain, and maintain the state of being new for a long time. The fabric made of it not only is soft and delicate, and bright in color, but also has a good wrinkle-resisting and enduring quality, suitable for the high-end market, enabling the apparel industry to have a potential for growth, and bringing obvious market advantages and high added value to the brand

Scope of application: Clothing

Representing enterprises: Wuxi First Cotton Spinning Group Co., Ltd.

Brand: TALAK

赛络紧密纺聚乳酸多组分混纺纱
COMPACT SIRO-SPUN POLYLACTIC ACID MULTI-COMPONENT BLENDED YARN

● **关键词**：纤维素、环保纤维、聚乳酸混纺

原料及规格：赛络紧密纺 黏胶/精梳棉/聚乳酸/蚕丝 45/30/19/6 40 英支

推荐理由：该纱线的生产过程成功解决了不同纤维性能差异及混合均匀的难题，技术含量高。它不仅具备纤维素纤维的吸湿舒适性、聚乳酸纤维的轻柔滑顺及吸湿透气性，以及天然棉纤维的保暖和自然传承的优点，还融合了天然桑蚕丝的养颜护肤等特点。该产品被应用于高端纺织品领域，满足了消费者对舒适、健康、时尚的穿着需求，具有较好的市场发展前景

适用范围：服装、家纺、产业用

代表企业：山东超越纺织有限公司

品牌：中鲁超越

Key words: cellulose, environment-friendly fiber, Polylactic Acid blendedd

Raw materials and specifications:
Compact siro-spinning viscose/combed cotton/Polylactic Acid/silk 45/30/19/6 40^S

Reasons for recommendation: The difficult problem of the difference in performance between different fibers and the uniformity of the blended is successfully solved in the manufacturing process for this yarn, which has a high technical content. It not only features a moisture-absorbing and comfortable quality that a cellulose fiber has, a soft, moisture-absorbing, and breathable quality that a Polylactic Acid fiber has, and a warmth-retaining close-to-nature quality that a natural cotton fiber has, but also combines a facially beautifying and skin-caring quality that a natural silk has. This product is applied in the high-end textile field, satisfying consumer demand for comfortableness, health, and fashion, having a good market prospect

Scope of application: Clothing, home textile, industrial textiles

Representing enterprises: Shandong Chaoyue Textile Co., Ltd.

Brand: Zhonglu Chaoyue

Excellent Quality

喷气涡流纺莱赛尔锦纶高支混纺纱
AIR-JET VORTEX SPUN LYOCELLNYLON HIGH-COUNT BLENDED YARN

● 关键词：绿色、环保、高性能、高档次、莱赛尔/锦纶

原料及规格： 喷气涡流纺 莱赛尔/锦纶 80/20 120 英支

推荐理由： 喷气涡流纺技术以其流程短、产量高、生产成本低和自动化程度高等优势，正成为纺纱业的后起之秀。其独特的纺纱原理使纱线毛羽少、光洁紧密，织成的面料具有优良的耐磨和抗起毛起球性能。该纱线实现了细分领域的技术突破，达到国际先进水平，同时为可降解绿色环保低碳产品，经济效益和社会效益显著

适用范围： 服装、家纺、产业用

代表企业： 吴江京奕特种纤维有限公司

Key words: green, environment-friendly, high-performance, top grade, Lyocell/nylon
Raw materials and specifications:
Jet vortex spinning Lyocell/nylon 80/20 120^S
Reasons for recommendation: With a short manufacturing process, high productivity, low production cost, and high level of atomization to its advantage, the Jet vortex spinning technology is becoming a rising star in the textile industry. Its unique theory about spinning enables yarn to be low in hairiness, shiny, clean, and tight, and the fabric made of it has a good wear-enduring and fluff- and piling-resisting quality. This yarn reflects a technical breakthrough in the segmented field, reaching the advanced international level, and meanwhile, it is a degradable green environment-friendly low-carbon product, having remarkable economic and social benefits
Scope of application: Clothing, home textile, Industrial textiles
Representing enterprises: Wujiang Jingyi Special Fiber Co., Ltd.

赛络紧密纺锦纶短纤纯纺纱
COMPACT SIRO-SPUN NYLON STAPLE MONO-FIBER YARN

● **关键词**：锦纶短纤纯纺、凉感、耐磨、质地柔软、透气性佳、顶破强力好

原料及规格：赛络紧密纺 锦纶短纤 100% 50 英支

推荐理由：无锡四棉凭借自主研发的"精密紧密纺"工艺，成功突破锦纶短纤纱纺技术难关，涵盖 N6、N66、PA56、再生 N6 等材质，适用于 21~50 英支纯纺，广泛应用于针织与机织领域。该纱线改变了原有锦纶长丝面料的穿着体验感，使面料在提高透气性的同时增强了棉感和亲肤感，保留了原有的贴肤凉感，吸湿速干性极佳，面料环保符合可持续要求，又契合了当前户外运动的潮流趋势。经权威检测机构圆轨迹法，590cN 加压重量，150 次起毛和 150 次起球后测试，其抗起毛起球达 3.5 级，适用于制作高端轻运动、轻商务 T 恤、高端内衣及瑜伽服饰

适用范围：服装（户外运动、商务、休闲、贴身内衣等）

代表企业：无锡四棉纺织有限公司

品牌：球鹤

Key words: nylon staple mono-fiber-spun, cool feel, wear-enduring, soft texture, good breathing performance, high bursting strength

Raw materials and specifications:
Compact siro-spinning nylon staple 100% 50^S

Reasons for recommendation: With its independently developed "precision compact-spinning" technology, Wuxi Fourth Cotton Spinning Co., Ltd. has successfully made a breakthrough in nylon staple spinning technology, which covers such materials as N6, N66, PA56, regenerated N6, applicable to 21-50^S mono-fiber-spinning, and widely used in the fields of knitted and woven products. This yarn has changed the feeling experienced with the original fabric made of nylon filament, so that while the fabric's freely breathing performance is improved, the feel of cotton that it gives and its skin-friendly quality has been enhanced, and it maintains the original cool feel to the touch, good at absorbing moisture and fast drying off, with its environment-friendliness in compliance with the requirements for sustainability, following the prevailing trend in outdoor sports. After being tested by an authoritative agency using the circle locus method with which the fabric is pressed at 590 cN, fluffed 150 times, and piled 150 times, its fluffing and piling have reached Grade 3.5, suitable for the T-shirts used in non-intensive sport and business activities, and for high-end underwear and the clothes used in Yoga

Scope of application: Clothing (outdoor sportswear, business wear, leisure wear, close-fitting underwear etc.)

Representing enterprises: Wuxi Fourth Cotton Spinning Co., Ltd.

Brand: Qiu He

检测报告
Test report

Excellent Quality

棉纺户外运动羊毛混纺纱线系列
COTTON OUTDOOR SPORTS WOOL BLENDED YARN SERIES

双弘 DOUBLE GREAT

● 关键词：环保、保暖、透气、高品质、羊毛

原料及规格：
①赛络纺 涤纶/羊毛 90/10 40 英支
②紧密纺 羊毛/锦纶 70/30 40 英支
③赛络紧密纺 莱赛尔/羊毛 70/30 40 英支

推荐理由： 近年来，随着室内与户外运动项目的增加，消费者对运动服饰的环境适应性、功能性和穿着舒适性提出了更高的要求。在现有棉纺设备基础上，利用细旦羊毛纤维，采用自主知识产权的新技术、新工艺，南通双弘纺织有限公司研发生产出各种羊毛纯纺纱、混纺纱，既满足运动领域用纱的亲肤舒适性与耐磨性，又具有优异的回弹性、吸湿排汗以及蓄热保暖等功能，且绿色环保

适用范围： 服装、家纺
代表企业： 南通双弘纺织有限公司
品牌： 双弘

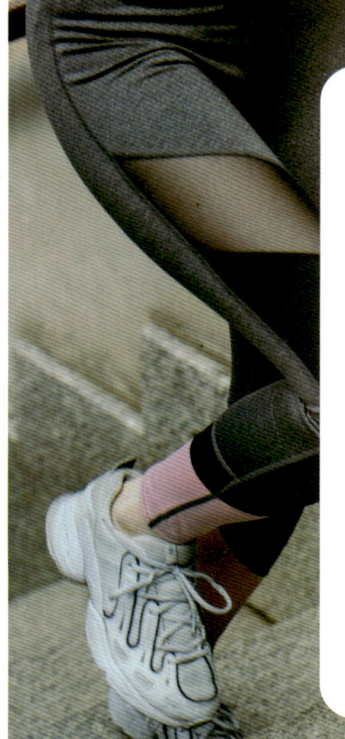

Key words: environment-friendly, warmth-retaining, breathable, high-quality, wool

Raw materials and specifications:
① Siro-spun polyester/wool 90/10 40^S
② compact-spun wool/nylon 70/30 40^S
③ compact siro-spinning Lyocell/wool 70/30 40^S

Reasons for recommendation: Recently, as indoor and outdoor sports items increased, consumers have additional requirements for sportswear's environmental adaptability, functionality, and comfortableness when being worn. Based on the existing cotton spinning equipment, using fine-denier wool fiber, and with the new techniques and technology that have independent intellectual property rights, Nantong Shuanghong Textile Co., ltd. has developed and produced various wool mono-fiber yarn and blended yarn, not only meeting the requirements for the skin-friendliness and wear-enduring quality of the yarn for use in the field of sports, but also featuring excellent rebound resilience, and moisture-absorbing, freely breathing, heat-storing, and warmth-retaining functions, as well as being green and environment-friendly

Scope of application: Clothing, Home textile
Representing enterprises: Nantong Shuanghong Textile Co., Ltd.
Brand: Shuanghong

赛络紧密纺莱赛尔腈纶混纺纱
COMPACT SIRO-SPUN LYOCELL ACRYLIC FIBER BLENDED YARN

● **关键词**：暖感、舒适、莱赛尔／腈纶

原料及规格：赛络紧密纺 莱赛尔／腈纶 70/30 40 英支

推荐理由：莱赛尔纤维有良好的吸湿透气，清爽舒适等特点，腈纶具有热弹性优异、蓬松性好、质地柔软、耐光性好、质轻、易洗快干等特点，将莱赛尔纤维与腈纶混纺，可实现纤维的性能互补，织成的面料具有暖感、柔软舒适的特点，满足休闲服、内衣、床上用品等对差别化的需求，是绿色、环保的差异化和功能性新型纤维纱线

适用范围：服装（休闲服、内衣）、家纺（床上用品等）

代表企业：福建新华源科技集团有限公司

产品获得认证／专利：经专家组鉴定达到国内领先水平

Key words: warm feel, comfortable, Lyocell/acrylic fiber

Raw materials and specifications:
Compact siro-spinning Lyocell/acrylic fiber70/30 40^S

Reasons for recommendation: Lyocell fiber is characterized by being able to absorb moisture, breathable, cool, and comfortable, while acrylic fiber is thermally elastic, fluffy, texturally soft, light-enduring, lightweight, easy to wash, and fast-drying. Lyocell fiber and acrylic fiber can functionally complement each other if they are blended together, and the blended fabric has a warm feel, being soft and comfortable, satisfying the differential requirements for casual wear, underwear, and bedding articles. This product is not only green, but also a new type of fiber yarn that is environment-friendly, differential, and functional

Scope of application: Clothing (casual wear, underwear), home textile (bedding articles etc.)

Representing enterprises: Fujian Xinhuayuan Scientific Group Co., Ltd.

Product certification/patent obtained: After evaluated by an expert panel, it has reached a level that is in the lead domestically

Excellent Quality

赛络紧密纺聚酯竹纤维混纺纱
COMPACT SIRO-SPUN PET BAMBOO FIBER BLENDED YARN

● 关键词：吸湿透气、抑菌

原料及规格： 赛络紧密纺 涤纶／竹纤维 50/50 50 英支

推荐理由： 竹纤维横截面布满大大小小椭圆形的孔隙，可以吸收并蒸发大量的水分，具有很好的吸放湿性能。在显微镜下观察，竹纤维制品上的细菌在 24h 后可被杀死 75% 以上，具有很好的抑菌功能；竹纤维的抗紫外线能力是棉的 41.7 倍，通过将竹纤维与涤纶混合后纺纱，使织物具备了竹纤维的优点的同时弥补了其脆弱、易破损的缺陷

适用范围： 服装

代表企业： 宜宾帛洋纺织科技有限公司

Key words: moisture-absorbing, breathable, antibacterial

Raw materials and specifications:
Compact siro-spinning polyester/bamboo fiber 50/50 50^S

Reasons for recommendation: Oval-shaped holes in various sizes are distributed throughout the cross-section of bamboo fiber, which can absorb and evaporate a great amount of water, having a good moisture-absorbing quality. When observed under a microscope, more than 75% of the bacteria in a bamboo fiber product can be eliminated within 24 hours, indicating that the product has a good bacteria-inhibiting quality. Bamboo fiber is 41.7 times the capability of cotton to resist UV light. By blending bamboo fiber with polyester, the fabric shares bamboo merits, but repairs the faults with it, which are weak, and easy to break

Scope of application: Clothing

Representing enterprises: Yibin Boyang Textile Scientific Co., Ltd.

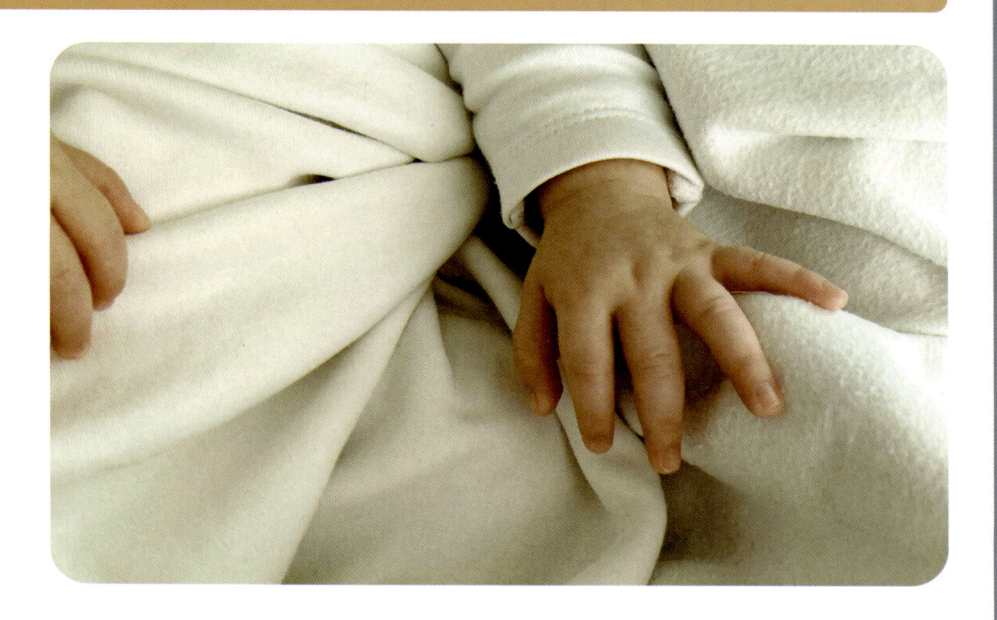

喷气涡流纺聚酯纤维纯纺纱
AIR-JET VORTEX SPUN PET FIBER MONO-FIBER YARN

● **关键词**：轻薄、柔软、抗起球、耐磨

原料及规格：喷气涡流纺 100% 涤纶 16~45 英支

推荐理由：喷气涡流纺纯涤纶纱线凭借其耐磨、高强度、弹性佳且不易变形的特性，以及织物易洗速干的优点，广泛应用于家纺、服装及工业用纱领域。该产品充分利用新疆本地涤纶短纤资源，实现产业链深度整合与就地加工，助力公司产品结构调整，提供高品质产品，满足市场需求，显著提升产品附加值

适用范围：服装、家纺

代表企业：新疆中泰金富特种纱业有限公司

品牌：金富

Key words: lightweight and thin, soft, anti-piling, wear-enduring

Raw materials and specifications:
Jet vortex spinning 100% polyester 16~45^S

Reasons for recommendation: it is able to endure wear, high in strength, elastic, and difficult to deform, with its fabric easy to wash, and fast to dry off, thus being widely used in the fields of home textile, apparel, and industrial yarn. By making better use of the local polyester staple resources in Xinjiang for this product, the industry chain integration and local processing are achieved, the company's product structure is adjusted, high-quality products are delivered, market demands are satisfied, and the product's added value has remarkably increased

Scope of application: Clothing, home textile

Representing enterprises: Xinjiang Zhongtai Jinfu Special Yarn Co., Ltd.

Brand: Jinfu

潮调
TRENDY TONE
Current of times, cutting quite a figure

关键词：个性化、多元、流行
Key words: Customized, Diverse, Popular

潮流涌动，尽显真我风采

在这个多元化与个性化的时代，纱线行业正经历着一场前所未有的变革。渐变、色纺等创新技术的应用，如同调色盘上的魔法，让纱线色彩与风格更加多元、独特，如同缤纷的笔触，勾勒出个性与时尚的画卷。这些创新技术不仅丰富了纱线的色彩和风格，更为消费者提供了更多个性化的选择，让每个人都能找到属于自己的那份独特与时尚。从艺术化定制到潮流单品，纱线以其独特的魅力和无限的可能性，成为消费者表达自我、追求创意生活的时尚符号，如同桥梁般连接着艺术与生活的彼岸。无论是追求时尚的年轻人，还是注重品质生活的消费者，都能在这里找到属于自己的那份独特与时尚，让纱线成为展现个性与风采的绚丽舞台。

In this diversification and personalization era, the yarn industry is undergoing an unprecedented revolution. Like a magic palette, the application of innovative technologies such as color-gradually-changed yarn and dye-spun yarn makes yarn's color and style more diversified and unique, as if a colorful pen is painting a personalized and fashionable picture. These innovative technologies not only enrich yarn's color and style, but also provide consumers with more personalized options, so that everyone can find their own uniqueness and fashionableness. From artistic customization to a single piece of fashionable clothing, with its unique charms and limitless potential, yarn becomes a fashionable symbol for consumers to express themselves and pursue an ingenuous life, and like a bridge to connect art with life. Whether young men in pursuit of fashion, or consumers paying attention to quality life, they both can find their own uniqueness and fashionableness here, because yarn has become a stage where personalities and fine qualities are displayed.

环锭纺渐变色纺纱系列
RING-SPUN COLOR-GRADUALLY-CHANGED YARN SERIES

● **关键词：渐变色**

原料及规格：
①环锭纺 再生涤纶/黏胶 70/30 32 英支
②环锭纺 黏胶/棉 60/40 32 英支
③环锭纺 100% 棉 32 英支
④环锭纺 黏胶/绢丝 92/8 32 英支

推荐理由： 渐变纱，作为一种全新的色纺风格，改变了传统染色、扎染、段染、吊染等烦琐工艺技术的限制，通过拼接同色系不同深浅度纱线来达成渐变效果的旧有方式。该渐变纱在织造过程即可创造渐变色彩，不仅简化了复杂的工艺流程，还显著降低了织造成本，同时摒弃了染色环节，有效减少了环境污染，极大地提升了产品的环保与节能特性。上海鸿骁实业有限公司率先研发出环锭纺渐变色纺纱系列，使单根纱线即可实现从一种颜色到另一种颜色的自然过渡，色彩渐变匀称自然，风格新颖独特。这一创新丰富了色纺纱线产品线，具有非常好的市场前景。

适用范围： 服装（无缝内衣、袜子）、家纺（毛巾）、机织纬纱、大圆机双面布
代表企业： 上海鸿骁实业有限公司
品牌： 鸿骁

Key words: color-gradually-changing
Raw materials and specifications:
① ring-spinning regenerated polyester/viscose 70/30 32^S
② ring-spinning viscose/cotton 60/40 32^S
③ ring-spinning 100%cotton 32^S
④ ring-spinning viscose/silk 92/8 32^S

Reasons for recommendation: As a new style of dye-spun yarn, color-gradually-changed yarn breaks through the constraints of the complicated technical processes such as traditional dyeing, tie-dyeing, space-dyeing, and dip-dyeing, in which yarns of different shades in the same color system are pieced together to achieve a color-gradually-changing effect. For this color-gradually-changed yarn, the color-gradually-changing effect can be created in the weaving process. Consequently, the complicated technical processes is streamlined to significantly reduce the cost of weaving, and the dyeing process is eliminated to effectively minimize environmental pollution, largely improving the product's environment-friendliness and energy-saving performance. Shanghai Hongxiao Industrial Co., Ltd. is the first to have developed the ring-spun color-gradually-changed yarn series, enabling a transition from one color to another in a single yarn, in a smooth and natural manner to exhibit a novel and unique style. This innovation has enriched the yarn product line, bringing a good market prospect

Scope of application: Clothing (seamless underwear, socks), home textile (towels), woven weft yarn, circular knitting machine double-knit fabric
Representing enterprises: Shanghai Hongxiao Industrial Co., Ltd.
Brand: Hongxiao

潮调 Trendy Tone

赛络紧密纺铜氨多组分混纺色纺纱
COMPACT SIRO-SPUN CUPRAMMONUIUM MULTI-COMPONENT BLENDED YARN

● **关键词**：舒适、天然、色泽、铜氨

原料及规格：赛络紧密纺 黏胶／腈纶／铜氨 50/30/20 40 英支

推荐理由：铜氨纤维是一种再生纤维素纤维，光泽适宜，上色性好，服用性能优良，吸湿性好，极具垂坠感，将铜氨纤维与再生纤维素纤维等混纺，织成的服装面料防尘防静电能力强，穿着舒适，能够形成自然的光泽，不易掉色，不霉变防虫蛀，可以降解、免烫、速干

适用范围：服装（保暖内衣、外装）、家纺、产业用

代表企业：沛县新丝路纺织有限公司

Key words: comfortable, natural, color and luster, copper ammonia

Raw materials and specifications:
Compact siro-spinning viscose/acrylic fiber/ cuprammonuium 50/30/20 40^S

Reasons for recommendation: Cuprammonuium fiber is a type of regenerated cellulose fiber, with suitable luster, easy coloration, excellent wearing properties, good moisture absorption, and a nice drapablity. The clothing fabric woven by blending cuproammonium fiber with regenerated cellulose fiber is dustproof, anti-static, comfortable to wear, naturally shiny, difficult to fade, resistant to mildew and moth damage, biodegradable, non-ironing, and fast drying

Scope of application: Clothing (warmth-retaining underwear, outerwear), home textile, industrial textiles

Representing enterprises: Peixian Xinsilu Textile Co., Ltd.

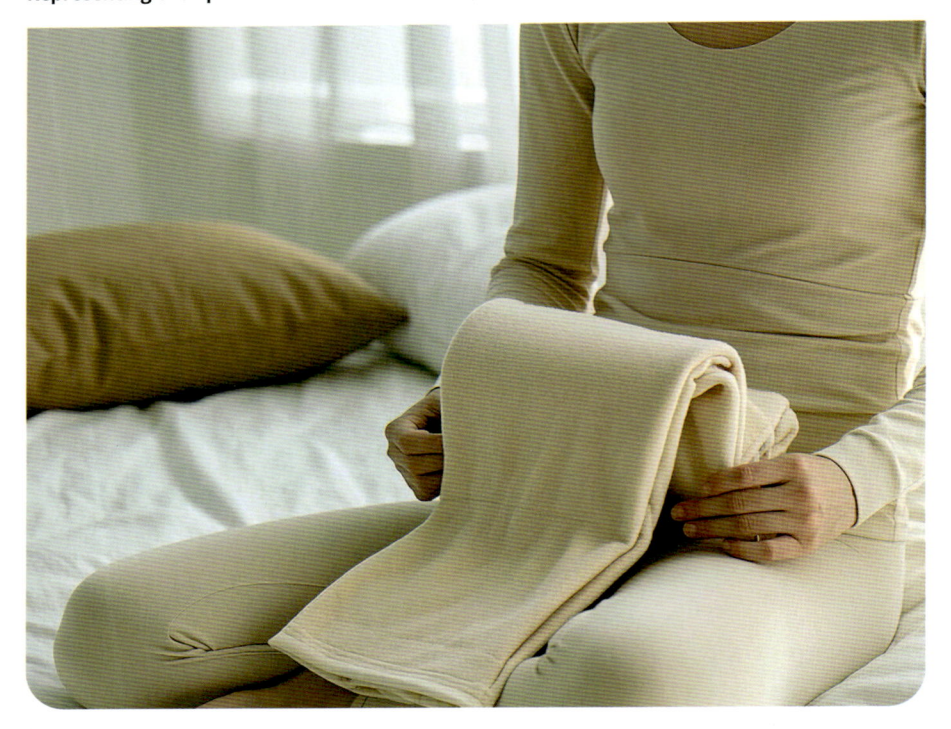

赛络纺莱赛尔亚麻混纺竹节纱
SIRO-SPUN LYOCELL FLAX BLENDED SLUB YARN

● **关键词**：绿色环保、吸湿排汗、抑菌、竹节

原料及规格：赛络纺 莱赛尔／亚麻 60/40 15 英支 竹节纱

推荐理由：该纱线兼具莱赛尔纤维吸湿透气、手感顺滑、亲肤舒适、易染色、耐磨、可纺性好的特点和亚麻纤维优异的吸湿排汗、抑菌、抗静电等优良特性，加上特殊设计的竹节工艺，呈现出天然的麻纤维风格。织成的面料既有穿着舒适性强、手感柔顺垂坠、绿色环保、透气性好等优点，又具有优异的吸湿排汗、耐热耐晒、防静电和独特的抑菌性能，可广泛用于休闲服装、童装、针织、家纺用品等领域

适用范围：服装、家纺、针织等

代表企业：河南平棉纺织集团股份有限公司

产品获得认证／专利：

①获得欧麻、再生农业、SRCCS、FSC 等全球绿色供应链可持续发展认证

②获得发明专利：《一种适纺亚麻赛络纱的细纱机牵伸机构》，ZL202210621807.1；《一种适纺亚麻赛络纱的细纱机断头自停装置》ZL2022 1 0621836.8

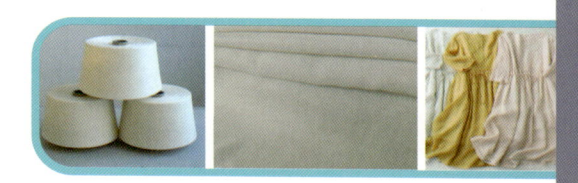

Key words: green environment-friendly, moisture-absorbing and breathable, antibacterial, slub
Raw materials and specifications:
Siro-spinning Lyocell/flax60/40 15^S slub yarn

Reasons for recommendation: This yarn combines the characteristics of Lyocell fiber, such as moisture absorption, breathability, smooth hand feel, skin-friendliness, ease of dyeing, wear resistance, and good spinnability, with the excellent properties of linen fiber, including superior moisture wicking, antibacterial properties, and antistatic capabilities. Coupled with a specially designed slub process, it presents a natural linen fiber style. The resulting fabric not only offers strong wearing comfort, a smooth and draping hand feel, environmental friendliness, and good breathability, but also possesses excellent moisture wicking, heat and sun resistance, antistatic and unique antibacterial properties. It can be widely used in high-end apparel areas such as casual wear, children's clothing, knitting, and home textile products

Scope of application: Clothing, home textile, textiles

Representing enterprises: Henan Pingmian Textile Group Co., Ltd.

Product certification/patent obtained:

① certified for sustainable development of global green supply chain by European Flax, Regenerative Agriculture, SRCCS, FSC etc.

② awarded the patent for innovation: "the spinning frame drafter for flax siro-spinning" ZL2022 1 0621807.1; "the spinning frame dropper automatic stopping mechanism for flax siro-spinning", ZL2022 1 0621836.8

纤·破界／无界

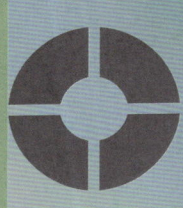

入选纤维应用趋势

ISSUE FIBER APPLICATION
TRENDS OF
FIBER·BEYOND THE LIMIT /
FIBER·WITHOUT LIMIT

China Fibers Fashion Trends
2025/2026

218 桐昆·中国纤维流行趋势报告 2025/2026 TONGKUN·CHINA FIBERS FASHION TRENDS REPORT 2025/2026

时尚趋势咨询机构 POP·趋势
程任姬

流行趋势研究与推广工作室
靳高岭　杨涛　王永生

Fashion Trend Consulting Agency POP·Trend
Cheng Renji

Fashion Trend Research and Promotion Studio
Jin Gaoling　Yang Tao　Wang Yongsheng

入选纤维应用趋势

时尚产业消费趋势关键词

温度 | 心态 | 体验

温度代替季节，随着气候变化与科技进步，时尚产业正经历从传统季节属性向温度适宜转变的趋势。**消费者越来越倾向于根据实时气温选择服装，而非遵循固定的季节更迭。**

心态通过影响情绪状态、认知过程和社会心理等多个方面，间接地塑造了消费者的购买决策和行为模式。**如何通过营销策略来激发正面的消费心态**，创造独特的购物体验，以赢得消费者的信任和支持，对于当下的企业至关重要。

体验式经济复兴，着重在实体零售业提供情感联系和沉浸式体验方面的独特价值，尽管这些体验较难量化，但它们对于吸引顾客至关重要。在竞争激烈的新细分和垂直市场中，企业须创造出**真实且富有吸引力的体验，才能脱颖而出。**

Keywords of fashion industry
consumption trends

KEYWORDS
Keywords of fashion industry consumption trends

TEMPERTURE | MINDSET | EXPERIENCE

Temperature replaces seasons with climate change and technological advancement, the fashion industry is experiencing a trend of shifting from traditional seasonal attributes to temperature sustainability. Consumers are increasingly inclined to choose clothing based on real-time temperature rather than following fixed seasonal changes.

Mindset indirectly shapes consumers' purchasing decisions and behavioral patterns by influencing multiple aspects such as emotional states, cognitive processes and psychosocial aspects. How to stimulate a positive consumer mindset and create a unique shopping experience through marketing strategies to win consumers' trust and support is crucial for businesses today.

The experiential economy resurgence focuses on the unique value of physical retail in providing emotional connections and immersive experiences, which, although difficult to quantify, are critical to attracting customers. In the fiercely competitive new segments and vertical markets, companies must create authentic and engaging experiences to stand out.

CONSUMPTION

入选纤维应用趋势

消费趋势材质偏好影响概述

环保可持续

随着社会对环境问题关注度的持续提升，当前全球消费者对消费品环保材料的认可度逐渐加强，在全球视野及政策导向的强力驱动下，采用环保材质正逐渐成为重要的行业风向标。

柔软舒适且耐用

在对抗年龄分层、强调时尚无界限的背景下，服装材质需兼顾各年龄段需求。柔软舒适的面料满足人们对穿着体验的基本追求，无论活力四射的青少年还是追求生活品质的长者均能从中受益。此外，耐用性同样重要，它不仅延长了衣物使用寿命，减少了因频繁更换导致的资源浪费，也与可持续发展的理念不谋而合。

科技赋能人体触感

纤维材料科技不断创新，通过多种形式对纤维材料进行改性处理：以共聚改性、共混改性、成型技术、表面构筑技术、纳米技术、智能技术等，一种或多种技术的融合，满足人体在**环境适应**（吸湿、导湿、防水透湿、暖感、凉感等）、**健康保健**（抑菌、消臭、抗紫外等）、**安全防护**（导电、阻燃、电磁防护等）、**运动休闲**（弹性、柔软、吸湿排汗等）、**便于养护**（机可洗、免烫、自清洁等）、**智能响应**（热舒适调控等）、**生物医学功能**等，实现多功能、多场景应用。

OVERVIEW OF THE IMPACT OF CONSUMER TRENDS ON MATERIAL PREFERENCES

Environmentally sustainable

With the increasing societal focus on environmental issues, global consumers are gradually placing greater emphasis on eco-friendly materials in consumer products. Driven by a global perspective and policy direction, the adoption of environmentally sustainable materials is becoming a significant industry trend.

Soft and comfortable

In the context of the fight against age stratification and the emphasis on fashion without boundaries, clothing materials need to cater to the needs of all age groups. Soft and comfortable fabrics meet the basic needs of the wearing experience, benefiting both energetic teenagers and senior citizens looking for quality of life. Durability is also important, as it not only extends the life of clothing and reduces the waste of resources caused by frequent replacement, but also fits in with the concept of sustainability.

Technology empowers physical sensation

Fiber material science and technology continues to innovate, through a variety of forms of fiber material modification treatment: copolymerization modification, blending modification, molding technology, surface construction technology, nanotechnology, intelligent technology, etc., the integration of one or more technologies. can satisfy the human body's needs in environmental adaptation (moisture absorption, moisture conductivity, waterproofing and permeability, warmth, coolness, etc.), health care (anti-bacteria, deodorization, UV-resistant, etc.), safety and protection (electrical conductivity, flame retardant, electromagnetic protection, etc.), sports and leisure (elasticity, softness, moisture absorption and perspiration, etc.), easy maintenance (machine washable, non-iron, self-cleaning, etc.), intelligent response (thermal comfort regulation, etc.), biomedical functions, etc., to achieve multi-functional, multi-scene applications.

入选纤维应用趋势

1 防透抗紫外循环再利用聚酯纤维

1.11dtex × 38mm 短纤

机织流行面料开发运用

APPLICATION OF ANTI-SEE-THROUGH & ANTI-ULTRAVIOLRT RECYCLED POLYESTER FIBER

1.11dtex × 38mm staple fiber
for the development of woven trend fabrics

时装领域 // Fashion clothes

纤维应用指导：

1. 织造运用： 选用该纤维与锦纶、氨纶混纺20~60英支纱线，结合机织三原组织结构开发棉型面料。建议成分占比超过30%。

2. 染整工艺： 涤、氨成分配比的平纹织物可以通过压花或者盐缩工艺开发泡泡纱外观的衬衫面料。

3. 面料特性： 面料手感柔滑细腻，防透抗皱。

4. 面料运用推荐：
女装——衬衫、连衣裙、西装套装；
男装——衬衫、裤装。

Fiber Application:

1. WEAVING TECHNIQUE: The fiber is selected to be blended with nylon and spandex in 20~60^S count yarns, and combined with woven Mihara tissue structure to develop cotton-type fabrics. The suggested composition is more than 30%.

2. DYEING AND FINISHING PROCESS: The polyester-ammonia ratio of plain fabrics can be embossed or salt-shrunk to develop bubble yarn-look shirting fabrics.

3. FABRIC PROPERTIES: The fabric has a smooth and delicate hand feel, and is impervious to light and wrinkles.

4. APPLICATION DIRECTION：
Women's clothing—shirts, dresses, suits;
Men's clothing—shirts, pants.

防透抗紫外循环再利用聚酯纤维

1.11dtex × 38mm 短纤

机织斜纹面料开发运用

APPLICATION OF ANTI-SEE-THROUGH & ANTI-ULTRAVIOLRT RECYCLED POLYESTER FIBER

1.11dtex × 38mm staple fiber
for the development of woven twill fabrics

制服领域 //Uniform

纤维运用指导：

1. 织造运用： 选用该纤维纯纺 20~60 英支纱线以斜纹结构或者变化斜纹结构开发克重在 90~200g/m² 机织面料。

2. 染整工艺： 常规染色染整理工艺，适当减缓水流速度。

3. 面料特性： 面料表面光洁、平整，手感柔滑，防透抗皱。

4. 面料运用推荐：
护士服、机长服。

Fiber Application：

1. WEAVING TECHNIQUE: The fiber is selected for the development of woven fabrics with a grammage of 90~200g/m² by spinning 20~60^S count yarns in twill or variegated twill structures.

2. FINISHING PROCESS: Conventional dyeing and finishing process to slow down the water flow appropriately.

3. FABRIC PROPERTIES: The surface of the fabric is smooth and even, with a silky hand feel, and is impervious to wrinkles.

4. APPLICATION DIRECTION：
Nurse's uniform, captain's uniform.

入选纤维应用趋势

防透抗紫外循环再利用聚酯纤维

84dtex/72f 长丝

机织防晒面料开发运用

APPLICATION OF ANTI-SEE-THROUGH & ANTI-ULTRAVIOLRT RECYCLED POLYESTER FIBER

84dtex/72f filament yarn
for the development of woven sun protection functional fabrics

户外运动领域 // Outdoors sports

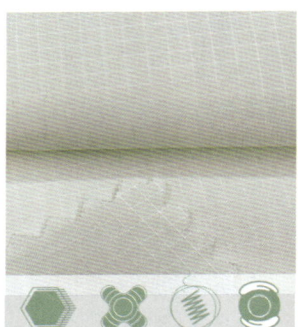

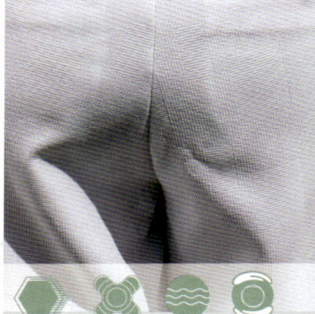

纤维应用指导：

1. 织造运用： 推荐 84dtex/72f 半消光长丝结合氨纶弹性纤维配合：（1）平纹开发轻薄高弹防护面料；（2）斜纹开发运动休闲面料；（3）几何提花结构开发时尚运动面料。

2. 染整工艺： 常规染整工艺。含氨纶面料注意控制染色温度，防止沾染氨纶组分降低面料色牢度。

3. 面料特性： 面料表面光洁、平整，手感柔滑细腻。

4. 面料运用推荐：
高尔夫运动裤装、休闲运动套装、防晒面罩。

Fiber Application:

1. WEAVING TECHNIQUE: Recommended 84dtex/72f semi-matte yarn combined with spandex elastic fiber with (1) plain weave to develop lightweight and high elasticity protective fabrics; (2) twill weave to develop sports and leisure fabrics; (3) geometric jacquard structure to develop fashionable sports fabrics.

2. DYEING FINISHING PROCESS: Conventional dyeing and finishing process. Pay attention to controlling the dyeing temperature for spandex-containing fabrics to prevent contamination with spandex components and reduce the color fastness of the fabric.

3. FABRIC PROPERTIES: The surface of the fabric is smooth and flat, and it feels soft and delicate.

4. APPLICATION DIRECTION :
Golf sports pants, casual sports suits, sunscreen masks.

防透抗紫外循环再利用聚酯纤维

84dtex/72f 长丝

针织圆机面料开发运用

APPLICATION OF ANTI-SEE-THROUGH & ANTI-ULTRAVIOLRT RECYCLED POLYESTER FIBER

84dtex/72f filament yarn
for the development of knitted sun protection functional fabrics

休闲运动领域 // Recreational sports

纤维运用指导：

1. 织造运用： 推荐 84dtex/72f 半消光长丝配合针织单罗纹结构、双罗纹结构开发坑条面料和棉毛布。

2. 染整工艺： 常规染整工艺。含氨纶面料注意控制染色温度，防止沾染氨纶组分降低面料色牢度。

3. 面料特性： 面料表面光洁、手感柔滑，弹性优良。

4. 面料运用推荐：
高尔夫裤装、POLO 衫、打底衫、防晒面罩。

Fiber Application:

1. WEAVING TECHNIQUE: It is recommended to use 84dtex/72f semi-dull yarn in combination with knitted rib structure and double rib structure to develop ribbed fabrics and interlock fabrics.

2. DYEING FINISHING PROCESS: Conventional dyeing and finishing process. Pay attention to controlling the dyeing temperature for spandex-containing fabrics to prevent contamination with spandex components and reduce the color fastness of the fabric.

3. FABRIC PROPERTIES: The fabric has a smooth surface, soft touch and excellent elasticity.

4. APPLICATION DIRECTION:
Golf pants, POLO shirts, base shirts, sunscreen masks.

2 遮热抗紫外聚酰胺6纤维

44dtex/34f 长丝

经编柔弹防晒面料开发运用

APPLICATION OF HEAT-SHIELDING &ANTI-ULTRAVIOLRT POLYAMIDE 6 FIBER
44dtex/34f filament yarn
for the development of warp knitted sun protection fabrics

运动休闲领域 // Sports & Leisure

纤维应用指导：

1. 织造运用： 推荐 44dtex/44f FDY 长丝搭配氨纶结合：（1）提花组织在拉舍尔经编机上织造镂空透孔面料；（2）经平以及变化组织开发弹力布。

2. 染整工艺： 常规染整工艺。

3. 面料特性： 面料表面光洁、细滑、四面弹力，保留原纱的抗紫外凉感性能。

4. 面料运用推荐： 运动训练服、瑜伽服、防晒衣。

Fiber Application:

1.WEAVING TECHNIQUE: It is recommended to use 44dtex/34f FDY yarn with spandex in combination with (1) jacquard weaves to weave open-texture fabrics on Raschel machines ; (2) warp plain and variable weaves to develop stretch fabrics.

2. F DYEING INISHING PROCESS: General dyeing and finishing process.

3. FABRIC PROPERTIES: The surface of the fabric is smooth, fine and elastic on all sides, retaining the cool UV-resistant sensory properties of the original yarn.

4. APPLICATION DIRECTION : Sports training clothes, yoga clothes, sun protection clothes.

遮热抗紫外
聚酰胺 6 纤维
22dtex/24f 长丝

机织锦氨面料开发运用

APPLICATION OF HEAT-SHIELDING &ANTI-ULTRAVIOLRT POLYAMIDE 6 FIBER
22dtex/24f filament yarn
for the development of woven fabrics

潮流运动领域 //Trend sports

纤维运用指导：

1. 织造运用： 推荐 22dtex/24f ACY 机包纱线结合机织平纹以及平纹变化组织织造高密织物。

2. 染整工艺： 常规染整工艺。

3. 面料特性： 微肌理结构设计，布面富有层次，手感柔滑细腻，质地紧实挺括。

4. 面料运用推荐：
休闲运动套装、防晒服。

Fiber Application:

1. WEAVING TECHNIQUE: 22dtex/24f ACY machine-wrapped yarns are recommended for weaving high density fabrics in combination with woven plain weave and plain weave variations.

2. F DYEING INISHING PROCESS: General dyeing and finishing process.

3. FABRIC PROPERTIES: Micro-muscle structure design, the fabric surface is rich in layers, smooth and delicate handfeel, and the texture is tight and firm.

4. APPLICATION DIRECTION :
Casual sports suits, sun protection clothing.

3. 防勾丝抗紫外聚酰胺6纤维

44dtex/34f 长丝

经编舒柔防晒面料开发运用

APPLICATION OF ANTI-SNAGGING&ANTI-ULTRAVIOLRT POLYAMIDE 6 FIBER

44dtex/34f filament yarn
for the development of warp knitted sun protection fabrics

时尚运动领域 //Fashion sports

纤维应用指导：

1. 织造运用： 推荐44dtex/34f 长丝搭配氨纶结合（1）经编缺垫组织开发提花织物；（2）经平组织与变化结构复合开发微肌理弹性面料。

2. 染整工艺： 常规染整工艺。

3. 面料特性： 面料手感柔糯细腻，具有防勾丝、耐磨的服用性能。

4. 面料运用推荐：
休闲运动套装、针织上衣、防晒服。

Fiber Application:

1.WEAVING TECHNIQUE: Recommended 44dtex/34f yarn with spandex combined with (1) warp knitting lack of padding organization to develop jacquard fabrics; (2) warp flat organization to develop stretch fabrics.

2. F DYEING INISHING PROCESS: General dyeing and finishing process.

3. FABRIC PROPERTIES: Fabrics feel soft and delicate, with anti-hooking, wear-resistant taking performance.

4. APPLICATION DIRECTION：
Casual sports suits, knitted tops, sun protection clothing.

防勾丝抗紫外聚酰胺 6 纤维

77dtex/48f 长纤

机织防晒耐磨面料开发运用

APPLICATION OF ANTI-SNAGGING&ANTI-ULTRAVIOLRT POLYAMIDE 6 FIBER

77dtex/48f filament yarn
for the development of woven sun protection functional fabrics

户外运动领域 // Outdoors sports

纤维运用指导：

1. **织造运用**：推荐 77dtex/48f 长丝结合三原变化组织开发微肌理机织织物。

2. **染整工艺**：防水透气膜贴膜整理，保持原有性能的基础上提升防水透气性能。

3. **面料特性**：面料表面呈现微肌理纹样，兼具耐磨、防紫外、防勾丝性能。

4. **面料运用推荐**：
冲锋衣、防晒夹克、滑雪服。

Fiber Application :

1. **WEAVING TECHNIQUE:** Recommended 77dtex/48f yarns combined with three original variations of organization for the development of micro-muscle textured woven fabrics.

2. **FINISHING PROCESS:** Waterproof and breathable membrane pasting finishing, increasing the waterproof and breathable performance while maintaining the original performance.

3. **FABRIC PROPERTIES:** The surface of the fabric has a micro-texture pattern and is wear-resistant, UV-resistant and anti-snagging.

4. **APPLICATION DIRECTION :**
Jackets, sun protection jackets, ski suits.

入选纤维应用趋势

4 高中空异形聚酯纤维
55.6dtex/12f 长丝

针织圆机保暖面料开发运用

APPLICATION OF HIGH HOLLOW DEFORMED POLYESTER FIBER
55.6dtex/12f filament yarn
for the development of knitted thermal functional fabrics

保暖内衣领域 // Thermal underwear

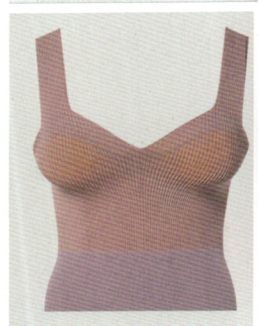

纤维应用指导：

1. 织造运用： 推荐 55.6dtex/12f 长丝与含有棉、毛成分的纱线交织结合：（1）双罗纹组织开发针织棉毛布；（2）衬垫组织开发起绒针织布；（3）单面提花组织开发提花棉毛布。

2. 染整工艺： 常规染整工艺，定形过程中减小压辊压力以防影响纤维以及织物的中空率。

3. 面料特性： 面料丰满柔软、轻盈、保暖性优异。

4. 面料运用推荐：
保暖套装、贴身内衣。

Fiber Application：

1. WEAVING TECHNIQUE: It is recommended to interweave 55.6dtex/12f yarn with yarn containing cotton and wool components: (1) double rib structure to develop interlock fabric; (2) cushioning structure to develop fleece knit fabric; (3) single-sided jacquard structure to develop jacquard interlock fabric.

2. FINISHING PROCESS: In general finishing process, reduce the roller pressure during the shaping process to prevent affecting the fiber and fabric hollow rate.

3. FABRIC PROPERTIES: The fabric is rich, soft, light and has excellent warmth retention.

4. APPLICATION DIRECTION:
Thermal suits, underwear.

高中空异形聚酯纤维

55.6dtex/12f 长丝

机织轻量化面料开发运用

APPLICATION OF HIGH HOLLOW DEFORMED POLYESTER FIBER
55.6dtex/12f filament yarn
for the development of woven lightweight fabrics

运动、休闲领域 // Sports & leisure

纤维运用指导：

1. 织造运用： 推荐经纬纱均使用55.6dtex/12f 长丝结合梭织小提花组织结构开发运动面料。

2. 染整工艺： 常规染整工艺，注意控制张力和压力以防影响面料的中空率。

3. 面料特性： 面料轻暖、干爽透湿。

4. 面料运用推荐： 休闲运动套装、商务夹克、滑雪服。

Fiber Application:

1. WEAVING TECHNIQUE: It is recommended to use 55.6dtex/12f yarn for both warp and weft yarns combined with woven small jacquard structure to develop sports fabrics.

2. FINISHING PROCESS: For general finishing process, pay attention to controlling the tension and pressure to avoid affecting the hollow rate of the fabric.

3. FABRIC PROPERTIES: Lightweight, warm, dry and breathable fabric.

4. APPLICATION DIRECTION: Leisure sports suit, jacket, ski suit.

入选纤维应用趋势

5 蓄热锁温抑菌聚酯纤维

1.33dtex × 38mm 短纤

针织圆机保暖面料开发运用

APPLICATION OF THERMAL-STORAGE & HEAT-RETAINING & ANTI-BACTERIA POLYESTER FIBER

1.33dtex × 38mm staple fiber
for the development of knitted thermal functional fabrics

保暖内衣领域 // Thermal underwear

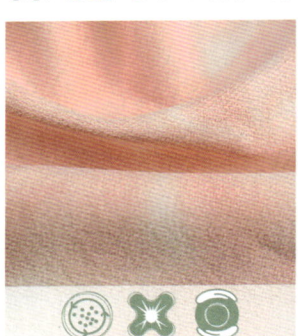

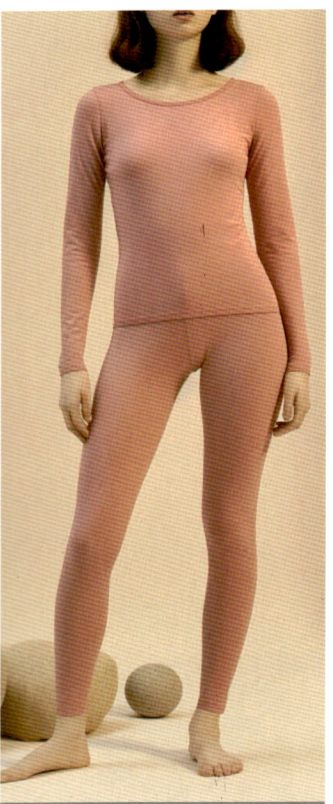

纤维应用指导：

1. 织造运用：推荐 1.33dtexX38mm 棉型短纤与棉、腈纶、氨纶混纺结合双罗纹结构开发棉毛布。建议该纤维配比超过 30%，以增加面料的保暖性能。

2. 染整工艺：常规染整工艺。

3. 面料特性：具备传统棉毛布柔糯丰满、弹性优异的性能，同时增加面料的保暖性能。

4. 面料运用推荐：
棉毛衫 / 裤等内衣产品。

Fiber Application:

1. WEAVING TECHNIQUE: It is recommend 1.33dtex×38mm cotton staple fiber and cotton, acrylic, spandex blended yarn combined with double rib knitting structure to develop cotton wool fabric. It is recommended that the ratio of this fiber is more than 30% to increase the warmth of the fabric.

2. FINISHING PROCESS: General finishing process.

3. FABRIC PROPERTIES: It has the performance of traditional cotton wool fabrics with softness, fullness and excellent elasticity; at the same time, it increases the warmth of the fabric.

4. APPLICATION DIRECTION :
Underwear products such as bottoms/pants.

蓄热锁温抑菌聚酯纤维

84dtex/72f 长丝

针织保暖功能面料开发运用

APPLICATION OF THERMAL-STORAGE & HEAT-RETAINING & ANTI-BACTERIA POLYESTER FIBER
84dtex/72f filament yarn
for the development of Knitted warm functional fabrics

运动基础领域 //Basic Sports

纤维运用指导：

1. 织造运用： 84dtex/72f 长丝可直接用于针织圆机的编织生产：（1）使用纱罗组织开发移圈针织面料；（2）以半畦编组织开发摇粒绒面料；（3）与棉纱等混纺纱结合单面毛圈组织或者双罗纹与集圈的复合组织开发休闲运动套装面料。

2. 染整工艺： 常规染整工艺。

3. 面料特性：（1）移圈针织面料表面具有凹凸立体的花纹纹样，手感柔滑细腻；（2）摇粒绒面料手感柔暖，绒面丰满；（3）运动套装面料紧实柔滑挺拔。

4. 面料运用推荐：
休闲运动套装、冲锋衣、打底层上衣。

Fiber Application：

1. WEAVING TECHNIQUE: 84dtex/72f yarn can be directly used for knitting production of circular knitting machines: (1) Use leno weave to develop transfer knitted fabrics; (2) Use half-rib knitted weave to develop polar fleece fabrics; (3) Use it with blended yarns such as cotton yarn to combine single-sided terry weave or double rib and tuck weave composite weave to develop casual suit fabrics.

2. FINISHING PROCESS: General finishing process.

3. FABRIC PROPERTIES: (1) The surface of the transfer knitted fabric has a concave and convex three-dimensional pattern, and feels smooth and delicate; (2) Soft and warm hand feeling, plush velvet surface; (3) The sports suit fabric is tight, smooth and crisp.

4. APPLICATION DIRECTION：
Leisure sports suit, jackets, baselayers.

蓄热锁温抑菌聚酯纤维
1.67dtex × 51mm 短纤

填充料开发运用
APPLICATION OF THERMAL-STORAGE & HEAT-RETAINING & ANTI-BACTERIA POLYESTER FIBER
1.67dtex × 51mm staple fiber
for filling flakes

保暖外套领域 //insulated jacket

纤维应用指导：

1. 产品优势： 羽绒棉状絮片、耐水洗不结团、轻盈保暖、防湿透气、抑菌、蓬松。

2. 应用场景： 雪域畅行、城市运动、都市休闲、活力学院、婴幼呵护。

3. 成品开发推荐：
运动服类——滑雪服、冲锋衣；
时装类——棉服、夹棉马甲；
童装类——校服、连体衣。

Fiber Application:

1. Product Advantages: Down cotton state flocculent, resistant to washing without clumping, lightweight and warm, moisture-proof and breathable, anti-bacterial, fluffy.

2. Application Scenario: Snow-covered travel, urban sports, city leisure, vitality academy, and infant care.

3. Product Development:
Sportswear—skiwear, punching jacket;
Fashion—Cotton clothes, cotton vests;
Children's clothing—school uniforms, jumpsuits.

蓄热锁温抑菌聚酯纤维

1.67dtex × 51mm 短纤

填充料开发运用

APPLICATION OF THERMAL-STORAGE & HEAT-RETAINING & ANTI-BACTERIA POLYESTER FIBER

1.67dtex × 51mm staple fiber for filling flakes

户外、家居领域 //Outdoors&Home

纤维运用指导：

1. 产品优势：羽绒棉状絮片、耐水洗不结团、轻盈保暖、防湿透气、抑菌、蓬松。

2. 应用场景：郊野户外、实用居家、萌趣婴童。

3. 成品开发推荐：

户外类——露营睡袋；

家居类——棉被、绗棉绣花被罩；

婴童类——包被、睡袋。

Fiber Application:

1. Product Advantages: Down cotton state flocculent, resistant to washing without clumping, lightweight and warm, moisture-proof and breathable, anti-bacterial, fluffy.

2. Application Scenario: Outdoor, Practical, Cute for Babies and Kids.

3. Product Development:

Outdoor category—Camping sleeping bags;

Home category—Quilts, Embroidered Quilt Covers;

Baby category—Swaddles, Sleeping Bags.

6 低温易染生物基呋喃聚酯纤维
56dtex/48f 长丝

机织提花面料开发运用

APPLICATION OF LOW TEMPERATURE EASY-TO-DYE BIO-BASED POLYESTER FIBER
55.5dtex/72f filament yarn
for the development of woven jacquard fabric

时尚休闲领域 // Fashion & Leisure

纤维应用指导：

1. 织造运用：（1）在大提花织机上经纬纱全部使用 56dtex/48f 长丝开发各类图案纹理的染色提花织物；（2）与棉纱或者棉型混纺纱交织开发色织纹理效果的提花织物。

2. 染整工艺： 常规染整工艺。

3. 面料特性：（1）面料兼具紧实挺括与柔滑悬垂的质地。因提花图案的不同展现出不同的纹理效果；（2）常压 100°C 条件下低温易染，纤维上染率高，布面颜色艳丽均匀。

4. 面料运用推荐：

女装——外套、裙装、衬衫、裤装；
男装——西装、冲锋衣、裤装。

Fiber Application：

1. WEAVING TECHNIQUE: (1) Using 56dtex/48f filament yarns for all warp and weft yarns on jacquard looms to develop dyed jacquard fabrics with various patterns and textures; (2) Interweaving with cotton yarn or cotton blended yarn to develop jacquard fabrics with yarn-dyed texture effects.

2. FINISHING PROCESS: General finishing process.

3. FABRIC PROPERTIES: (1) The fabric is both firm and drapey. The jacquard pattern gives a different textural effect. (2) normal pressure 100°C under the conditions of low-temperature dyeing, fiber dyeing rate is high, the color of the fabric is bright and uniform.

4. APPLICATION DIRECTION:

Womenswear—coats, dresses, blouses, pants;
Menswear—suits, jackets, pants.

低温易染生物基呋喃聚酯纤维

84dtex/72f 长丝

针织珠地面料开发运用

APPLICATION OF LOW TEMPERATURE EASY-TO-DYE BIO-BASED POLYESTER FIBER
84dtex/72f filament yarn
for the development of knitted pique fabric

运动时尚领域 // Sports & Fashion

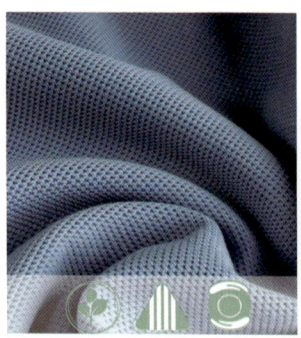

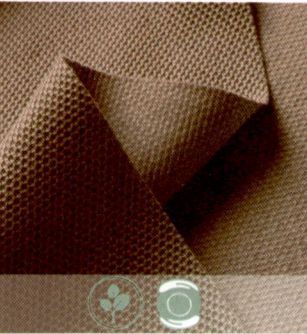

纤维应用指导：

1. 织造运用： 84dtex/72f 长丝（1）直接用于针织圆机织造结合单面集圈结构开发网眼镂空珠地面料；（2）与棉纱或者棉型混纺纱交织配合元宝针开发双面珠地面料。

2. 染整工艺： 常规染整工艺。

3. 面料特性：（1）面料表面光洁、有细微肌理变化，手感柔滑细腻，质地紧实挺括；（2）常压 100℃条件下低温易染，纤维上染率高，布面颜色艳丽均匀。

4. 面料运用推荐：
休闲运动套装、POLO 衫、T 恤。

Fiber Application:

1. WEAVING TECHNIQUE: 84dtex/72f filament (1) Directly used for circular knitting machine weaving combined with single-sided tuck structure to develop mesh hollow pique fabric (2) Interwoven with cotton yarn or cotton blended yarn to develop pique fabric with rib structure.

2. FINISHING PROCESS: General finishing process.

3. FABRIC PROPERTIES: (1) The surface of the fabric is smooth, with subtle texture changes, smooth and delicate handfeel, and tight and firm texture. (2) normal pressure 100℃ under the conditions of low-temperature dyeing, fiber dyeing rate is high, the color of the fabric is bright and uniform.

4. APPLICATION DIRECTION:
Leisure sports suits, POLO shirts, T-shirts.

低温易染生物基呋喃聚酯纤维
135dtex/72f 长丝

机织粗粝化纤面料开发运用

APPLICATION OF LOW TEMPERATURE EASY-TO-DYE BIO-BASED POLYESTER FIBER
135dtex/72f filament yarn
for the development of woven coarse chemical fiber fabrics

机能运动领域 // Pioneer Sports

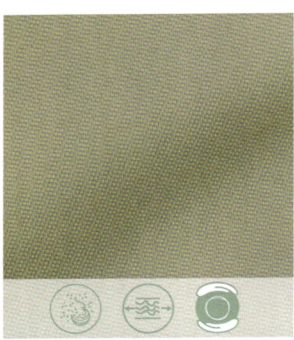

纤维运用指导：

1. 织造运用： 推荐135dtex/72f 长丝结合：(1) 机织变化平纹组织结构开发表面颗粒感织物；(2) 机织变化斜纹组织结构开发各种斜度的粗斜纹织物。

2. 染整工艺： 常规染整工艺。

3. 面料特性： (1) 面料表面具有粗粝的微肌理结构，手感滑爽有身骨；(2) 常压100℃条件下低温易染，纤维上染率高，布面颜色艳丽均匀。

4. 面料运用推荐： 休闲运动套装、冲锋衣、半裙、裤装。

Fiber Application:

1. WEAVING TECHNIQUE: Recommended 135dtex/72f filaments combined with: (1) woven variegated plain weave tissue structure to develop surface graininess fabrics; (2) woven variegated twill tissue structure to develop coarse twill fabrics with various slant.

2. FINISHING PROCESS: General finishing.

3. FABRIC PROPERTIES: (1) The surface of the fabric has a coarse micro-muscle texture structure and feels smooth with body and bones. (2) normal pressure 100℃ under the conditions of low-temperature dyeing, fiber dyeing rate is high, the color of the fabric is bright and uniform.

4. APPLICATION DIRECTION： Leisure sports suit, jackets, skirts, trousers.

7 二氧化碳基乙二醇聚酯纤维

148dtex/108f 长丝

机织棉感化纤面料开发运用

APPLICATION OF CARBON OXIDE-BASED GLYCOL POLYESTER FIBER
148dtex/108f filament yarn
for the development of woven cotton-type chemical fiber fabrics

户外运动领域 // Outdoors sports

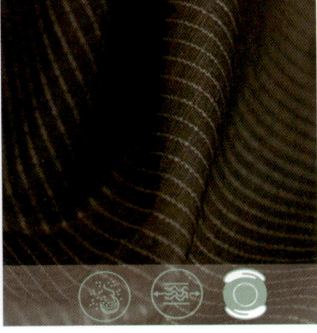

纤维运用指导：

1. **织造运用**：推荐 148dtex/72f 长丝与 30 旦氨纶空包结合机织三原组织结构开发纬弹或者四面弹户外运动化纤面料。

2. **染整工艺**：常规染整工艺。

3. **面料特性**：面料表面光洁、平整，棉型织物，质地紧实挺括。

4. **面料运用推荐**：
休闲运动套装、冲锋衣、滑雪服。

Fiber Application:

1. **WEAVING TECHNIQUE:** It is recommended to combine 148dtex/72f filament and 30D spandex covered yarn with woven three-original structure to develop weft-stretch or four-way-stretch outdoor sports chemical fiber fabrics.

2. **FINISHING PROCESS:** General finishing process.

3. **FABRIC PROPERTIES:** The surface of the fabric is glossy and flat, cotton type fabric with a firm and stiff texture.

4. **APPLICATION DIRECTION :**
Leisure sports suit, jacket, ski suit.

二氧化碳基乙二醇聚酯纤维

66dtex/72f 长丝

针织运动面料开发运用

APPLICATION OF CARBON OXIDE-BASED GLYCOL POLYESTER FIBER

66dtex/72f filament yarn
for the development of knitted sports fabrics

训练服领域 // Training suit

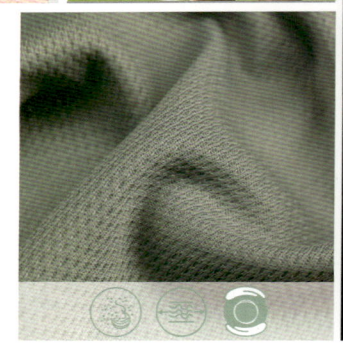

纤维应用指导：

1. 织造运用：推荐 66dtex/72f 消光长丝结合针织提花组织、纱罗组织或者菠萝组织开发针织提花面料。

2. 染整工艺：常规染整工艺。

3. 面料特性：面料表面光洁，因组织结构的差异有不同的纹理效果，柔弹棉型手感。

4. 面料运用推荐：
休闲运动套装、训练服。

Fiber Application：

1. WEAVING TECHNIQUE: 66dtex/72f matte yarn is recommended for the development of knitted jacquard fabrics in combination with knitted jacquard, leno or pineapple tissue.

2. FINISHING PROCESS: General finishing process.

3. FABRIC PROPERTIES: The surface of the fabric is smooth and has different texture effects due to the differences in the organization structure, and the soft elastic cotton type handfeel.

4. APPLICATION DIRECTION:
Leisure sports suits, training suits.

二氧化碳基乙二醇聚酯纤维

66dtex/72f 长丝

梭织时装面料开发运用

APPLICATION OF CARBON OXIDE-BASED GLYCOL POLYESTER FIBER

66dtex/72f filament yarn
or the development of woven fashion fabric

时尚成衣领域 // Ready-to-wear

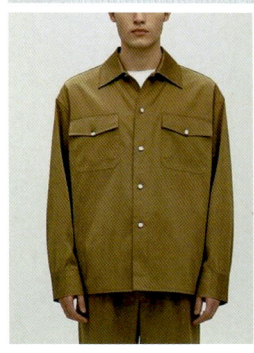

纤维运用指导：

1. 织造运用： 推荐 66dtex/72f 消光 DTY 长丝：(1) 直接用于机织基础组织以及三原变化组织丝绸型面料开发；(2) 结合机器空包工艺或者纬纱使用同种类型 SSY 型纱线开发机织纬弹面料。

2. 染整工艺： 常规染整工艺。

3. 面料特性：(1) 丝绸型面料表面光泽柔和，手感柔滑细腻，悬垂性优异；(2) 空包纱开发的面料表面肌理变化丰富，手感多样。

4. 面料运用推荐：

休闲时尚套装、衬衫式夹克、连衣裙。

Fiber Application :

1. WEAVING TECHNIQUE: It is recommended that 66dtex/72f matte DTY yarn: (1) be used directly in the development of woven basic structure and three-original variation structure silk fabrics; (2) be used in combination with machine empty bag process or weft yarn using the same type of SSY yarn to develop woven weft elastic fabrics.

2. FINISHING PROCESS: General finishing process.

3. FABRIC PROPERTIES: (1) Silk-type fabrics have soft surface luster, smooth and delicate handfeel, and excellent drape; (2) The surface texture of fabrics developed by air-covered yarns is rich in texture changes, and the handfeel is varied.

4. APPLICATION DIRECTION :
Leisure fashion suits, shirt jackets, dresses.

8 黑色循环再利用再生纤维素纤维
1.33dtex × 38mm 短纤

机织 TR 混纺面料开发运用

APPLICATION OF BLACK RECYCLED REGENERATED CELLULOSE FIBER
1.33dtex × 38mm staple fiber
for the development of woven TR blended fabrics

时尚成衣领域 // Ready-to-wear

纤维应用指导：

1. 织造运用：推荐使用配比成分超过 30% 的该纤维与棉、麻、涤纶等纤维混纺制备纱线，结合机织基础组织结构开发 TR 面料。

2. 染整工艺：常规染整工艺。

3. 面料特性：面料可以纯色也可以模拟精纺混纺花灰色系，抗皱易打理，表面具有棉麻天然肌理效果。

4. 面料运用推荐：
休闲时尚套装、西装套装、连衣裙、衬衫。

Fiber Application：

1. WEAVING TECHNIQUE: It is recommended to develop TR fabrics by blending the fiber with cotton, linen, polyester and other fibers to prepare yarns with the basic structure of woven fabrics with a proportionate composition of more than 30%.

2. FINISHING PROCESS: General finishing process.

3. FABRIC PROPERTIES: The fabric can be solid color or simulate a worsted blend floral gray system, wrinkle-resistant and easy to care, the surface has a natural texture effect of cotton and linen.

4. APPLICATION DIRECTION:
Casual fashion suits, suits, dresses, shirts.

黑色循环再利用再生纤维素纤维

1.67dtex × 38mm 短纤

经编混纺面料开发运用

APPLICATION OF BLACK RECYCLED REGENERATED CELLULOSE FIBER

1.67dtex × 8mm staple fiber
for the development of warp knit blended fabrics

休闲领域 // Leisure wear

纤维运用指导：

1. **织造运用**：推荐使用超过 30% 该成分的纤维与涤纶、尼龙混纺，结合经编经平斜组织开发双面异色或者双层面料。
2. **染整工艺**：常规染整工艺。
3. **面料特性**：面料正反面具有不同的服用性能，整体抗皱、透气、舒弹。
4. **面料运用推荐**：
休闲运动套装、冲锋衣、时装裤料。

Fiber Application :

1. **WEAVING TECHNIQUE:** It is recommended to use more than 30% of the fibers with polyester and nylon blends in combination with warp knitting and flat twill organization to develop double-sided heterochromatic or double-layer fabrics.
2. **FINISHING PROCESS:** General finishing process.
3. **FABRIC PROPERTIES:** The front and back of the fabric have different taking properties, overall anti-wrinkle, breathable and soothing elasticity.
4. **APPLICATION DIRECTION :**
Leisure sports suits, jackets, fashion pants.

9 rPET 基化学法再生氨纶

40D/3f 长丝

梭织涤弹面料开发运用

APPLICATION OF rPET-BASED CHEMICALLY REGENERATED ELASTANE
40D/3f filament
for the development of woven TR blended fabrics

商务通勤领域 // Business commuting

纤维应用指导：

1. 织造运用： 推荐使用40旦/3f长丝与再生涤纶、尼龙结合升级传统机织时装面料的环保属性。

2. 染整工艺： 常规染整工艺。

3. 面料特性：（1）具备传统氨纶的舒弹性能及该纤维赋予面料的高回弹性；（2）可在常压低温条件下使用分散染料染色且布面上染率均匀，颜色饱满。

4. 面料运用推荐：
西装套装、商务夹克、裤装。

Fiber Application：

1. WEAVING TECHNIQUE: It is recommended to use 40D/3f filament yarn combed with recycled polyester and nylon to upgrade the environmental properties of traditional woven fashion fabrics.

2. FINISHING PROCESS: General finishing process.

3. FABRIC PROPERTIES: (1) The comfortable elasticity of traditional spandex fiber and the high resilience that the fiber gives to the fabric. (2) It can be dyed with disperse dyes under normal pressure and low temperature and the dyeing rate on the fabric is even and the color is full.

4. APPLICATION DIRECTION:
Suits, business jackets, pants.

rPET 基化学法再生氨纶

40D/3f 长丝

针织涤弹面料开发运用

APPLICATION OF rPET-BASED CHEMICALLY REGENERATED ELASTANE
40D/3f filament
for the development of knitted polyester elastic fabrics

休闲运动领域 // Leisure sports

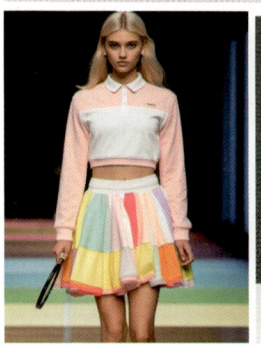

纤维运用指导：

1. 织造运用：（1）织造过程中可以使用半添纱或者全添纱组织开发弹力针织面料；（2）将该纤维与棉、涤纶、尼龙等混纺纱包覆开发针织弹力面料。

2. 染整工艺： 常规染整工艺。

3. 面料特性：（1）根据弹性纤维含量的多少以及组织结构的纹样设计表现不同的弹性效果和纹理面观。（2）可在常压低温条件下使用分散染料染色且布面上染率均匀，颜色饱满。

4. 面料运用推荐：

休闲运动套装、T恤、卫衣、打底衫。

Fiber Application:

1. WEAVING TECHNIQUE: (1) The weaving process can use half-added yarn or full-added yarn organization to develop elastic knitted fabrics; (2) The fiber will be blended with cotton, polyester, nylon and other blended yarns to develop knitted elastic fabrics.

2. FINISHING PROCESS: General finishing process.

3. FABRIC PROPERTIES: (1) Depending on the amount of elastic fiber content and the organizational structure of the pattern design to show different elastic effects and texture appearance. (2) It can be dyed with disperse dyes under normal pressure and low temperature and the dyeing rate on the fabric is even and the color is full.

4. APPLICATION DIRECTION:

Leisure sports suits, T-shirts, sweatshirts, baselayers.

rPET 基化学法再生氨纶

2D/1f 长丝

针织高弹产品开发运用

APPLICATION OF rPET-BASED CHEMICALLY REGENERATED ELASTANE
20D/1f filament for sock development

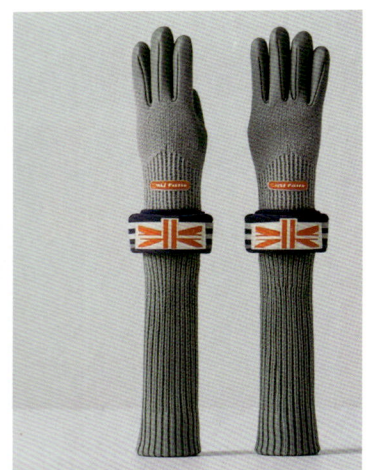

服饰领域 // Clothing accessories products

纤维运用指导：

1. 产品优势：（1）减少二氧化碳排放，有效降低能耗，弹性效果与传统氨纶一致。（2）可在常压低温条件下使用分散染料染色且上染率均匀，颜色饱满。

2. 成品开发推荐：
连体裤袜、丝袜、袜子、针织帽、装饰手套。

Fiber Application：

1. Product Advantages: (1) Reduced carbon dioxide emissions, effective reduction of energy consumption, elastic effect is consistent with traditional spandex. (2) It can be dyed with disperse dyes under normal pressure and low temperature and the dyeing rate on the fabric is even and the color is full.

2. Product Development:
Jumpsuits, stockings, socks, knit hats, decorative gloves.

入选、入围纤维表及下游应用推荐表

ISSUE AND RECOMMENDED FIBERS LIST AND DOWNSTREAM APPLICATION FORM

桐昆·中国纤维流行趋势 2025/2026
入选纤维

分类	纤维名称	企业	品牌
纤·境界			
舒感纤维	热湿舒适性调控聚酯纤维	中国石化仪征化纤有限责任公司	怡爽
舒感纤维	抑菌消臭高强低伸再生纤维素纤维	上海正家牛奶丝科技有限公司	淼卡
舒感纤维	阳离子/原液着色聚酯混纺	桐昆集团股份有限公司	桐昆
舒感纤维	超高异形仿兔毛聚酯纤维	苏州龙杰特种纤维股份有限公司	龙杰
舒感纤维	超细旦抗起球聚丙烯腈纤维	吉林奇峰化纤股份有限公司	华绒
柔弹纤维	生物基聚酰胺 PA5X 双组分复合弹性纤维	上海凯赛生物技术股份有限公司	泰纶
柔弹纤维	rPET/PTT 双中空复合弹性纤维	江苏三联新材料股份有限公司	坦佩罗
柔弹纤维	双组分复合聚酰胺纤维	黑龙江伊品新材料有限公司	伊纶
柔弹纤维	PTT 复合弹性纤维	上海华灏化学有限公司	柏黛尔
柔弹纤维	超低温易定形氨纶	华峰化学股份有限公司	千禧
柔弹纤维	超低温易定形氨纶	河北邦泰氨纶科技有限公司	安优卡
纤·破界			
抗紫外纤维	吸湿速干抗紫外聚酯纤维	杭州天科纺织有限公司	天科
抗紫外纤维	吸湿速干抗紫外聚酯纤维	三六一度（中国）有限公司	三六一度
抗紫外纤维	防透抗紫外循环再利用聚酯纤维	上海德福伦新材料科技有限公司	舒莱棉
抗紫外纤维	防透抗紫外循环再利用聚酯纤维	浙江佳人新材料有限公司	佳人
抗紫外纤维	遮热抗紫外聚酰胺 6 纤维	福建永荣锦江股份有限公司	锦康纱
抗紫外纤维	防勾丝抗紫外聚酰胺 6 纤维	义乌华鼎锦纶股份有限公司	华鼎锦纶
保暖纤维	高中空异形聚酯纤维	苏州春盛环保纤维有限公司	超中空
保暖纤维	蓄热锁温抑菌聚酯纤维	山东稀有科技发展有限公司	热湃
保暖纤维	蓄热锁温抑菌聚酯纤维	江苏康溢臣生命科技有限公司	白焰
保暖纤维	稀土改性蓄热聚酰胺 6 纤维	镧明材料技术（上海）有限公司	镧明
保暖纤维	保暖聚丙烯腈改性纤维	佛山市安芯纤维科技有限公司	安芯纤维
纤·跨界			
防护用阻燃纤维	阻燃抗熔滴聚酯纤维	浙江恒逸石化研究院有限公司	恒逸
防护用阻燃纤维	阻燃抗熔滴原液着色聚酰胺 6 纤维	广东恒申美达新材料股份有限公司	恒申新材
防护用阻燃纤维	阻燃抗熔滴原液着色聚酰胺 6 纤维	上海安凸塑料添加剂有限公司	安凸阻燃
产业用纤维	高模量循环再利用聚酯工业丝	浙江尤夫高新纤维股份有限公司	尤夫
产业用纤维	熔纺型中强超高分子量聚乙烯纤维	九州星际科技有限公司	九星纱
产业用纤维	原液着色高强型间位芳纶	泰和新材集团股份有限公司	泰美达
产业用纤维	HM50E 高强高模聚丙烯腈基碳纤维	江苏恒神股份有限公司	恒神股份
纤·无界			
绿色纤维	低温易染生物基呋喃聚酯纤维	浙江桐昆新材料研究院有限公司	桐昆
绿色纤维	二氧化碳基乙二醇聚酯纤维	江苏国望高科纤维有限公司	芮控
绿色纤维	黑色循环再利用再生纤维素纤维	唐山三友集团兴达化纤有限公司	唐丝
绿色纤维	rPET 基化学法再生氨纶	连云港杜钟新奥神氨纶有限公司	奥神
低温热黏合纤维	微细旦皮芯复合热黏合纤维	福建闽瑞新合纤股份有限公司	闽瑞股份
低温热黏合纤维	多组分复合改性聚乳酸纤维	苏州金泉新材料股份有限公司	绿纶

Tongkun · China Fibers Fashion Trends 2025/2026
ISSUE FIBERS

Category	Fiber Name	Company	Brand
Fiber · at the limit			
Comfortable Fiber	Heat-humidity Comfortable Regulating Polyester Fiber	SINOPEC Yizheng Chemical Fibre Co., Ltd.	YISUN
	Anti-bacteria and Deodorizing Regenerated Cellulose Fiber with High Strength and Low Elongation	Shanghai Zhengjia Milk Fiber Sci & Tech Co., Ltd.	MILD CARE
	Cationic Ion/Dope-dyed Polyester Blended Fiber	Tongkun Group Co., Ltd.	TONGKUN
	Ultra-high Deformed Faux Rabbit Fur Polyester Fiber	Suzhou Longjie Special Fiber Co., Ltd.	Loo Jee
	Ultra-fine Denier Anti-pilling Polyacrylonitrile Fiber	Jilin Qifeng Chemical Fiber Co., Ltd.	WALON
The Flexible and Elastic Fiber	Bio-based Polyamide PA5X Bicomponent Composite Elastic Fiber	Cathay Biotech Inc.	TERRYL
	rPET/PTT Double-hollow Composite Elastic Fiber	Jiangsu Sanlian New Material Co., Ltd.	TEMPERO
	Bicomponent Composite Polyamide Fiber	Heilongjiang Eppen New Materials Co., Ltd.	EYLON
	PTT Composite Elastic Fiber	HH Chemical Co., Ltd.	BIODEX
	Ultra-low Temperature Easy-to-set Elastane	Huafeng Chemical Co., Ltd.	QIANXI
		Hebei Bangtai Spandex Technology Co., Ltd.	ANYOUKA
Fiber · beyond the limit			
Anti-ultraviolet Fiber	Moisture-absorption and Quick-drying Anti-ultraviolet Polyester Fiber	Hangzhou Tianke Textile Co., Ltd.	TIANKE
		361° (CHINA) Co., Ltd.	361°
	Anti-see-through and Anti-ultraviolet Recycled Polyester Fiber	Shanghai Different Advanced Material Co., Ltd.	cellulook
		Zhejiang Jiaren New Materials Co., Ltd.	JIAREN
	Heat-shielding and Anti-ultraviolet Polyamide 6 Fiber	Fujian Eversun Jinjiang Co., Ltd.	JIN KANG SHA
	Anti-snagging and Anti-ultraviolet Polyamide 6 Fiber	Yiwu Huading Nylon Co., Ltd.	Huading
Thermal Fiber	High Hollow Deformed Polyester Fiber	Suzhou Chunsheng Environmental Protection Fiber Co., Ltd.	SUPPER HOLLOW
	Thermal-storage, Heat-retaining and Anti-bacteria Polyester Fiber	Shandong Rare Technology Development Co., Ltd.	AIREPAI
		Jiangsu KECens Life Science&Tenchnology Co., Ltd.	White-flame
	Rare Earth Modified Thermal-storage Polyamide 6 Fiber	RM Nano Material Technology (Shanghai) Co., Ltd.	RM
	Modified Thermal Polyacrylonitrile Fiber	Foshan Anxin Fiber Technology Co., Ltd.	ANSINGH
Fiber · outside the limit			
Flame-retardant Fiber for Protection	Flame-retardant and Anti-melt-drop Polyester Fiber	Zhejiang HENGYI Petrochemical Research Institute Co., Ltd.	HENGYI
	Flame-retardant and Anti-melt-drop Dope-dyed Polyamide 6 Fiber	Guangdong Highsun Meida New Materials Co., Ltd.	H-tech
		Shanghai ANTU Masterbatch Co., Ltd.	CESALON
Industrial Fiber	High-modulus Recycled Polyester Industrial Yarn	Zhejiang Unifull Industrial Fiber Co., Ltd.	UNIFULL
	Melt-spun Medium-strength Ultra-high Molecular Weight Polyethylene Fiber	Xingi Technology Co., Ltd.	JIUXINGSHA
	Dope-dyed High-strength Meta-Aramid	Tayho Advanced Materials Group Co., Ltd.	Tametar
	HM50E High-strength and High-modulus Polyacrylonitrile-based Carbon Fiber	Jiangsu Hengshen Co., Ltd.	HENGSHEN
Fiber · without limit			
Green Fiber	Low Temperature Easy-to-Dye Bio-based Furan Polyester Fiber	Tongkun Institute for Advanced Materials Co., Ltd.	TONGKUN
	Carbon Oxide-based Glycol Polyester Fiber	Jiangsu Guowang Hi-Tech Fiber Co., Ltd.	REOCOER
	Black Recycled Regenerated Cellulose Fiber	Tangshan Sanyou Group Xingda Chemical Fiber Co., Ltd.	TangCell
	rPET-based Chemically Regenerated Elastane	LDZ New Aoshen Spandex Co., Ltd.	AOSHEN
Low-temperature Heat-bondable Fiber	Micro-denier Leather Core Composite Heat-bondable Fiber	Fujian Mr Fiber Joint Co., Ltd.	MR
	Multi-component Composite Modified Polylactic Acid Fiber	Suzhou Kingcharm New Materials Co., Ltd.	PLON

桐昆·中国纤维流行趋势 2025/2026
入围纤维

分类	纤维名称	企业	品牌
生物基化学纤维	DT新溶剂法再生纤维素纤维	新乡化纤股份有限公司	瑞赛尔
	沙棘改性再生纤维素纤维	宜宾惠美纤维新材料股份有限公司	果维多
	可追溯低碳再生纤维素纤维	宜宾丝丽雅集团有限公司	宜可雅
	胶原蛋白改性竹莱赛尔纤维	上海里奥纤维企业发展有限公司	里奥
	导湿快干原液着色聚乳酸纤维	绍兴迈宝科技有限公司 现代纺织技术创新中心（鉴湖实验室）	玉绫丝
循环再利用化学纤维	海洋再生聚酯纤维	苏州佳海特种纤维有限公司	鑫鸣远
原液着色化学纤维	亮彩轻柔聚酯纤维	江苏桐昆恒阳化纤有限公司	桐昆
	原位聚合超黑聚酯纤维	纤丝纺环保材料科技（苏州）有限公司	纤丝纺
	原液着色仿麂皮海岛聚酯纤维	绍兴诚邦高新纤维科技有限公司	兴发
抗静电纤维	白色皮芯复合抗静电聚酯纤维	苏州凡虎导电纤维有限公司	凡虎
抑菌纤维	稀土改性抑菌聚酯纤维	中纺院（天津）科技发展有限公司	稀贝丝
	抑菌可降解再生纤维素纤维	太极石股份有限公司	兰丝尔
	姜多酚改性抑菌再生纤维素纤维	青岛邦特纤维有限公司	暖姜
	细旦多孔抑菌聚酯纤维	江苏桐昆恒欣新材料有限公司	桐昆
低熔点纤维	异形双组分低熔点聚酯纤维	凯泰特种纤维科技有限公司	DP110
抗紫外纤维	无锑遮热聚酯纤维	上海洁宜康化工科技有限公司	洁宜康
	抗紫外中空聚酰胺6纤维	烟台华润锦纶有限公司	雅达
舒感纤维	C形扁平聚酯纤维	桐昆集团浙江恒腾差别化纤维有限公司	桐昆
	异形抗起球聚酯纤维	江苏埄恒复合材料有限公司	柔软聚酯纤维
	亲水速干异形聚酯纤维	青岛新维纺织开发有限公司	麻丽
	仿醋酸聚酯纤维	江苏嘉通能源有限公司	桐昆
	桉树驱蚊防紫外聚酰胺6纤维	青岛尼希米生物科技有限公司	桉树驱蚊纤维
	抗起球干法聚丙烯腈纤维	中国石化齐鲁石化公司	中国石化
	调温抑菌再生纤维素纤维	杭州尚选科技有限公司	度可可
	大豆牛奶蛋白复合改性聚乙烯醇纤维	上海全宇生物科技遂平有限公司	天绒
石墨烯改性纤维	石墨烯原位聚合改性异形有色聚酯纤维	常州恒利宝纳米新材料科技有限公司	烯纳斯
	石墨烯改性循环再利用聚酯纤维	江苏海科纤维有限公司	海科云绒
	石墨烯改性聚丙烯腈纤维	绍兴泰鼎石墨烯科技有限公司	泰鼎
阻燃纤维	原位聚合阻燃有色聚酯纤维	诸暨市新丝维纤维有限公司	新丝维
	原液着色阻燃循环再利用聚酯纤维	杭州奔马化纤纺丝有限公司	奔马

Tongkun · China Fibers Fashion Trends 2025/2026
RECOMMENDED FIBERS

Category	Fiber Name	Company	Brand
Bio-Based Chemical Fiber	DT New Solvent Method-regenerated Cellulose Fiber	Xinxiang Chemical Fiber Co., Ltd.	ByluRecel
	Sea Buckthorn-modified Regenerated Cellulose Fiber	Yibin Hmei New Fiber Co., Ltd.	G.VITO
	Traceable Low-carbon Regenerated Cellulose Fiber	Yibin Grace Group Co., Ltd.	Ecosliya
	Collagen-modified Bamboo Lyocell Fiber	Shanghai Lyocell Fiber Development Co., Ltd.	LYO
	Moisture-conductive Fast-Drying Dope-dyed PLA Fiber	Marlboro Technologies (Shaoxing) Limited Zhejiang Modern Textile Technology Innovation Center (Jianhu Laboratory)	BMC
Recycled Chemical Fiber	Marine Regenerated Polyester Fiber	Suzhou Jiahai Special Fiber Co., Ltd.	XINMINGYUAN
Dope-dyed Chemical Fiber	Bright-colored Lightweight Soft Polyester Fiber	Jiangsu Tongkun Hengyang Chemical Fiber Co., Ltd.	TONGKUN
	In-situ-polymerized Ultra-Black Polyester Fiber	Suzhou Avant Environmental Sci-Tech Co., Ltd.	QSF
	Dope-dyed Imitation Suede Sea-Island Polyester Fiber	Shaoxing Chengbang High-Tech Fiber Technology Co., Ltd.	Xingfa
Anti-static Fiber	White Leather-core Composite Polyester Fiber	Suzhou Vistiger Fiber Co., Ltd.	Vistiger
Antibacterial Fiber	Rare Earth-modified Antibacterial Polyester Fiber	China Textile Academy (Tianjin) Technology Development Co., Ltd.	REbase
	Antibacterial Degradable Regenerated Cellulose Fiber	Tai Chi Stone Co., Ltd.	Iansir
	Gingerol-modified Antibacterial Regenerated Cellulose Fiber	Qingdao BetterTex Fiber Co., Ltd.	WarmGinger
	Fine-denier Porous Antibacterial Polyester Fiber	Jiangsu Tongkun Hengxin New Materials Co., Ltd.	TONGKUN
Low-melting Point Fiber	Profiled Double-component Low-melting Point Polyester Fiber	CTA High-tech Fibre Co., Ltd.	DP110
Anti-UV Fiber	Stibium-free Heat-isolating Polymerized Fiber	Shanghai Jiecon Chemicals Hi-tech Co., Ltd.	JIECON
	Anti-UV Hollow Polyamide 6 Fiber	China Resources Yantai Nylon Co., Ltd.	YADA
Pleasant-feel Fiber	C-Shaped Flat Polyester Fiber	Tongkun Group Zhejiang Hengteng Differential Fiber Co., Ltd.	TONGKUN
	Profiled Anti-piling Polyester Fiber	Jiangsu Xingheng Composite Material Co., Ltd.	Ternura
	Hydrophilic Fast-drying Profiled Polyester Fiber	Qing Dao XINWEI Textile Development Co., Ltd.	MALI
	Imitation of Cellulose Acetate Polyester Fiber	Jiangsu Jiatong Energy Co., Ltd.	TONGKUN
	Eucalypt Mosquito-dispelling Anti-UV Polyamide 6 Fiber	Qingdao Niximi Biotechnology Co., Ltd.	MosquitoSpell
	Anti-piling Polyacrylonitrile Fiber Prepared by Dry-Jet Wet Spinning Technique	SINOPEC Qilu Petrochemical Company	SINOPEC
	Temperature-regulating Antibacterial Regenerated Cellulose Fiber	Hangzhou Shangxuan Technology Co., Ltd.	Dukk
	Soybean and Milk Protein Composite PVA Fiber	Shanghai Quanyu Biotechnology Suiping Co., Ltd.	TIANRONG
Graphene Modified Fiber	Graphene In-situ Polymerized Modified Profiled Colored Polyester Fiber	Changzhou Highbery New Nano Materials Technology Co., Ltd.	PHENAX
	Graphene Modified Recycled Polyester Fiber	Jiangsu Oceantex Fiber Co., Ltd.	OCEANTEX
	Graphene Modified Polyacrylonitrile Fiber	Shaoxing Taiding Graphene Technology Co., Ltd.	TAIDING
Fire-resistant Fiber	In-situ Polymerized Fire-resistant Colored Polyester Fiber	Zhuji Xinsiwei Fiber Co., Ltd.	Sansiwell
	Dope-dyed Fire-resistant Recycled Polyester Fiber	Hangzhou Benma Chemfibre and Spinning Co., Ltd.	BENMARPET

桐昆·中国纤维流行趋势 2025/2026 下游应用推荐表

服装用纺织品

应用领域	推荐纤维品种	企业
休闲服	抑菌消臭高强低伸再生纤维素纤维	上海正家牛奶丝科技有限公司
	阳离子/原液着色聚酯混纤	桐昆集团股份有限公司
	生物基聚酰胺 PA5X 双组分复合弹性纤维	上海凯赛生物技术股份有限公司
	rPET/PTT 双中空复合弹性纤维	江苏三联新材料股份有限公司
	双组分复合聚酰胺纤维	黑龙江伊品新材料有限公司
	PTT 复合弹性纤维	上海华灏化学有限公司
	高中空异形聚酯纤维	苏州春盛环保纤维有限公司
	低温易染生物基呋喃聚酯纤维	浙江桐昆新材料研究院有限公司
	二氧化碳基乙二醇聚酯纤维	江苏国望高科纤维有限公司
	DT 新溶剂法再生纤维素纤维	新乡化纤股份有限公司
	可追溯低碳再生纤维素纤维	宜宾丝丽雅集团有限公司
	导湿快干原液着色聚乳酸纤维	绍兴迈宝科技有限公司
		现代纺织技术创新中心（鉴湖实验室）
	无锑遮热聚酯纤维	上海洁宜康化工科技有限公司
	异形抗起球聚酯纤维	江苏垶恒复合材料有限公司
	亲水速干异形聚酯纤维	青岛新维纺织开发有限公司
运动服	热湿舒适性调控聚酯纤维	中国石化仪征化纤有限责任公司
	抑菌消臭高强低伸再生纤维素纤维	上海正家牛奶丝科技有限公司
	阳离子/原液着色聚酯混纤	桐昆集团股份有限公司
	生物基聚酰胺 PA5X 双组分复合弹性纤维	上海凯赛生物技术股份有限公司
	rPET/PTT 双中空复合弹性纤维	江苏三联新材料股份有限公司
	双组分复合聚酰胺纤维	黑龙江伊品新材料有限公司
	PTT 复合弹性纤维	上海华灏化学有限公司
	超低温易定形氨纶	华峰化学股份有限公司
		河北邦泰氨纶科技有限公司
	吸湿速干抗紫外聚酯纤维	杭州天科纺织有限公司
		三六一度（中国）有限公司
	遮热抗紫外聚酰胺 6 纤维	福建永荣锦江股份有限公司
	防勾丝抗紫外聚酰胺 6 纤维	义乌华鼎锦纶股份有限公司
	高中空异形聚酯纤维	苏州春盛环保纤维有限公司
	低温易染生物基呋喃聚酯纤维	浙江桐昆新材料研究院有限公司
	二氧化碳基乙二醇聚酯纤维	江苏国望高科纤维有限公司
	rPET 基化学法再生氨纶	连云港杜钟新奥神氨纶有限公司
	导湿快干原液着色聚乳酸纤维	绍兴迈宝科技有限公司
		现代纺织技术创新中心（鉴湖实验室）
	亮彩轻柔聚酯纤维	江苏桐昆恒阳化纤有限公司
	石墨烯原位聚合改性异形有色聚酯纤维	常州恒利宝纳米新材料科技有限公司
	细旦多孔抑菌聚酯纤维	江苏桐昆恒欣新材料有限公司
	无锑遮热聚酯纤维	上海洁宜康化工科技有限公司
	抗紫外中空聚酰胺 6 纤维	烟台华润锦纶有限公司
	亲水速干异形聚酯纤维	青岛新维纺织开发有限公司

Tongkun · China Fibers Fashion Trends 2025/2026 Downstream Application Form
CLOTHING TEXTILES

Application Fields	Fiber Variety for Recommendation	Company
Leisure wear	Anti-bacterial and Deodorizing Regenerated Cellulose Fiber with High Strength and Low Elongation	Shanghai Zhengjia Milk Fiber Sci & Tech Co., Ltd.
	Cationic/Dope-dyed Polyester Blended Fiber	Tongkun Group Co., Ltd.
	Bio-based Polyamide PA5X Two-component Composite Elastic Fiber	Cathay Biotech Inc.
	rPET/PTT Bicomponent Hollow Composite Elastic Fiber	Jiangsu Sanlian New Material Co., Ltd.
	Two-component Composite Polyamide Fiber	Heilongjiang Eppen New Materials Co., Ltd.
	PTT Composite Elastic Fiber	HH Chemical Co., Ltd.
	Super Hollow Profiled Polyester Fiber	Suzhou Chunsheng Environmental Protection Fiber Co., Ltd.
	Low-Temperature Easy-to-dye Bio-based Furan Polyester Fiber	Tongkun Institute for Advanced Materials Co., Ltd.
	Carbon Dioxide-based Glycol Polyester Fiber	Jiangsu Guowang Hi-Tech Fiber Co., Ltd.
	DT New Solvent Method-regenerated Cellulose Fiber	Xinxiang Chemical Fiber Co., Ltd.
	Traceable Low-carbon Regenerated Cellulose Fiber	Yibin Grace Group Co., Ltd.
	Moisture-conductive Fast-drying Dope-dyed PlA Fiber	Marlboro Technologies (Shaoxing) Limited
		Zhejiang Modern Textile Technology Innovation Center (Jianhu Laboratory)
	Antimony-free Heat-shielding Polyester Fiber	Shanghai Jiecon Chemicals Hi-tech Co., Ltd.
	Profiled Anti-pilling Polyester Fiber	Jiangsu Xingheng Composite Material Co., Ltd.
	Hydrophilic Fast-drying Profiled Polyester Fiber	Qing Dao XINWEI Textile Development Co., Ltd.
Sportswear	Thermal and Moisture Comfort Control Polyester Fiber	SINOPEC Yizheng Chemical Fibre Co., Ltd.
	Anti-bacterial and Deodorizing Regenerated Cellulose Fiber with High Strength and Low Elongation	Shanghai Zhengjia Milk Fiber Sci & Tech Co., Ltd.
	Positive Ion/Dope-dyed Polyester Blended Fiber	Tongkun Group Co., Ltd.
	Bio-based Polyamide PA5X Two-component Composite Elastic Fiber	Cathay Biotech Inc.
	rPET/PTT Bicomponent Hollow Composite Elastic Fiber	Jiangsu Sanlian New Material Co., Ltd.
	Two-component Composite Polyamide Fiber	Heilongjiang Eppen New Materials Co., Ltd.
	PTT Composite Elastic Fiber	HH Chemical Co., Ltd.
	Ultra-low Temperature Easy-shaping Elastane	Huafon Chemical Co., Ltd.
		Hebei Bangtai Spandex Technology Co., Ltd.
	Moisture-absorption and Quick-drying Anti-ultraviolet Polyester Fiber	Hangzhou Tianke Textile Co., Ltd.
		361° (CHINA) Co., Ltd.
	Heat-shielding and Anti-ultraviolet Polyamide 6 Fiber	Fujian Eversun Jinjiang Co., Ltd.
	Anti-snagging and Anti-ultraviolet Polyamide 6 Fiber	Yiwu Huading Nylon Co., Ltd.
	Super Hollow Profiled Polyester Fiber	Suzhou Chunsheng Environmental Protection Fiber Co., Ltd.
	Low Temperature Easy-to-dye Bio-based Furan Polyester Fiber	Tongkun Institute for Advanced Materials Co., Ltd.
	Carbon Oxide-based Glycol Polyester Fiber	Jiangsu Guowang Hi-Tech Fiber Co., Ltd.
	rPET-based Chemically Regenerated Elastane	LDZ New Aoshen Spandex Co., Ltd.
	Moisture-conductive Fast-drying Dope-dyed PLA Fiber	Marlboro Technologies (Shaoxing) Limited
		Zhejiang Modern Textile Technology Innovation Center (Jianhu Laboratory)
	Bright-colored Lightweight Soft Polyester Fiber	Jiangsu Tongkun Hengyang Chemical Fiber Co., Ltd.
	Graphene In-situ Polymerized Modified Profiled Colored Polyester Fiber	Changzhou Highbery New Nano Materials Technology Co., Ltd.
	Fine-denier Porous Antibacterial Polyester Fiber	Jiangsu Tongkun Hengxin New Materials Co., Ltd.
	Stibium-free Heat-isolating Polymerized Fiber	Shanghai Jiecon Chemicals Hi-tech Co., Ltd.
	Anti-UV Hollow Polyamide 6 Fiber	China Resources Yantai Nylon Co., Ltd.
	Hydrophilic Fast-drying Profiled Polyester Fiber	Qing Dao XINWEI Textile Development Co., Ltd.

桐昆·中国纤维流行趋势 2025/2026 下游应用推荐表

服装用纺织品

应用领域	推荐纤维品种	企业
家居服	超细旦抗起球聚丙烯腈纤维	吉林奇峰化纤股份有限公司
	保暖聚丙烯腈改性纤维	佛山市安芯纤维科技有限公司
	可追溯低碳再生纤维素纤维	宜宾丝丽雅集团有限公司
	沙棘改性再生纤维素纤维	宜宾惠美纤维新材料股份有限公司
	稀土改性抑菌聚酯纤维	中纺院（天津）科技发展有限公司
	胶原蛋白改性竹莱赛尔纤维	上海里奥纤维企业发展有限公司
	抑菌可降解再生纤维素纤维	太极石股份有限公司
	异形抗起球聚酯纤维	江苏垶恒复合材料有限公司
	大豆牛奶蛋白复合改性聚乙烯醇纤维	上海全宇生物科技遂平有限公司
童装	黑色循环再利用再生纤维素纤维	唐山三友集团兴达化纤有限公司
	超细旦抗起球聚丙烯腈纤维	吉林奇峰化纤股份有限公司
	桉树驱蚊防紫外聚酰胺 6 纤维	青岛尼希米生物科技有限公司
	可追溯低碳再生纤维素纤维	宜宾丝丽雅集团有限公司
	姜多酚改性抑菌再生纤维素纤维	青岛邦特纤维有限公司
西装	亮彩轻柔聚酯纤维	江苏桐昆恒阳化纤有限公司
	石墨烯改性聚丙烯腈纤维	绍兴泰鼎石墨烯科技有限公司
牛仔	黑色循环再利用再生纤维素纤维	唐山三友集团兴达化纤有限公司
	rPET 基化学法再生氨纶	连云港杜钟新奥神氨纶有限公司
	抑菌可降解再生纤维素纤维	太极石股份有限公司
	异形抗起球聚酯纤维	江苏垶恒复合材料有限公司
工装	阻燃抗熔滴聚酯纤维	浙江恒逸石化研究院有限公司
	阻燃抗熔滴原液着色聚酰胺 6 纤维	广东恒申美达新材料股份有限公司
		上海安凸塑料添加剂有限公司
	原液着色高强型间位芳纶	泰和新材集团股份有限公司
	原位聚合阻燃有色聚酯纤维	诸暨市新丝维纤维有限公司
	导湿快干原液着色聚乳酸纤维	绍兴迈宝科技有限公司
		现代纺织技术创新中心（鉴湖实验室）
	白色皮芯复合抗静电聚酯纤维	苏州凡虎导电纤维有限公司
	稀土改性抑菌聚酯纤维	中纺院（天津）科技发展有限公司
	无锑遮热聚酯纤维	上海洁宜康化工科技有限公司
贴身内衣	蓄热锁温抑菌聚酯纤维	山东稀有科技发展有限公司
		江苏康溢臣生命科技有限公司
	姜多酚改性抑菌再生纤维素纤维	青岛邦特纤维有限公司
	抗起球干法聚丙烯腈纤维	中国石化集团齐鲁石化
	调温抑菌再生纤维素纤维	杭州尚选科技有限公司
	热湿舒适性调控聚酯纤维	中国石化仪征化纤有限责任公司
	超细旦抗起球聚丙烯腈纤维	吉林奇峰化纤股份有限公司
	双组分复合聚酰胺纤维	黑龙江伊品新材料有限公司
	高中空异形聚酯纤维	苏州春盛环保纤维有限公司
	保暖聚丙烯腈改性纤维	佛山市安芯纤维科技有限公司
	沙棘改性再生纤维素纤维	宜宾惠美纤维新材料股份有限公司

Tongkun · China Fibers Fashion Trends 2025/2026 Downstream Application Form
CLOTHING TEXTILES

Application Fields	Fiber Variety for Recommendation	Company
Home wear	Ultra-Fine Denier Anti-pilling Polyacrylonitrile Fiber	Jilin Qifeng Chemical Fiber Co., Ltd.
	Thermal Polyacrylonitrile Modified Fiber	Foshan Anxin Fiber Technology Co., Ltd.
	Traceable Low-carbon Regenerated Cellulose Fiber	Yibin Grace Group Co., Ltd.
	Sea Buckthorn-modified Regenerated Cellulose Fiber	Yibin Hmei New Fiber Co., Ltd.
	Rare Earth-modified Antibacterial Polyester Fiber	China Textile Academy (Tianjin) Technology Development Co., Ltd.
	Collagen-modified Bamboo Lyocell Fiber	Shanghai Lyocell Fiber Development Co., Ltd.
	Degradable Antibacterial Regenerated Cellulose Fiber	Tai Chi Stone Co., Ltd.
	Profiled Anti-pilling Polyester Fiber	Jiangsu Xingheng Composite Material Co., Ltd.
	Soybean and Milk Protein Composite Modified Poval Fiber	Shanghai Quanyu Biotechnology Ping Co., Ltd.
Kids	Black Recycled Regenerated Cellulose Fiber	Tangshan Sanyou Group Xingda Chemical Fibre Co., Ltd.
	Ultra-fine Denier Anti-pilling Polyacrylonitrile Fiber	Jilin Qifeng Chemical Fiber Co., Ltd.
	Eucalypt Mosquito-dispelling Anti-UV Polyamide 6 Fiber	Qingdao Niximi Biotechnology Co., Ltd.
	Traceable Low-carbon Regenerated Cellulose Fiber	Yibin Grace Group Co., Ltd.
	Gingerol-modified Antibacterial Regenerated Cellulose Fiber	Qingdao BetterTex Fiber Co., Ltd.
Suit	Bright-colored Lightweight Soft Polyester Fiber	Jiangsu Tongkun Hengyang Chemical Fiber Co., Ltd.
	Graphene Modified Polyacrylonitrile Fiber	Shaoxing Taiding Graphene Technology Co., Ltd.
Jeans	Black Recycled Regenerated Cellulose Fiber	Tangshan Sanyou Group Xingda Chemical Fibre Co., Ltd.
	rpet-based Chemically Regenerated Elastane	LDZ New Aoshen Spandex Co., Ltd.
	Degradable Antibacterial Regenerated Cellulose Fiber	Tai Chi Stone Co., Ltd.
	Profiled Anti-piling Polyester Fiber	Jiangsu Xingheng Composite Material Co., Ltd.
Overalls	Flame-retardant and Anti-melt-drop Polyester Fiber	Zhejiang HENGYI Petrochemical Research Institute Co., Ltd.
	Flame-retardant and Anti-melt-drop Dope-dyed Polyamide 6 Fiber	Guangdong Highsun Meida New Materials Co., Ltd.
		Shanghai ANTU Masterbatch Co., Ltd.
	Dope-dyed High-strength Meta-aramid	Tayho Advanced Materials Group Co., Ltd.
	In-situ Polymerized Fire-resistant Colored Polyester Fiber	Zhuji Xinsiwei Fiber Co., Ltd.
	Moisture-conductive Fast-drying Dope-dyed PLA Fiber	Marlboro Technologies (Shaoxing) Limited
		Zhejiang Modern Textile Technology Innovation Center (Jianhu Laboratory)
	White Sheath-core Composite Polyester Fiber	Suzhou Vistiger fiber Co., Ltd.
	Rare Earth-modified Antibacterial Polyester Fiber	China Textile Academy (Tianjin) Technology Development Co., Ltd.
	Stibium-free Heat-Isolating Polymerized Fiber	Shanghai Jiecon Chemicals Hi-tech Co., Ltd.
Lingerie	Thermal-storage, Heat-retaining and Anti-bacterial Polyester Fiber	Shandong Rare Technology Development Co., Ltd.
		Jiangsu KECens Life Science&Tenchnology Co., Ltd.
	Gingerol-modified Antibacterial Regenerated Cellulose Fiber	Qingdao BetterTex Fiber Co., Ltd.
	Anti-piling Dry Method-enabled Polyacrylonitrile Fiber	Sinopec Qilu Petrochemical Company
	Temperature-regulating Antibacterial Regenerated Cellulose Fiber	Hangzhou Shangxuan Technology Co., Ltd.
	Thermal and Wet Comfort Control Polyester Fiber	SINOPEC Yizheng Chemical Fibre Co., Ltd.
	Ultra-Fine Denier Anti-pilling Polyacrylonitrile Fiber	Jilin Qifeng Chemical Fiber Co., Ltd.
	Two-component Composite Polyamide Fiber	Heilongjiang Eppen New Materials Co., Ltd.
	Super Hollow Profiled Polyester Fiber	Suzhou Chunsheng Environmental Protection Fiber Co., Ltd.
	Thermal Polyacrylonitrile Modified Fiber	Foshan Anxin Fiber Technology Co., Ltd.
	Sea Buckthorn-modified Regenerated Cellulose Fiber	Yibin Hmei New Fiber Co., Ltd.

桐昆·中国纤维流行趋势 2025/2026 下游应用推荐表

服装用纺织品

应用领域	推荐纤维品种	企业
贴身内衣	可追溯低碳再生纤维素纤维	宜宾丝丽雅集团有限公司
	胶原蛋白改性竹莱赛尔纤维	上海里奥纤维企业发展有限公司
	稀土改性抑菌聚酯纤维	中纺院（天津）科技发展有限公司
	细旦多孔抑菌聚酯纤维	江苏桐昆恒欣新材料有限公司
	抑菌可降解再生纤维素纤维	太极石股份有限公司
	C 形扁平聚酯纤维	桐昆集团浙江恒腾差别化纤维有限公司
	抑菌消臭高强低伸再生纤维素纤维	上海正家牛奶丝科技有限公司
	超低温易定形氨纶	华峰化学股份有限公司
		河北邦泰氨纶科技有限公司
	大豆牛奶蛋白复合改性聚乙烯醇纤维	上海全宇生物科技遂平有限公司
衬衣	防透抗紫外循环再利用聚酯纤维	上海德福伦新材料科技有限公司
		浙江佳人新材料有限公司
	低温易染生物基呋喃聚酯纤维	浙江桐昆新材料研究院有限公司
	二氧化碳基乙二醇聚酯纤维	江苏国望高科纤维有限公司
	导湿快干原液着色聚乳酸纤维	绍兴迈宝科技有限公司
		现代纺织技术创新中心（鉴湖实验室）
	海洋再生聚酯纤维	苏州佳海特种纤维有限公司
	姜多酚改性抑菌再生纤维素纤维	青岛邦特纤维有限公司
	C 形扁平聚酯纤维	桐昆集团浙江恒腾差别化纤维有限公司
	异形抗起球聚酯纤维	江苏垶恒复合材料有限公司
	亲水速干异形聚酯纤维	青岛新维纺织开发有限公司
	仿醋酸聚酯纤维	江苏嘉通能源有限公司
	大豆牛奶蛋白复合改性聚乙烯醇纤维	上海全宇生物科技遂平有限公司
毛衣	黑色循环再利用再生纤维素纤维	唐山三友集团兴达化纤有限公司
	异形抗起球聚酯纤维	江苏垶恒复合材料有限公司
	石墨烯改性聚丙烯腈纤维	绍兴泰鼎石墨烯科技有限公司
羽绒服	生物基聚酰胺 PA5X 双组分复合弹性纤维	上海凯赛生物技术股份有限公司
	rPET/PTT 双中空复合弹性纤维	江苏三联新材料股份有限公司
	稀土改性蓄热聚酰胺 6 纤维	镧明材料技术（上海）有限公司
防晒服	遮热抗紫外聚酰胺 6 纤维	福建永荣锦江股份有限公司
	抗紫外中空聚酰胺 6 纤维	烟台华润锦纶有限公司
	防勾丝抗紫外聚酰胺 6 纤维	义乌华鼎锦纶股份有限公司
	无锑遮热聚酯纤维	上海洁宜康化工科技有限公司
瑜伽服	超低温易定形氨纶	华峰化学股份有限公司
		河北邦泰氨纶科技有限公司
	遮热抗紫外聚酰胺 6 纤维	福建永荣锦江股份有限公司
	rPET 基化学法再生氨纶	连云港杜钟新奥神氨纶有限公司
	抗紫外中空聚酰胺 6 纤维	烟台华润锦纶有限公司
泳衣	超低温易定形氨纶	华峰化学股份有限公司
		河北邦泰氨纶科技有限公司

Tongkun · China Fibers Fashion Trends 2025/2026 Downstream Application Form
CLOTHING TEXTILES

Application Fields	Fiber Variety for Recommendation	Company
Lingerie	Traceable Low-carbon Regenerated Cellulose Fiber	Yibin Grace Group Co., Ltd.
	Collagen-modified Bamboo Lyocell Fiber	Shanghai Lyocell Fiber Development Co., Ltd.
	Rare Earth-modified Antibacterial Polyester Fiber	China Textile Academy (Tianjin) Technology Development Co., Ltd.
	Fine-denier Porous Antibacterial Polyester Fiber	Jiangsu Tongkun Hengxin New Materials Co., Ltd.
	Degradable Antibacterial Regenerated Cellulose Fiber	Tai Chi Stone Co., Ltd.
	C-shaped Flat Polyester Fiber	Tongkun Group Zhejiang Hengteng Differential Fiber Co., Ltd.
	Anti-Bacterial and Deodorizing Regenerated Cellulose Fiber With High Strength and Low Elongation	Shanghai Zhengjia Milk Fiber Sci & Tech Co., Ltd.
	Ultra-low Temperature Easy-to-set Spandex	Huafon Chemical Co., Ltd.
		Hebei Bangtai Spandex Technology Co., Ltd.
	Soybean and Milk Protein Composite Modified Poval Fiber	Shanghai Quanyu Biotechnology Ping Co., Ltd.
Shirt	Anti-see-through and Anti-Ultraviolet Recycled Polyester Fiber	Shanghai Different Advanced Material Co., Ltd.
		Zhejiang Jiaren New Materials Co., Ltd.
	Low Temperature Easy-to-dye Bio-based Furan Polyester Fiber	Tongkun Institute for Advanced Materials Co., Ltd.
	Carbon Oxide-based Glycol Polyester Fiber	Jiangsu Guowang Hi-Tech Fiber Co., Ltd.
	Moisture-conductive Fast-drying Dope-dyed PLA Fiber	Marlboro Technologies (Shaoxing) Limited
		Zhejiang Modern Textile Technology Innovation Center (Jianhu Laboratory)
	Marine Regenerated Polyester Fiber	Suzhou Jiahai Special Fiber Co., Ltd.
	Gingerol-modified Antibacterial Regenerated Cellulose Fiber	Qingdao BetterTex Fiber Co., Ltd.
	C-Shaped Flat Polyester Fiber	Tongkun Group Zhejiang Hengteng Differential Fiber Co. Ltd.
	Profiled Anti-piling Polyester Fiber	Jiangsu Xingheng Composite Material Co., Ltd.
	Hydrophilic Fast-drying Profiled Polyester Fiber	Qing Dao XINWEI Textile Development Co., Ltd.
	Imitation Acetate Polyester Fiber	Jiangsu Jiatong Energy Co., Ltd.
	Soybean and Milk Protein Composite Modified Poval Fiber	Shanghai Quanyu Biotechnology Ping Co., Ltd.
Sweater	Black Recycled Regenerated Cellulose Fiber	Tangshan Sanyou Group Xingda Chemical Fibre Co., Ltd.
	Profiled Anti-piling Polyester Fiber	Jiangsu Xingheng Composite Material Co., Ltd.
	Graphene Modified Polyacrylonitrile Fiber	Shaoxing Taiding Graphene Technology Co., Ltd.
Down jacket	Bio-Based Polyamide Pa5x Two-component Composite Elastic Fiber	Cathay Biotech Inc.
	rpet/Ptt Bicomponent Hollow Composite Elastic Fiber	Jiangsu Sanlian New Material Co., Ltd.
	Rare Earth-modified Thermal-storage Polyamide 6 Fiber	RM Nano Material Technology (Shanghai) Co., Ltd.
Sun-proof clothing	Heat-Shielding and Anti-ultraviolet Polyamide 6 Fiber	Fujian Eversun Jinjiang Co., Ltd.
	Anti-UV Hollow Polyamide 6 Fiber	China Resources Yantai Nylon Co., Ltd.
	Anti-snagging and Anti-ultraviolet Polyamide 6 Fiber	Yiwu Huading Nylon Co., Ltd.
	Stibium-free Heat-isolating Polymerized Fiber	Shanghai Jiecon Chemicals Hi-tech Co., Ltd.
Yoga clothes	Ultra-low Temperature Easy-to-set Elastane	Huafon Chemical Co., Ltd.
		Hebei Bangtai Spandex Technology Co., Ltd.
	Heat-shielding and Anti-ultraviolet Polyamide 6 Fiber	Fujian Eversun Jinjiang Co., Ltd.
	Rpet-based Chemically Regenerated Elastane	LDZ New Aoshen Spandex Co., Ltd.
	Anti-UV Hollow Polyamide 6 Fiber	China Resources Yantai Nylon Co., Ltd.
Swimsuit	Ultra-low Temperature Easy-to-set Spandex	Huafon Chemical Co., Ltd.
		Hebei Bangtai Spandex Technology Co., Ltd.

桐昆·中国纤维流行趋势 2025/2026 下游应用推荐表

服装用纺织品

应用领域	推荐纤维品种	企业
泳衣	防透抗紫外循环再利用聚酯纤维	浙江佳人新材料有限公司
	rPET 基化学法再生氨纶	连云港杜钟新奥神氨纶有限公司
登山服	超细旦抗起球聚丙烯腈纤维	吉林奇峰化纤股份有限公司
	防勾丝抗紫外聚酰胺 6 纤维	义乌华鼎锦纶股份有限公司
	rPET/PTT 双中空复合弹性纤维	江苏三联新材料股份有限公司
	保暖聚丙烯腈改性纤维	佛山市安芯纤维科技有限公司
	石墨烯原位聚合改性异形有色聚酯纤维	常州恒利宝纳米新材料科技有限公司
	蓄热锁温抑菌聚酯纤维	山东稀有科技发展有限公司
		江苏康溢臣生命科技有限公司
	二氧化碳基乙二醇聚酯纤维	江苏国望高科纤维有限公司
	调温抑菌再生纤维素纤维	杭州尚选科技有限公司
舞台服/礼服	仿醋酸聚酯纤维	江苏嘉通能源有限公司
	细旦多孔抑菌聚酯纤维	江苏桐昆恒欣新材料有限公司
	超高异形仿兔毛聚酯纤维	苏州龙杰特种纤维股份有限公司
	亮彩轻柔聚酯纤维	江苏桐昆恒阳化纤有限公司
	黑色循环再利用再生纤维素纤维	唐山三友集团兴达化纤有限公司
T 恤	吸湿速干抗紫外聚酯纤维	杭州天科纺织有限公司
		三六一度（中国）有限公司
	海洋再生聚酯纤维	苏州佳海特种纤维有限公司
	姜多酚改性抑菌再生纤维素纤维	青岛邦特纤维有限公司
	抗紫外中空聚酰胺 6 纤维	烟台华润锦纶有限公司
裤装	防透抗紫外循环再利用聚酯纤维	上海德福伦新材料科技有限公司
		浙江佳人新材料有限公司
	稀土改性蓄热聚酰胺 6 纤维	镧明材料技术（上海）有限公司
护士服	防透抗紫外循环再利用聚酯纤维	上海德福伦新材料科技有限公司
		浙江佳人新材料有限公司
帽子	超高异形仿兔毛聚酯纤维	苏州龙杰特种纤维股份有限公司
	原液着色仿麂皮海岛聚酯纤维	绍兴诚邦高新纤维科技有限公司
袜子	抑菌消臭高强低伸再生纤维素纤维	上海正家牛奶丝科技有限公司
	超低温易定形氨纶	华峰化学股份有限公司
		河北邦泰氨纶科技有限公司
	保暖聚丙烯腈改性纤维	佛山市安芯纤维科技有限公司
	rPET 基化学法再生氨纶	连云港杜钟新奥神氨纶有限公司
	稀土改性抑菌聚酯纤维	中纺院（天津）科技发展有限公司
	调温抑菌再生纤维素纤维	杭州尚选科技有限公司
鞋材	超高异形仿兔毛聚酯纤维	苏州龙杰特种纤维股份有限公司
	rPET/PTT 双中空复合弹性纤维	江苏三联新材料股份有限公司
	蓄热锁温抑菌聚酯纤维	山东稀有科技发展有限公司
		江苏康溢臣生命科技有限公司
	原液着色仿麂皮海岛聚酯纤维	绍兴诚邦高新纤维科技有限公司

Tongkun · China Fibers Fashion Trends 2025/2026 Downstream Application Form
CLOTHING TEXTILES

Application Fields	Fiber Variety for Recommendation	Company
Swimsuit	Anti-see-through and Anti-ultraviolet Recycled Polyester Fiber	Zhejiang Jiaren New Materials Co., Ltd.
	rPET-based Chemically Regenerated Elastane	LDZ New Aoshen Spandex Co., Ltd.
Climbing clothes	Ultra-fine Denier Anti-pilling Polyacrylonitrile Fiber	Jilin Qifeng Chemical Fiber Co., Ltd.
	Anti-snagging and Anti-ultraviolet Polyamide 6 Fiber	Yiwu Huading Nylon Co., Ltd.
	rPET/PTT Bicomponent Hollow Composite Elastic Fiber	Jiangsu Sanlian New Material Co., Ltd.
	Thermal Polyacrylonitrile Modified Fiber	Foshan Anxin Fiber Technology Co., Ltd.
	Graphene In-situ Polymerized Modified Profiled Colored Polyester Fiber	Changzhou Highbery New Nano Materials Technology Co., Ltd.
	Thermal-storage, Heat-retaining and Anti-bacterial Polyester Fiber	Shandong Rare Technology Development Co., Ltd.
		Jiangsu KECens Life Science&Tenchnology Co., Ltd
	Carbon Oxide-based Glycol Polyester Fiber	Jiangsu Guowang Hi-Tech Fiber Co., Ltd.
	Temperature-regulating Antibacterial Regenerated Cellulose Fiber	Hangzhou Shangxuan Technology Co., Ltd.
Dramatic gowns/party frocks	Imitation Acetate Polyester Fiber	Jiangsu Jiatong Energy Co., Ltd.
	Fine-denier Porous Antibacterial Polyester Fiber	Jiangsu Tongkun Hengxin New Materials Co., Ltd.
	Ultra-high Deformed Faux Rabbit Fur Polyester Fiber	Suzhou Longjie Special Fiber Co., Ltd.
	Bright-colored Lightweight Soft Polyester Fiber	Jiangsu Tongkun Hengyang Chemical Fiber Co., Ltd.
	Black Recycled Regenerated Cellulose Fiber	Tangshan Sanyou Group Xingda Chemical Fibre Co., Ltd.
T-shirt	Moisture-absorption and Quick-drying Anti-ultraviolet Polyester Fiber	Hangzhou Tianke Textile Co., Ltd.
		361° (CHINA) Co., Ltd.
	Marine Regenerated Polyester Fiber	Suzhou Jiahai Special Fiber Co., Ltd.
	Gingerol-modified Antibacterial Regenerated Cellulose Fiber	Qingdao BetterTex Fiber Co., Ltd.
	Anti-UV Hollow Polyamide 6 Fiber	China Resources Yantai Nylon Co., Ltd.
Pants	Anti-see-through and Anti-ultraviolet Recycled Polyester Fiber	Shanghai Different Advanced Material Co., Ltd.
		Zhejiang Jiaren New Materials Co., Ltd.
	Rare Earth Modified Thermal-storage Polyamide 6 Fiber	RM Nano Material Technology (Shanghai) Co., Ltd.
Nurse clothes	Anti-see-through and Anti-ultraviolet Recycled Polyester Fiber	Shanghai Different Advanced Material Co., Ltd.
		Zhejiang Jiaren New Materials Co., Ltd.
Cap	Ultra-high Deformed Sunday Angora Yarn Polyester Fiber	Suzhou Longjie Special Fiber Co., Ltd.
	Dope-dyed Imitation Suede Sea-island Polyester Fiber	Shaoxing Chengbang High-Tech Fiber Technology Co., Ltd.
Socks	Anti-bacteria and Deodorizing Regenerated Cellulose Fiber with High Strength and Low Elongation	Shanghai Zhengjia Milk Fiber Sci & Tech Co., Ltd.
	Ultra-low Temperature Easy-to-set Elastane	Huafon Chemical Co., Ltd.
		Hebei Bangtai Spandex Technology Co., Ltd.
	Thermal Polyacrylonitrile Modified Fiber	Foshan Anxin Fiber Technology Co., Ltd.
	rPET-based Chemically Regenerated Elastane	LDZ New Aoshen Spandex Co., Ltd.
	Rare Earth-modified Antibacterial Polyester Fiber	China Textile Academy (Tianjin) Technology Development Co., Ltd.
	Temperature-regulating Antibacterial Regenerated Cellulose Fiber	Hangzhou Shangxuan Technology Co., Ltd.
Shoe materials	Ultra-high Deformed Sunday Angora Yarn Polyester Fiber	Suzhou Longjie Special Fiber Co., Ltd.
	rPET/PTT Bicomponent Hollow Composite Elastic Fiber	Jiangsu Sanlian New Material Co., Ltd.
	Thermal-storage, Heat-retaining and Anti-bacterial Polyester Fiber	Shandong Rare Technology Development Co., Ltd.
		Jiangsu KECens Life Science&Tenchnology Co., Ltd.
	Dope-dyed Imitation Suede sea-island Polyester Fiber	Shaoxing Chengbang High-Tech Fiber Technology Co., Ltd.

桐昆·中国纤维流行趋势 2025/2026
下游应用推荐表

家用纺织品

应用领域	推荐纤维品种	企业
床品	超高异形仿兔毛聚酯纤维	苏州龙杰特种纤维股份有限公司
	超细旦抗起球聚丙烯腈纤维	吉林奇峰化纤股份有限公司
	PTT 复合弹性纤维	上海华灏化学有限公司
	DT 新溶剂法再生纤维素纤维	新乡化纤股份有限公司
	可追溯低碳再生纤维素纤维	宜宾丝丽雅集团有限公司
	胶原蛋白改性竹莱赛尔纤维	上海里奥纤维企业发展有限公司
	高中空异形聚酯纤维	苏州春盛环保纤维有限公司
	稀土改性抑菌聚酯纤维	中纺院（天津）科技发展有限公司
	抑菌可降解再生纤维素纤维	太极石股份有限公司
	调温抑菌再生纤维素纤维	杭州尚选科技有限公司
	石墨烯原位聚合改性异形有色聚酯纤维	常州恒利宝纳米新材料科技有限公司
窗帘	阳离子/原液着色聚酯混纤	桐昆集团股份有限公司
	防透抗紫外循环再利用聚酯纤维	上海德福伦新材料科技有限公司
		浙江佳人新材料有限公司
	阻燃抗熔滴聚酯纤维	浙江恒逸石化研究院有限公司
	阻燃抗熔滴原液着色聚酰胺 6 纤维	广东恒申美达新材料股份公司
		上海安凸塑料添加剂有限公司
	原液着色高强型间位芳纶	泰和新材集团股份有限公司
	亮彩轻柔聚酯纤维	江苏桐昆恒阳化纤有限公司
	原位聚合阻燃有色聚酯纤维	诸暨市新丝维纤维有限公司
地毯	超高异形仿兔毛聚酯纤维	苏州龙杰特种纤维股份有限公司
	阻燃抗熔滴原液着色聚酰胺 6 纤维	广东恒申美达新材料股份公司
		上海安凸塑料添加剂有限公司
	C 形扁平聚酯纤维	桐昆集团浙江恒腾差别化纤维有限公司
	原位聚合阻燃有色聚酯纤维	诸暨市新丝维纤维有限公司
	原液着色阻燃循环再利用聚酯纤维	杭州奔马化纤纺丝有限公司
沙发布	rPET/PTT 双中空复合弹性纤维	江苏三联新材料股份有限公司
	阻燃抗熔滴聚酯纤维	浙江恒逸石化研究院有限公司
	阻燃抗熔滴原液着色聚酰胺 6 纤维	广东恒申美达新材料股份公司
		上海安凸塑料添加剂有限公司
	原液着色仿麂皮海岛聚酯纤维	绍兴诚邦高新纤维科技有限公司
	稀土改性抑菌聚酯纤维	中纺院（天津）科技发展有限公司
填充物	超细旦抗起球聚丙烯腈纤维	吉林奇峰化纤股份有限公司
	蓄热锁温抑菌聚酯纤维	山东稀有科技发展有限公司
		江苏康溢臣生命科技有限公司
	保暖聚丙烯腈改性纤维	佛山市安芯纤维科技有限公司
	大豆牛奶蛋白复合改性聚乙烯醇纤维	上海全宇生物科技遂平有限公司
	石墨烯改性循环再利用聚酯纤维	江苏海科纤维有限公司
玩具	超高异形仿兔毛聚酯纤维	苏州龙杰特种纤维股份有限公司
	海洋再生聚酯纤维	苏州佳海特种纤维有限公司
墙纸	原位聚合阻燃有色聚酯纤维	诸暨市新丝维纤维有限公司
装饰物	亮彩轻柔聚酯纤维	江苏桐昆恒阳化纤有限公司
	原液着色阻燃循环再利用聚酯纤维	杭州奔马化纤纺丝有限公司
凉席	调温抑菌再生纤维素纤维	杭州尚选科技有限公司

Tongkun · China Fibers Fashion Trends 2025/2026 Downstream Application Form
HOME TEXTILES

Application Fields	Fiber Variety for recommendation	Company
Bedding	Ultra-high Deformed Sunday Angora Yarn Polyester Fiber	Suzhou Longjie Special Fiber Co., Ltd.
	Ultra-fine Denier Anti-pilling Polyacrylonitrile Fiber	Jilin Qifeng Chemical Fiber Co., Ltd.
	PTT Composite Elastic Fiber	HH Chemical Co., Ltd.
	DT New Solvent Method-regenerated Cellulose Fiber	Xinxiang Chemical Fiber Co., Ltd.
	Traceable Low-carbon Regenerated Cellulose Fiber	Yibin Grace Group Co., Ltd.
	Collagen-modified Bamboo Lyocell Fiber	Shanghai Lyocell Fibre Development Co., Ltd.
	Super Hollow Profiled Polyester Fiber	Suzhou Chunsheng Environmental Protection Fiber Co., Ltd.
	Rare Earth-modified Antibacterial Polyester Fiber	China Textile Academy (Tianjin) Technology Development Co., Ltd.
	Degradable Antibacterial Regenerated Cellulose Fiber	Tai Chi Stone Co., Ltd.
	Temperature-regulating Antibacterial Regenerated Cellulose Fiber	Hangzhou Shangxuan Technology Co., Ltd.
	Graphene In-situ Polymerized Modified Profiled Colored Polyester Fiber	Changzhou Highbery New Nano Materials Technology Co., Ltd.
Curtain	Positive Ion/Dope-dyed Polyester Blended Fiber	Tongkun Group Co., Ltd.
	Anti-see-through and Anti-ultraviolet Recycled Polyester Fiber	Shanghai Different Advanced Material Co., Ltd.
		Zhejiang Jiaren New Materials Co., Ltd.
	Flame-retardant and Anti-melt-drop Polyester Fiber	Zhejiang HENGYI Petrochemical Research Institute Co., Ltd.
	Flame-retardant and Anti-melt-drop Dope-dyed Polyamide 6 Fiber	Guangdong Highsun Meida New Materials Co., Ltd.
		Shanghai ANTU Masterbatch Co., Ltd.
	Dope-dyed High-strength Meta-aramid	Tayho Advanced Materials Group Co., Ltd.
	Bright-colored Lightweight Soft Polyester Fiber	Jiangsu Tongkun Hengyang Chemical Fiber Co., Ltd.
	In-situ Polymerized Fire-resistant Colored Polyester Fiber	Zhuji Xinsiwei Fiber Co., Ltd.
Carpet	Ultra-high Deformed Sunday Angora Yarn Polyester Fiber	Suzhou Longjie Special Fiber Co., Ltd.
	Flame-retardant and Anti-melt-drop Dope-dyed Polyamide 6 Fiber	Guangdong Highsun Meida New Materials Co., Ltd.
		Shanghai ANTU Masterbatch Co., Ltd.
	C-shaped Flat Polyester Fiber	Tongkun Group Zhejiang Hengteng Differential Fiber Co., Ltd.
	In-situ Polymerized Fire-resistant Colored Polyester Fiber	Zhuji Xinsiwei Fiber Co., Ltd.
	Dope-dyed Fire-resistant Recycled Polyester Fiber	Hangzhou Benma Chemfibre and Spinning Co., Ltd.
Sofa fabric	rPET/PTT Double-hollow Composite Elastic Fiber	Jiangsu Sanlian New Material Co., Ltd.
	Flame-retardant and Anti-melt-drop Polyester Fiber	Zhejiang HENGYI Petrochemical Research Institute Co., Ltd.
	Flame-retardant and Anti-melt-drop Dope-dyed Polyamide 6 Fiber	Guangdong Highsun Meida New Materials Co., Ltd.
		Shanghai ANTU Masterbatch Co., Ltd.
	Dope-dyed Imitation Suede Sea-island Polyester Fiber	Shaoxing Chengbang High-Tech Fiber Technology Co., Ltd.
	Rare Earth-modified Antibacterial Polyester Fiber	China Textile Academy (Tianjin) Technology Development Co., Ltd.
Filler	Ultra-fine Denier Anti-pilling Polyacrylonitrile Fiber	Jilin Qifeng Chemical Fiber Co., Ltd.
	Thermal-storage, Heat-retaining and Anti-bacteria Polyester Fiber	Shandong Rare Technology Development Co., Ltd.
		Jiangsu KECens Life Science&Tecnnology Co., Ltd.
	Thermal Polyacrylonitrile Modified Fiber	Foshan Anxin Fiber Technology Co., Ltd.
	Soybean and Milk Protein Composite Modified Poval Fiber	Shanghai Quanyu Biotechnology Suiping Co., Ltd.
	Graphene Modified Recycled Polyester Fiber	Jiangsu Oceantex Fiber Co., Ltd.
Toys	Ultra-high Deformed Sunday Angora Yarn Polyester Fiber	Suzhou Longjie Special Fiber Co., Ltd.
	Marine Regenerated Polyester Fiber	Suzhou Jiahai Special Fiber Co., Ltd.
Wallpaper	In-situ Polymerized Fire-resistant Colored Polyester Fiber	Zhuji Xinsiwei Fiber Co., Ltd.
Trimming	Bright-colored Lightweight Soft Polyester Fiber	Jiangsu Tongkun Hengyang Chemical Fiber Co., Ltd.
	Dope-dyed Fire-resistant Recycled Polyester Fiber	Hangzhou Benma Chemfibre and Spinning Co., Ltd.
Mat	Temperature-Regulating Antibacterial Regenerated Cellulose Fiber	Hangzhou Shangxuan Technology Co., Ltd.

桐昆·中国纤维流行趋势 2025/2026 下游应用推荐表

产业用纺织品

应用领域	推荐纤维品种	企业
汽车内饰及配件	阻燃抗熔滴聚酯纤维	浙江恒逸石化研究院有限公司
	阻燃抗熔滴原液着色聚酰胺6纤维	广东恒申美达新材料股份有限公司
		上海安凸塑料添加剂有限公司
	高模量循环再利用聚酯工业丝	浙江尤夫高新纤维股份有限公司
	原位聚合超黑聚酯纤维	纤丝纺环保材料科技（苏州）有限公司
	原液着色仿麂皮海岛聚酯纤维	绍兴诚邦高新纤维科技有限公司
	原液着色阻燃循环再利用聚酯纤维	杭州奔马化纤纺丝有限公司
过滤用品	超细旦抗起球聚丙烯腈纤维	吉林奇峰化纤股份有限公司
	异形双组分低熔点聚酯纤维	凯泰特种纤维科技有限公司
睡袋	rPET/PTT双中空复合弹性纤维	江苏三联新材料股份有限公司
	蓄热锁温抑菌聚酯纤维	山东稀有科技发展有限公司
		江苏康溢臣生命科技有限公司
	保暖聚丙烯腈改性纤维	佛山市安芯纤维科技有限公司
	石墨烯原位聚合改性异形有色聚酯纤维	常州恒利宝纳米新材料科技有限公司
遮阳布	超细旦抗起球聚丙烯腈纤维	吉林奇峰化纤股份有限公司
	石墨烯原位聚合改性异形有色聚酯纤维	常州恒利宝纳米新材料科技有限公司
	亮彩轻柔聚酯纤维	江苏桐昆恒阳化纤有限公司
	原位聚合超黑聚酯纤维	纤丝纺环保材料科技（苏州）有限公司
	原位聚合阻燃有色聚酯纤维	诸暨市新丝维纤维有限公司
面膜	微细旦皮芯复合热黏合纤维	福建闽瑞新合纤股份有限公司
	大豆牛奶蛋白复合改性聚乙烯醇纤维	上海全宇生物科技遂平有限公司
医用纺织品	微细旦皮芯复合热黏合纤维	福建闽瑞新合纤股份有限公司
纸尿裤	微细旦皮芯复合热黏合纤维	福建闽瑞新合纤股份有限公司
	多组分复合改性聚乳酸纤维	苏州金泉新材料股份有限公司
防护手套	熔纺型中强超高分子量聚乙烯纤维	九州星际科技有限公司
无人机	HM50E高强高模聚丙烯腈基碳纤维	江苏恒神股份有限公司
发动机壳体	HM50E高强高模聚丙烯腈基碳纤维	江苏恒神股份有限公司
橡胶制品	高模量循环再利用聚酯工业丝	浙江尤夫高新纤维股份有限公司
绳缆	熔纺型中强超高分子量聚乙烯纤维	九州星际科技有限公司
	白色皮芯复合抗静电聚酯纤维	苏州凡虎导电纤维有限公司
电子烟储油棉	异形双组分低熔点聚酯纤维	凯泰特种纤维科技有限公司
马克笔笔头	异形双组分低熔点聚酯纤维	凯泰特种纤维科技有限公司